Christie Derbes
833-8693

SO-CVL-753

Health Care of Mothers and Children in National Health Services: Implications for the United States

Health Care of Mothers and Children in National Health Services:
Implication for the United States

Editor
Helen M. Wallace, M.D., M.P.H.

Professor and Chairman
Maternal and Child Health Program
and
Family Health Program

University of California School of Public Health, Berkeley

Ballinger Publishing Company ● **Cambridge, Mass.**
A Subsidiary of J.B. Lippincott Company

RG
960
.H33

 This book is printed on recycled paper.

Copyright © 1975 by Ballinger Publishing Company. All rights reserved. No part of this publication may be reproduced, stored in a retrieval system, or transmitted in any form or by any means, electronic mechanical photocopy, recording or otherwise, without the prior written consent of the publisher.

International Standard Book Number: 0-88410-130-4

Library of Congress Catalog Card Number: 75-19162

Printed in the United States of America

Library of Congress Cataloging in Publication Data

Main entry under title:

Health care of mothers and children in national health services.

      1. Maternal health services—United States. 2. Great Britain—National Health Service. 3. Maternal health services—Sweden. I. Wallace, Helen M. [DNLM: 1. Child health services. 2. Maternal health services. 3. State medicine. WA310 H434]
RG960.H33   362.1'9'8200941   75-19162
ISBN 0-88410-130-4

Contents

Preface   ix

Part I   *The United Kingdom*

Chapter One
The National Health Service in the United Kingdom, 1973
Helen M. Wallace   3

Chapter Two
Maternal and Child Health in the United Kingdom
Helen M. Wallace   13

Maternal Health, Family Planning, and Abortion   13
Child Health   22
School Health   36
Handicapped Children   41

Chapter Three
Child Health Services in the United Kingdom—Present and Future
Ross G. Mitchell   51

Chapter Four
Social Pediatrics: Aspect or Attitude?
Fred J.W. Miller   65

Chapter Five
Family Planning and Abortion in the United Kingdom
Michael V. Smith   85

Chapter Six
Perinatal Care in the United Kingdom
Beryl D. Corner   95

Chapter Seven
Longitudinal Studies in the United Kingdom
J.W.B. Douglas   113

Chapter Eight
Services for the Adolescent in the United Kingdom
S.T. Morton and I. Kolvin   135

Chapter Nine
**The Care of the Handicapped Child in the United
Kingdom**
Kenneth S. Holt   155

Part II   Sweden

Chapter Ten
The National Health Service in Sweden
Malcolm Tottie and Helen M. Wallace   169

Chapter Eleven
Maternal and Child Health in Sweden
Helen M. Wallace   193

Maternal Health, Family Planning, and Abortion   193
Child Health   202
School Health   212
Handicapped Children   216

Chapter Twelve
Infant Mortality in Sweden
Stig Sjölin   229

Chapter Thirteen
Day Care of Children in Sweden
Bodil Rosengren   241

Chapter Fourteen
Sex Education in Sweden
Thorsten Sjovall   261

Part III   *Implications for the United States*

Chapter Fifteen
**Maternal and Child Health in a National Health
Service: Implications for the United States**
Helen M. Wallace   297

Chapter Sixteen
**Child Health Care in the United States—Expenditures
and Extent of Coverage With Selected Comprehensive
Services**
Helen M. Wallace and Hyman Goldstein   311

Index   321

About the Editor   327

About the Contributors   329

Preface

The United States is on the threshold of significant changes in the delivery of medical and health care. There is considerable public dissatisfaction with many aspects—the lack of personal care, the increasing costs, the difficulty in securing medical and hospital care, the unevenness in quality, and the inequality in distribution, availability, and accessibility of medical and health care. These problems are not limited to the United States; they are all problems which most countries have been facing for decades.

During the early 1930s in the United States, a great debate took place about the problems of medical and health care. Out of this debate was enacted the Social Security Act of 1935, legislation combining income maintenance, assistance for needy families, and health services, including Title V which contains special provisions for mothers and children. The 1940s witnessed some national discussion about the need for national health insurance.

In 1946, the Hill-Burton Act was enacted, in an effort to improve hospital facilities and later to include chronic disease facilities and health centers. After a dormant period during the 1950s, the Kennedy-Johnson period made it possible for a number of steps to be taken in the field of health legislation and medical care. Under the aegis of interest in the field of mental retardation, two innovative pieces of legislation were enacted, making possible the Maternity and Infant Care Projects (1963) and the Children and Youth Projects (1965), both experiments in the delivering of special health services for high risk mothers and children. The Economic Opportunity Act of 1964 brought a chain of neighborhood health centers to the poor, largely in urban ghettos, as well as requiring consumer participation and community action, and providing legal services for the poor. Each of these pieces of health and social legislation has been an expression of concern about the need to strengthen and extend our heatlh resources, and to reach high risk populations in great need. Some of the legislation has attempted to experiment with the health care delivery system, in specific efforts for specific groups, rather than in an overall effort. At the same time, there has been interest in experimenting with the pattern of group practice. Examples of this are the Health Insurance Plan of New York and the Kaiser Permanente Plan. Out of this grew the concept of the health maintenance organization, an effort to combine preventive, diagnostic, and treatment services to maintain health. Most recently, versions of proposed national health insurance are again being introduced into Congress.

During these decades the United Kingdom and many countries of Western Europe have moved ahead and have developed well-advanced social and health experiments. Both the United Kingdom and Sweden, as well as some other countries, have a national health service and a national health insurance program. It is clear that there are basic differences between national health insurance (the system of collecting funds and paying bills for health care), and national health service (the system of planning, providing, and evaluating the delivery of health care to people). Each of the two countries is attempting to provide primary health care to all of its people, and is trying to make it freely and easily accessible to all, backed up by medical specialists, paramedical personnel, and hospitals.

In addition to concern for the health and social needs of the total population, there needs to be equal concern with the special needs of certain specific population groups. Among them are mothers and children, the chronically ill and disabled, and the elderly. One of the issues is the question of how the special needs of a special population group, such as mothers and children, fit into an overall program. It is clear that in both the United Kingdom and Sweden mothers and children are given high priority, special funds are made available for their care, and special services are provided for them. It is pertinent to study the experience of these two countries which have well-advanced social and health experiments, to study the methods they tried, their successes, and their remaining problems.

I want to gratefully acknowledge the support of the National Institute of Child Health and Human Development and of the Ford Foundation which made it possible for me to spend a three-month study tour in Sweden and the United Kingdom. I also wish to acknowledge the constructive criticism and assistance of Dr. William Bennett of the Harvard University Press and of Anna M. Fillmore in the preparation of this manuscript.

Part I:

The United Kingdom

Chapter 1

The National Health Service in the United Kingdom

Helen M. Wallace

BRIEF HISTORY OF THE NATIONAL HEALTH SERVICE IN THE UNITED KINGDOM [1, 3]

The National Health Service was enacted in the National Health Service Act of 1946, and began to operate on July 5, 1948. It was built on a long history and tradition of providing care for the sick, the needy, and the homeless, which began under the Poor Law Act of 1601. During this time, steps were also taken to control water supplies and epidemics. In the eighteenth and nineteenth centuries, British medical services developed. Hospitals were built and began to be made available to the general population on a charitable basis. The provident poor began to insure against the cost of illness by subscribing to provident and friendly societies and sick clubs. Rapid growth of towns in the nineteenth century led to problems with the control of communicable diseases, and then to the program of sanitary reform in 1848 which first established the Public Health Act.

In the twentieth century, provision for personal health services began to be developed. The National Health Insurance Act of 1912 introduced a program whereby all people earning a modest annual income (less than £160, later raised to £420[a]) were entitled to the services of a general practitioner, in return for regular contributions made by themselves and their employers to certain insurance organizations, known as approved societies. The doctors who participated were paid a capitation fee for patients who had asked to be on their list and who were accepted. This plan covered most of the poorer half of the population, while the other half was dependent for their medical care either on paying fees as private patients or on a number of voluntary sick clubs (a type of voluntary insurance whereby people paid the doctor a small amount a week).

---

[a]Current currency conversion rate: £1 is equivalent to $2.40.

At the same time, voluntary hospitals expanded their free services for the poor, with the aid of fees from other patients and from voluntary donations. After 1929 the Poor Law infirmaries began to develop into local authority (local government) general hospitals. Some local authorities began to provide improved social and health services, mainly for mothers, children, and schools. The Second World War paved the way for further development. The Emergency Hospital Service was developed to deal with the war wounded; welfare food service was introduced; school meal services and industrial canteens were expanded; the feeding of mothers and children as the most vulnerable part of the population was given high priority. The Beveridge report in 1942 recommended changes which involved a considerable extension of both health and social security services and formed the basis of much postwar social legislation [2].

At this writing, plans and discussions are under way for a revision of the National Health Service to take place in April 1974.

ORGANIZATION OF THE NATIONAL HEALTH SERVICE [3, 5]

The Acts setting up the National Health Service—the National Health Service Act 1946, the National Health Service (Scotland) Act 1947, and the Health Services Act (Northern Ireland) 1948—became effective July 5, 1948. The services operating in England, Wales, Scotland, and Northern Ireland are similar, though there are differences in their administration.

Aims and Scope

The objective of the National Health Service Act 1946 was "to promote the establishment in England and Wales of a comprehensive health service designed to secure improvement in the physical and mental health of the people of England and Wales and the prevention, diagnosis, and treatment of illness, and for that purpose to provide or secure the effective provision of services." The services are available to people normally resident in Britain according to medical need without any regard to insurance qualification. National insurance contributors are required to pay a weekly contribution, but contributors and non-contributors are entitled to the same range of services. All the services were originally free to users, but various charges for certain of the services have been introduced under subsequent legislation, though these can be waived under certain conditions. All but a very small proportion of the population use the services, though a number of people also occasionally pay for a private consultation and for treatment. Nearly all doctors and dentists participate in the service, but this does not prevent them from also taking private patients. Only a small number of specialist consultants, about 2 percent of general practitioners, and a small number of dentists, pharmacists, ophthalmologists and opticians do not participate. A small number of hospitals remain outside the service.

Organization in England

Essentially the National Health Service has a tripartite structure, composed of the general practitioner service, the hospital service, and the local health authority services. The Secretary of State for Social Services has direct responsibility for the provision on a national basis of all hospital and specialist services, the conduct of research work, a Public Health Laboratory Service, and a Blood Transfusion Service. He has indirect responsibility for the family practitioner and local health authority services. He discharges his responsibilities through executive councils, regional hospital boards, boards of governors of teaching hospitals, and local health authorities.

1. *Administrative Organization.*

Executive Councils. These are responsible for the administration of family practitioner services given by family doctors, dentists, pharmacists, and opticians. The responsibilities include consideration of applications to practice in their area and investigation of complaints against any of the practitioners. There are 119 in England, usually one for each administrative county and county borough. Membership consists of representatives of the professions concerned and local health authority.

Regional Hospital Boards. There are fourteen in England, responsible for planning and coordinating the development of hospital and specialist services.

Boards of Governors of Teaching Hospitals. There are thirty-five teaching hospitals, each with its own board of governors.

Local Authorities. There are 174 local authorities, which are responsible for a wide variety of personal health services covering domiciliary midwifery, health visiting, home nursing, child health services, welfare food services, care of premature infants, family planning, immunization, ambulance service, health centers. They operate school health services (through the local school authority) and personal social services (through local social service departments).

2. *Practitioner Services.*

Family Doctor Service. The general practitioner (GP) plays a key role in the National Health Service. He is the one who provides primary health care. Anyone sixteen years or over may choose his own doctor, who is free to accept any patient. A person may change doctor if he wishes, and a mechanism exists for this. The general practitioner, also called family doctor, may call a consultant or refer a patient to a hospital, if he feels this is indicated. A doctor in solo practice may have up to 3,500 patients on his National Health Service list: if he is practicing in partnership, he or any of his partners may have up to 4,500 patients, as long as the average of the combined lists does not exceed

3,500 for each partner. There is a trend toward doctors practicing in groups, and this is in turn accompanied by the attachment, by local health authorities, of health visitors and nurses to the groups. There is also some trend toward doctors locating their offices in health centers provided by the local authorities. The family doctor usually has no hospital appointment.

General Dental Service. Through the general dental service, patients are provided with all forms of treatment. Dentists may take private as well as National Health Service patients. Dentists provide treatment in their offices on a prescribed scale of fees. Dental care is provided free of charge for expectant mothers and mothers within the first year after delivery of a child; for children under sixteen years; for those under twenty-one and still full time in school. All dental care is available, including filling and extraction. Orthodontia care requires approval of the Dental Estimates Board. About three and one-half million people (5 percent) are covered by fluoridation of the community water supply.

General Ophthalmic Services. These services provide for the testing of sight and supplying of spectacles. Anyone found to require treatment is referred to his family doctor. There are three kinds of personnel: (1) Ophthalmic medical practitioners (doctors who test sight and prescribe glasses); (2) Ophthalmic opticians (non-physicians who test sight, prescribe, and supply glasses); (3) Dispensing opticians (who supply glasses). The provision of glasses is available at cost, except that children receive them free. Ophthalmic medical practitioners and ophthalmic opticians are paid prescribed fees for testing sight by the National Health Service. Payment by the National Health Service is also made for the supply of spectacles plus a dispensing fee.

Pharmaceutical Service. Everyone under care of a general practitioner is entitled to medicines and certain appliances. There is a small charge (20 pence or $.50) for each prescription item. There is no such charge for children, the elderly, expectant mothers, or mothers for one year after delivery. Pharmacists are paid, for each prescription, the cost of the ingredients plus a professional fee. Most appliances (braces, crutches, wheelchairs) are available. Hearing aids present a current special problem.

3. *Hospital and Specialist Services.* The hospital and specialist services provide all forms of hospital care and treatment in general and special hospitals for inpatients, outpatients, and day patients. They also provide specialists' opinion and treatment, in hospitals, clinics, or in the patient's home. Hospital and specialist services are obtained through the patient's family doctor, who makes the arrangements. Most patients are accommodated in general wards, but single or small wards are available without charge for those needing them on medical grounds.

FINANCE [3]

General

Expenditure in the health and welfare services in Britain was estimated at £2,835 million in 1971-1972.

Table 1-1.   Authorities Responsible for National Health Service

Regional Hospital Boards	15
Board of Governors of Teaching Hospitals	36
Hospital Management Committees	330
Local Health Authorities	175
Executive Councils	134
Total	690

Table 1-2.   National Health Service Manpower Survey

	1965	*1969*	*1971*
HOSPITAL SERVICES			
Medical staff	22,123	25,674	27,867
Hospital dental staff	663	840	904
Hospital nursing staff	264,683	300,598	331,165
Hospital midwifery staff	17,333	19,438	19,923
Hospital professional and technical staff	31,659	37,930	41,770
Hospital ancillary staff	241,037	257,351	269,889
Hospital admin. & clerical staff	41,767	48,392	53,606
Regional hospital boards	5,755	7,314	9,374
Mass radiography & blood transfusion staffs	3,414	3,762	3,941
GENERAL PRACTITIONER SERVICES			
General medical practitioners	24,260	24,239	24,668
General dental practitioners	11,572	11,761	12,054
Ophthalmic medical practitioners	887	950	986
Opticians	7,317	6,729	6,694
Executive councils staff	4,467	5,266	5,354
Dental estimates board	1,435	1,387	1,476
Joint pricing committees & pay accounts committee	2,102	2,266	2,201
LOCAL AUTHORITY SERVICES			
Nursing staff	23,354	25,211	27.109
Home help	35,929	37,720	NA
Mental health training center staff	3,657	5,501	NA
Day nursing staff	5,137	5,501	NA
Social workers	3,737	NA	NA

Source: *Health Services in Britain* (London: Her Majesty's Stationery Office, 1973), p. 72.

The greater part of the funds comes from the central government and is met from general taxation; a small part is met from local rates (taxes). Other income is from the national health service contribution paid with the national insurance contribution, and from charges paid by people using certain services.

There are charges for prescriptions (10 pence), except for children up to sixteen years; expectant and nursing mothers; the elderly (over sixty-five); patients with certain medical conditions; war pensioners; and people in receipt of supplementary benefits and family income supplement. There are charges for treatment in the dental service (but not for examination only, or for treatment given to people under 21 or to expectant or nursing mothers). There are charges for dentures (except for children under sixteen or still at school, and expectant and nursing mothers). There are charges for spectacles (except childrens' standard spectacles). There are charges for some local authority services.

Dentists providing treatment in their own offices are paid on a prescribed scale of fees according to the treatment they have provided; they are paid on a fee-for-service basis.

Pharmacists dispensing on their own premises are paid on the basis of the prescriptions they dispense.

Ophthalmic medical practitioners and ophthalmic opticians are paid approved fees for each sight test made. Opticians who dispense spectacles are paid according to the number and type of pairs supplied.

Payment of General Practitioners

Remuneration was originally based almost entirely on a capitation system, according to the number of patients on the doctor's list; a maximum of 3,500 patients is permitted per individual (single-handed) doctor. Higher fees are provided for patients sixty-five years and over. A basic practice allowance is paid in recognition of basic practice expenses and commitments. Additional payment is made to doctors practicing in areas short of doctors, for seniority, and for refresher-type (vocational) training. There are also additional payments made for accepting responsibilities out of normal hours; for visits to patients at night; for maternity services (prenatal care, delivery, postnatal care); for immunizations; for taking cervical smears; for emergency care for patients not on their list. Direct payments are made for rent and rates of practice premises, and for expenditure on ancillary staff (receptionist, etc.). General practitioners are now paid a basic practice allowance of £1,540 a year, plus an additional allowance per each extra group of patients. They may also obtain grants to improve their practice premises, and loans are available for the purchase, erection, and improvement of premises [3].

Thus, the method used to renumerate general practitioners is that of the basic capitation system, plus additional payments on a fee-for-service basis.

Payment of Consultants

Consultants have a choice of either of two systems of remuneration. The first is that of the full-time consultant, who has a hospital appointment for eleven sessions a week (5-1/2 days), and has no private practice. The second is that of the maximum part-time consultant, who has a hospital appointment for nine sessions a week (4-1/2 days). For the other day, he may see private patients, or be shared with several other hospitals as a consultant. The present basic

Table 1-3. Public Expenditure on the Health and Personal Social Service in Britain

	£ million			
Current Expenditure	*1951-52*	*1961-62*	*1969-70*	*1971-72*
Hospital, etc. services	275	551	1,076	1,458
less receipts from patients	−3	−6	−11	−14
General medical, etc. services	166	274	483	613
less receipts from patients	−4	−41	−47	−67
Pharmaceutical services	53	100	204	249
General dental services	38	63	92	121
General ophthalmic services	12	17	28	31
General medical services	59	88	148	197
Local Authority Services				
Health	38	82	117	149
Personal social services	29	56	205	263
School meals and milk				
School milk	10	14	14	11
School meals	42	85	180	206
less payment by parents	−16	−35	−69	−94
Welfare foods	32	−29	39	18
Dept. Admin., other expenses	7	19	41	60
Total	576	1,028	2,028	2,603
Capital Expenditures				
Hospital, etc. services	15	44	131	174
Local authority health & personal social services	7	14	37	53
Other services	6	3	5	5
Total	28	62	173	232
Total public expenditure on health & personal social services	604	1,090	2,201	2,835

Source: *Health Services in Britain* (London: Her Majesty's Stationery Office, 1973), p. 62.

annual salary of the fulltime ordinary consultant is £6,500; in addition there is a system of awards (C, B, A, A+); the A+ award would mean essentially a doubling of the basic annual salary.

REORGANIZATION OF THE NATIONAL HEALTH SERVICE

One of the recognized main problems of the National Health Service has been that it is administered in three parts—the Hospital and Specialist Services, the General Practitioner Services, and the Local Health Authority Services. These are now being unified under the National Health Service Reorganization Bill, effective April 1, 1974. In addition, the school health services are part of this unification. The new reorganization consists of the following:

1. *Regional Health Authorities.* There are fourteen in number, each staffed by a regional medical officer, nurse, administrator, and financial officer. They are responsible for planning and deployment of staff.

2. *Area Health Authorities.* There are ninety in number, each staffed by an area medical officer, nurse, administrator, and financial officer. They are responsible for planning, monitoring, research, and evaluation. An area with a university with a medical school is known as a teaching area, with more representation by the university in policy decisions. The responsibility of the local school health program is being moved from the local education authority to the area health authority.

3. *District.* This consists of a population of 200,000-500,000 with a general hospital. This is to bring together the general practitioner, hospital, and preventive services. Each district has a community health council.

4. *Central.* Among the changes, central responsibility for the school health service was moved from the Department of Education and Science to the Department of Health and Social Security; within the Department of Health and Social Security (DHSS), it is a part of the Maternal and Child Health Unit.

MAJOR ISSUES

In considering the provision and delivery of medical and health care, based on observations in the United Kingdom and Sweden, certain issues are primary and need solution. They include:

1. *The Delivery of Primary Health Care.* The alternatives for this include the following:
a.   The general practitioner or family physician
b.   The nurse in an extended role, backed up by physicians
c.   The internist for adults, and the pediatrician for children
d.   Group or team practice
   i. Groups of general practitioners

    ii. Groups of general practitioners and specialists

   iii. Interdisciplinary groups of general practitioners, medical specialists, nurses and others.

Related to this is the question of solo versus group practice, and the composition of the group. Because there is no clear answer to this, there is need for opportunity to experiment with and evaluate various methods.

      2. *The Method(s) of Payment.* In an organized program, the alternatives are (a) salary; (b) fee-for-service; (c) capitation. The program in the United Kingdom uses the salary method for specialists. It began with the capitation method for general practitioners, and has added fee-for-service to it.

      3. *The Relationship of Treatment Services.* Included in this are such aspects as:

a. The relationship of general practitioners to consultants, and vice versa

b. The relationship of general practitioners to hospitals. Should they all have a hospital appointment?

c. The relationship of specialists to hospitals

d. Determination of the best way to provide continuous coverage for patients, twenty-four hours a day, seven days a week.

      4. *The Relationship of Preventive and Treatment Services.* Included in this issue are such aspects as:

a. Can preventive and treatment be combined and delivered by one person or one group of people?

b. How can the hospital move out into the community?

c. How can community preventive services be more closely related to hospitals and physicians?

      5. *The Role of the Generalist in Specialty Services.* Included in this issue are such aspects as:

a. How far can the general practitioner play a role in:

      Maternity Care

      Child Health Care—preventive and treatment

      Family Planning

      Handicapped Children

b. What special preparation is needed—basic and refresher

      6. *Care of Vulnerable High Risk Groups.* Within a general health service for the total population, do certain groups of high risk need special emphasis and care? Examples might include:

a. All mothers and children, because they are more vulnerable

b. Special groups of high risk mothers; infants; children; handicapped children.

      7. *Evaluation.* Operational research is needed to evaluate the outcome or effects of various methods of delivering health care.

REFERENCES

1. Anderson, O.W. *Health Care: Can There Be Equity?* New York: John Wiley & Sons, 1972.
2. Beveridge, William. *Social Insurance and Allied Services.* New York: MacMillan Company, 1942.
3. *Health Services in Britain.* London: Her Majesty's Stationery Office, 1973.
4. Klein, R. "An Anatomy of the NHS." *New Society* (June 28, 1973): 739-741.
5. Ministry of Health, National Health Service. *The Administrative Structure of the Medical and Related Services in England and Wales.* London: Her Majesty's Stationery Office, 1968.
6. *National Health Service Reorganization: England.* Presented to Parliament by the Secretary of State for Social Services by Command of Her Majesty. London: Her Majesty's Stationery Office, August 1972.

Chapter 2

Maternal and Child Health in the United Kingdom

Helen M. Wallace

MATERNAL HEALTH, FAMILY PLANNING, AND ABORTION

Organization of Services

At the central level, the Department of Health and Social Security is responsible for maternal and child health services. It has thirteen divisions, one of which is the Maternal and Child Health Division headed by a pediatrician. Also in this division are a deputy; a physician responsible for adoptions, child abuse, and institutions for juvenile delinquents; the present head of the school health program, now in the Department of Education and Science, has joined this division in the reorganization of the National Health Service. Also at the central level is an obstetrician in charge of maternal health and family planning.

All large cities and counties and each borough of London have a medical officer in charge of maternal and child health. They may also be in charge of family planning. There are about 200 in all. Some may also have a medical officer in charge of school health.

Fertility

The live birthrate has been gradually declining since 1965. In 1971, it was 16.1 per 1,000 population. The fertility rate (per 1,000 women 15-44 years of age) has been gradually declining since 1964; in 1970, it was 83.3 (Tables 2-1 and 2-2).

At present, approximately 90 percent of all live births occur in hospitals in the United Kingdom, most of them in National Health Service hospitals (Table 2-1).

The incidence of low birth weight (5-1/2 pounds or less at birth) has

Table 2-1.   Live Birth, Fertility, and Illegitimacy Rates, Incidence of Low Birth Weight, and Percentage of Hospital Deliveries England and Wales

| Year | Live Birthrate | Percentage of Total Confinement in: | | Live Births Per 1,000 Women 15-44 Years | Illegitimate Births Per 1,000 Live Births | Percentage Live Births 2500 Grams or Less |
		All Institutions	NHS Hospitals			
1955	15.0	64.3	60.2	72.8	47	6.9
1956	15.7			77.6	48	6.8
1957	16.1			80.0	48	6.9
1958	16.4			82.1	49	6.9
1959	16.5			83.0	51	6.7
1960	17.2			86.8	54	6.7
1961	17.6			89.1	60	6.7
1962	18.0			90.5	66	6.7
1963	18.2			90.9	69	6.6
1964	18.5	70.0	67.1	92.5	72	6.4
1965	18.1	72.5	69.8	91.2	77	6.3
1966	17.7	75.0	75.4	90.1	79	6.5
1967	17.2	78.9	65.4	88.4	84	6.5
1968	16.9	80.6	78.6	87.0	85	6.6
1969	16.4	83.1	81.2	84.7	84	6.7
1970	16.0	86.0	84.2	83.3	83	6.8
1971	16.1	88.9				
1972	14.8					

Source: Department of Health and Social Security, *On the State of the Public Health* (London: Her Majesty's Stationery Office, 1972).

Table 2-2.   Percentage of Births Which Are Illegitimate

Year	United States White	United States Non-White	United States Total	Sweden	England
1950	1.7	18.0	4.0	9.8	4.9
1960	2.3	21.6	5.3	11.3	5.8
1966	4.4	27.6	8.4	14.6	7.7
1968	5.3	31.2	9.7	15.1	8.4
1969	5.5	32.5	10.0		8.4
1970				19.4	8.3
1971				21.6	8.2

Sources: (1) O.W. Anderson, *Health Care: Can There Be Equity?* (New York: J. Wiley and Sons, 1972), p. 145. (2) PKSU Statistik. *Befolkningen, Sexualvanor, Aborter, Gonore, Sexualbrott, Internationalellt.* Stockholm, May 1973.

been from 6.3-6.9 percent. In 1971, it was 6.4 percent (Tables 2-1 and 2-3).

The birthrates in the United Kingdom and the United States are similar; they are higher than Sweden's. The illegitimacy rate in the United Kingdom is lower than that of the United States, which in turn is lower than Sweden's. The incidence of low birth weight in the United Kingdom is higher than that in Sweden and lower than that in the United States (Tables 2-1 through 2-4).

Registration of births is done by the local health authority; one of the purposes is to alert health visitors to visit the home. There is special interest in infants of low birth weight, or those with a congenital malformation. If the mother has been discharged within forty-eight hours after delivery, she is visited by a nurse-midwife.

Screening for phenylketonuria is done at six to fourteen days of age in the home by the health visitor. About 80 percent of live births are screened.

Table 2-3.   Percentage of Live Births Premature, by Birth Weight

United States (1968)	
White	7.1
Non-White	13.7
Total	8.2
Sweden (1968)	5.0
England and Wales (1968)	6.6

Source: O.W. Anderson, *Health Care: Can There Be Equity?* (New York: J. Wiley and Sons, 1972), p. 241.

Maternal Mortality

In 1967-68, England and Wales ranked seventh in maternal mortality among the nations of the world. In 1969, the rate was 1.9 per 10,000 live births [2a].

In 1971, the maternal mortality rate for England was 1.4 per 10,000 total births. One-fourth of the 103 maternal deaths were associated with abortion.

Major causes of death in 1971 were abortion, toxemia, hemorrhage, and infection.

Of the 455 deaths directly due to pregnancy in 1967-69, 56.0 percent were found to have avoidable factors. In 1967-69, there were 243 additional maternal deaths not directly due to pregnancy or childbirth; of this number 15 percent had avoidable factors [2a].

Maternity Care

There are approximately 23,000 maternity beds in England, of which 18,000 are "consultant" beds, and 5,000 are "general practitioner" beds. The latter are in smaller hospitals, primarily in rural areas.

Prenatal care is shared by the general practitioner in his office, and the nurse-midwife and the obstetrician in the hospital. Thus, the maternity patient may receive prenatal care from the general practitioner until 30-32-34

Table 2-4. Birthrate Per 1,000 Population in United States, Sweden, and England

| Year | United States | | | Sweden | England |
	White	Non-White	Total		
1935	17.9	25.8	18.8	13.8	14.8
1945	19.7	26.5	20.8	20.2	18.3
1950	23.0	33.3	24.5	16.5	15.8
1955	23.8	34.7	25.3	14.8	15.0
1960	22.7	32.1	23.9	13.7	17.1
1965	18.3	27.6	19.4	15.9	18.1
1966	17.4	26.1	18.4	15.8	17.7
1967	16.8	25.0	17.8	15.4	17.2
1968	16.6	24.2	17.5	14.2	16.9
1969	16.9	24.4	17.7	13.5	16.4
1970			18.2	13.6	16.0
1971			17.3	14.1	16.1
1972				13.8	14.8

Source: O.W. Anderson, *Health Care: Can There Be Equity?* New York: J. Wiley and Sons, 1972), p. 144.

Table 2-5. Maternal Mortality—Selected Countries

Country	Year	Rank	Maternal Mortality Rate Per 100,000 Live Births
Australia	1968	12	28.2
Belgium	1967	3	17.8
Czechoslovakia	1967	9	26.9
Denmark	1966	4	19.2
England and Wales	1968	7	24.4
France	1968	13	28.9
Holland	1968	5	21.1
Japan	1967	15	70.5
North Ireland	1968	10	27.1
New Zealand	1968	6	24.1
Norway	1967	8	25.5
Scotland	1968	2	14.8
Sweden	1967	1	14.0
United States	1967	11	28.0
West Germany	1967	14	59.6

Table 2-6. Maternal Mortality Rate Per 10,000 Live Births

Year	United States			Sweden	England and Wales
	White	Non-White	Total		
1930	60.0	120.0	66.0		42.4
1957	2.1	12.5	4.1	3.6	4.8
1966	2.0	7.2	2.9	1.1	2.6
1967	2.0	7.0	2.8	1.4	2.0
1968	1.7	6.4	2.5		2.4
1969			2.7		1.9

Source: O.W. Anderson, *Health Care: Can There Be Equity?* (New York: J. Wiley and Sons, 1972), p. 242.

weeks of pregnancy; during that time, she will be referred to the hospital where she is seen by the nurse-midwife; if she has a medical problem, she will be seen by an obstetrician; after that time, the patient receives the remainder of her prenatal care at the hospital.

Hospital delivery of normal patients is performed by the nurse-midwife. The services of an obstetrician are available for patients with complications.

Table 2-7.   Maternal Mortality, England

Year	Total Births	Maternal Mortality		Maternal Mortality from Abortions		
		Number	Death Rate Per 1,000 Total Births	Number	Rate Per 1,000 Total Births	Rated Per Million Aged 15-44
1971	749,379	103	0.14	26	0.03	3
1970	751,707	108	0.14	29	0.04	3
1969	764,444	113	0.15	34	0.04	4
1968	786,201	143	0.18	48	0.06	5

Source: Department of Health and Social Security, *On the State of the Public Health* (London: Her Majesty's Stationery Office, 1972).

Table 2-8. Causes of Death Ascribed to Pregnancy and Childbirth in England

Cause	1957	1963	1965	1967	1970	1971
Ectopic Pregnancy	22	16	11	11	19	7
Hemorrhage	7	6	1			2
Other complications of pregnancy	12	25	15	18	13	14
Toxemia	88	46	48	44	25	23
Abortion	61	49	52	34	29	26
Placenta previa or antepartum hemorrhage	21	11	12	7	6	8
Postpartum hemorrhage	23	21	11	5	5	9
Other deaths from delivery	57	33	44	35	23	24
Puerperal phlebitis, thrombosis, and pulmonary	33	20	17	10	10	12
Other sepsis of pregnancy, childbirth, puerperium	19	8	5	3		4
Other complications of puerperium	6	8	5	5	7	
Total	349	243	221	172	137	129

Sources: (1) Department of Health and Social Security, *On the State of the Public Health* (London: Her Majesty's Stationery Office, 1972). (2) Department of Health and Social Security, *Domiciliary Midwifery and Maternity Bed Needs* (London: Her Majesty's Stationery Office, 1970).

The general practitioner was described as playing a decreasing role in delivery, but an increasing role in prenatal care. There is an "obstetric list" for general practitioners; to be on the obstetric list, they must individually present evidence of obstetric experience and/or training. To be on the obstetric list means that the general practitioner has certain privileges and is paid more by the National Health Service.

Domiciliary midwifery service is available from the local health authority; approximately 10 percent of women still deliver at home. Domiciliary midwifery is decreasing [2b]. Nurse-midwives and health visitors are being attached to general practitioners in their offices and in health centers.

The average length of hospital stay for maternity patients in 1971 was 7.3 days for consultant beds, and 5.8 days for general practitioner beds (compared with 7.6 days and 6.1 days respectively in 1970) [2c].

During 1971, there were approximately 1,900,000 tests for screening for cervical cancer. This number has increased steadily since cervical cancer screening was introduced in 1966. Smears are taken by general practitioners, and in hospital, local health authority and family planning clinics [2d].

Special Maternal Health Benefits

Maternity Grant. There is a maternity grant of £25 provided. It may be paid on either the mother's own insurance or her husband's, but not on both [2e].

Maternity Allowance. There is a maternity allowance of £6.75 a week for eighteen weeks, starting eleven weeks before the week in which the baby is expected. This is payable only to women who are or who have been employed or self-employed and have been paying full flat-rate national insurance contributions [2e].

Family Planning

Brief History of Family Planning in the United Kingdom. The family planning program was begun in the 1920s by the Family Planning Association (FPA). It established a separate group of family planning doctors. For many years, the major responsibility for providing family planning services was carried out by the Family Planning Association. When the Abortion Act was enacted in 1966, it became evident there was a need for both abortion and family planning services. General practitioners are gradually being brought in to play a greater role in family planning. When the National Health Service was reorganized in April 1974, the family planning clinics now operated by the Family Planning Association are gradually being taken over by the National Health Service.

Estimate of Extent of Coverage with Family Planning Service. Estimates indicate that, of ten million women aged 15-44 years, the coverage with family planning service is as follows:

Status	Number of Women
Pregnant at any one time	1 million
Subfertile	1 million
On some type of contraceptive	5.3 million
Condom—2.4 million	
Pill—2.25 million	
IUD—0.35 million	
Chemical—0.2 million	
Cap and chemical—0.2 million	
Remainder	3 million

Family Planning Services at Present. It is reported by the Department of Health and Social Security that two-thirds of the family planning is currently provided by general practitioners. Some of these have had training in family planning; others have not.

In 1972 the Family Planning Association [3] operated 1,016 clinics, providing 91,451 clinic sessions. They saw a total of 815,642 individuals, including 284,207 new patients. Included in this were 845 clinics in local health authority premises, and 139 clinics in hospital premises. Hospitals as a whole were reported to be playing a relatively small role in family planning.

There is a domiciliary family planning program for poorly motivated women. This consists of a visit to the home by a general practitioner, health visitor, and/or nurse. Advice and contraception service are provided to women in the home. Subsequent service and follow-up are then provided in family planning clinics.

There is considerable local variation in the free availability of family planning services. In some local authorities, everything may be free; in others, it may be free for women who are poor; in others, it may be free for the first year after the birth of the baby. There is a prescription charge of 20 pence ($.50) for oral contraceptives.

Training of Doctors and Other Personnel [1, 6]. The responsibility for training doctors and other personnel in the field of family planning has been carried out by the Family Planning Association. For doctors, this consists of a three-day course, plus six practical sessions. Training in the use of intrauterine devices is separate. A fee is charged by the Family Planning Association. In addition, the Family Planning Association has also had training courses (short term) for nurses, health visitors, social workers, teachers, etc. Eventually it is planned to turn this training over to the medical schools and hospitals.

Special Services for Teenagers. Two percent of the Family Planning Association Clinics have special sessions for teenagers. The number seen is large. The Family Planning Association also provides speakers for youth groups and schools. The Family Planning Association supports Grapevine, an experimental outreach program, which uses young volunteers attempting to reach youth wherever they are for the purposes of providing information, referral, etc.

The Brook Advisory Service, which has sixteen centers in the United Kingdom, serves a large number of unmarried teenagers. Services consist of contraception and counseling for the girl and her parents.

The Pregnancy Advisory Service also sees a large number of teenagers. They provide counseling, certification for an abortion, and they operate an abortion service. This costs £52 per person.

Abortion

In 1972, it was estimated that 150,000 abortions were done in the United Kingdom. Approximately one-third were done on women from other countries as private patients. Two-thirds were done on women from the United Kingdom; of this group, one-half were done in the National Health Service under the care of an obstetrician; the other half were done in the private sector under the care of a doctor.

A woman wanting an abortion must have a certificate signed by two doctors, and this has presented some problems. There is a restriction that abortion be done only for health reasons, but this is being interpreted liberally.

A study of 3,000 women coming to the Pregnancy Advisory Service indicated that failure to use a contraceptive accounted for two-thirds of the pregnancies [4].

Problems encountered in the abortion picture include the need for services (doctors and facilities) geographically available; a more enlightened attitude by some doctors; the need for standards to protect the patient; and the problem of large-scale volume on a commercial basis in some instances [5]. For these reasons, the Pregnancy Advisory Services have been established around the United Kingdom to provide counseling, referral, and abortion services. Most of the women served by them are single, and young (aged 18-24 years).

CHILD HEALTH

The Health Care of Children and Medical Manpower and Practice

The health care of children in the United Kingdom is broadly divided among the following groups: well child care of infants and preschool children is conducted largely by the child welfare centers, with a small volume done by physicians in general practice; well child care of school-age children and of school-age youth is conducted by the school health service; the care of sick infants and children and youth is provided by physicians in general practice; pediatric specialty care is available on referral by the general practitioner to the pediatrician, who is hospital-based and who serves as consultant.

The United Kingdom has 23,000 general practitioners, who provide the bulk of primary health care for illness in children. General practitioners are paid on a per capita basis, to provide year-round, 24-hour medical care of up to 3,500 patients per doctor. General practitioners are paid additionally for "out-of-hours" calls, for each patient in excess of 1,000 on the general practitioner's list, for each patient over age sixty-five, for each patient receiving complete maternity services, and for immunizations.

Pediatricians are mostly hospital-based, serving as a consultant and providing the medical care of children in hospitals. They are either on a full-time salary (for 5-1/2 days a week), or paid as part-time consultants (4-1/2 days a week); the remainder of the week, the part-time pediatrician may see private patients, or be shared with other hospitals as a consultant. There is a basic annual salary for the consultant, and a system of additional awards; the maximum award doubles the basic salary.

Table 2-9.   Whole-Time Academic Clinic Pediatric Staff in
the United Kingdom—1970

	Number
Medical Schools	23
Staff	
Professors/Readers	27
Senior Lecturers	21
Lecturers	35
Pediatric Staffing In the U.K.—1969-70	
Consultants	
Total	362
Honorary	53
Single-handed	83
Senior Registrars	
Total	84
Honorary	30
Registrars	211
Senior House Officers	351

Source: D. Court and A. Jackson, *Paediatrics in the Seventies* (London: Oxford University Press, 1972).

In 1972, the British Pediatric Association published a report "Paediatrics in the Seventies" [9]. Major recommendations include: (1) The development of a new type of pediatrician, the community pediatrician; (2) A substantial increase in the number of full-time pediatric faculty members in medical schools and university hospitals; (3) The further development of hospital services for children, at district and regional levels, increased use of day-hospital care, and studies to establish the needs of children for long-term care; (4) Provision of additional pediatric specialists in perinatology, handicapped children, malignant diseases, cardiology, neurology, nephrology, endocrinology, and hematology; (5) The expansion of assessment and treatment centers for handicapped children at regional and district levels; and (6) The provision of hospital services for adolescents. As a result of this, the Department of Health and Social Security has just appointed a new working group to consider and make recommendations about child health services for the future.

Special interest has been shown in the United Kingdom in problem of infant and perinatal mortality; in case finding, assessment and management of handicapped children; and in such problems as battered babies; care of the child with spina bifida; detection of congenital dislocation of the hip; genetics; hemolytic disease of the newborn; deafness; and hospital facilities for children. Each of these has been the subject of special working committee reports. [11]

Infant Mortality

In 1970-1971, Sweden ranked first in infant mortality, with a rate of 11.0. England and Wales ranked thirteenth with a rate of 17.6. The United States ranked sixteenth with a rate of 19.2. The infant mortality rates in England and Wales and in Sweden are lower than that for whites in the United States (Tables 2-10 through 2-14). Infant mortality in England and Wales has declined consistently since 1950.

Major causes of infant mortality in England and Wales are congenital anomalies, bronchitis and pneumonia, immaturity, and birth injury and asphyxia

Table 2-10. Infant Mortality Rate—Selected Countries (Per 1,000 Live Births)

Country	Year	Rate
Sweden	1971	11.1
Netherlands	1971	11.1
Finland	1971	11.8
Japan	1971	12.4
Iceland	1970	13.2
Norway	1969	13.8
Denmark	1970	14.2
France	1971	14.4
Switzerland	1970	15.1
Lichtenstein	1969	16.7
New Zealand	1970	16.7
Australia	1971	17.4
England & Wales	1971	17.6
Canada	1970	18.8
U.S.A.	1971	19.2
Iceland	1970	19.6
Singapore	1971	19.7
Scotland	1971	19.9
Belgium	1970	20.5
Czechoslovakia	1970	22.1
Luxembourg	1971	22.5
Israel	1970	22.9
U.S.S.R.	1971	22.9
N. Ireland	1971	23.0
West Germany	1971	23.2
Bulgaria	1971	24.9

Source: United Nations Statistical Yearbook, 1972. New York. 1973. Table 21, pag 89-94.

Table 2-11. Infant and Childhood Mortality—England and Wales

Year	Perinatal (SB + DR Under one week)	Infant Mortality Rate						Infant Mortality Rate Per 1,000	
		Total	Under 4 weeks	4 wks -one year	1-4 Years	5-9 Years	10-14 Years	Born In Wedlock	Born Out of Wedlock
1951	38.2	29.8	18.9	11.0	1.35	0.55	0.47		
1955	37.4	24.9	17.2	7.6	1.00	0.43	0.38	25	32
1960	32.8	21.8	15.5	6.3	0.87	0.44	0.32	22	26
1961	32.6	21.4	15.3	6.1	0.93	0.40	0.32	21	25
1962	20.8	21.7	15.1	6.6	0.86	0.38	0.34	21	27
1963	29.3	21.1	14.3	6.9	0.91	0.40	0.32	21	26
1964	28.2	19.9	13.8	6.1	0.81	0.39	0.33	19	26
1965	26.9	19.0	13.0	6.0	0.82	0.40	0.36	19	25
1966	26.2	19.0	12.9	6.1	0.84	0.37	0.34	19	25
1967	25.4	18.3	12.5	5.8	0.77	0.37	0.35	18	24
1968	24.7	18.3	12.4	5.9	0.80	0.37	0.33	18	23
1969	23.4	18.0	12.0	6.0	0.77	0.34	0.30	17	26
1970	23.5	18.2	12.3	5.9	0.72	0.33	0.30	17	26
1971	22.3	17.5	11.6	5.9	0.70	0.36	0.30		

Sources: (1) Department of Health and Social Security, *On the State of the Public Health* (London: HMSO, 1972). (2) National Council for the Unmarried Mother and Her Child. Annual Report, April 1971-March 1972. (London).

Table 2-12.   Infant Mortality Rates Per 1,000 Live Births in U.S.A., Sweden, and England

Year	U.S.A. Total	White	Non-White	Sweden	England
1950	29.2	26.8	44.5	21.0	31.4
1960	26.0	22.9	43.2	16.6	21.8
1965	24.7	21.5	40.3	13.3	19.0
1967	22.1	19.7	35.9	12.9	18.4
1968	21.8	19.2	34.5	13.0	18.3
1969	20.7	18.7	28.8	11.7	18.0
1970	19.8	17.4	31.4	11.0	18.2
1971	19.2	16.8	30.2		17.5
1972	18.2	16.3	29.0		

(Table 2-13). Almost two-thirds of all infant deaths occurred in infants of low birth weight.

One-third of infant mortality in England and Wales occurs in the postneonatal period (age from four weeks to first birthday). A special study of 679 postneonatal deaths 1964-66 of three Local Health Authorities [11e] showed that 187 deaths (28 percent) had avoidable factors. Social causes played

Table 2-13.   Causes of Infant Mortality—England 1970 and 1971-Death Rates Per 100,000 Live Births

Cause	1970	1971
Congenital Anomalies	371	372
Bronchitis and Pneumonia	297	278
Immaturity	201	183
Injury at Birth and Asphyxia	123	112
Hemolytic Disease of Newborn	27.0	25.3
Accidental Suffocation	15.6	12.6
Whooping Cough	1.75	2.57
Measles	1.08	0.68
Gastritis and Duodenitis	0.13	0.14
Tuberculosis	0.13	
All Other Causes	779	760
All Causes	1,816	1,747

Source: Department of Health and Social Security, *On the State of the Public Health* (London: HMSO, 1972).

Table 2-14.   Reported Live Births and Deaths in Low Birth
Weight Infants, England—1971

Birth Weight Group	Live Births	Deaths Within 28 Days	Deaths Per 1,000 Live Births in Birth Weight Group
Under 1000 Gm	1,803	1,442	799.7
1000-1500 Gm	3,278	1,432	436.8
1501-2000 Gm	8,375	1,170	139.7
2001-2250 Gm	10,452	503	48.1
2251-2500 Gm	23,294	550	23.6
	47,202	5,097	108.1

Source: Department of Health and Social Security, *On the State of the Public Health* (London: HMSO, 1972).

a role in 36 percent of the 187 deaths, largely related to housing, broken families, parental desertion, etc. Parents played a role in 35 percent of the 187 deaths, largely related to inadequacy, failure to summon medical aid, mental subnormality, failure to appreciate the seriousness of the situation, neglect, etc. General practitioners played a role in 17 percent of the 187 deaths, largely related to failure to realize the severity of the situation, diagnostic delay or failure, delay in visiting, slowness in referral to hospital, etc. The hospital played a role in 6 percent of the 187 deaths, largely related to diagnostic failure or delay, hospital-acquired infection, management, etc.

The infant mortality rate was 50 percent higher in babies born out of wedlock than in those born in wedlock (Table 2-11).

A report of the Expert Group on Special Care for Babies [11h] covered such aspects as present facilities for special care of babies, future organization of special care for babies, research, staffing of special care nurseries, design and equipment of special care nurseries. As a tentative guide to planning, they recommended six special care cots per 1,000 live births; such factors as local population density, birthrate, social class distribution, and incidence of low birth weight also need to be considered. Steps are actively being taken to develop regional intensive care centers for newborn infants with special needs.

A special committee has considered the problems of sudden death in infants [16d].

Health Care of Infants and Preschool Children

Mortality. Mortality in preschool children ared 1-4 years is lowest in Sweden. The mortality rate is lower in England and Wales than in the United States for children of all ethnic groups. The mortality rate in this age group in

Sweden is lower than white children in the United States; the rate in England and Wales is the same as that for white children in the United States (Table 2-15).

The Child Welfare Centers [16c]

The local health authorities operate child welfare centers. In 1965, there were 6,376 child welfare centers in operation; they saw 76.7 percent of all infants born in England and Wales, 69.6 percent of children aged 1-2 years, and 20.7 percent of those aged 2-5 years. Most of the children receiving health supervision did so at these local authority child welfare centers. The highest percentage of users at child welfare centers are social class 3 (71.5 percent), followed by social class 5 (63.7 percent), social class 4 (61.9 percent), and social classes 1 and 2 (54.9 percent). There was higher utilization for first births, and the rate of utilization decreased for each subsequent birth (Tables 2-16 through 2-19).

Table 2-15.   Mortality of Children 1-4 Years of Age Rate Per 1,000

Country	Rate	Period
Sweden	2.4	1965-67
Denmark	3.1	1966-67
England & Wales	3.2	1965-67
Ireland	3.4	1965-67
U.S.A. White—3.2 Non-White—6.0	3.6	1965-67
Norway	3.6	1965-67
Scotland	3.6	1965-67
France	3.6	1965-67
Belgium	3.7	1965-66
Netherlands	3.8	1966-67
Australia	3.8	1965-67
Israel	3.8	1965-67
Canada	3.9	1965-67
W. Germany	4.2	1965-67
N. Zealand	4.3	1965-67
Italy	5.0	1965-67
Japan	5.1	1965-67
Poland	5.1	1965-66
U.S.S.R.	9.6	1966-67

Source: Metropolitan Life Insurance Company, *Statistical Bulletin*, March 1971.

Table 2-16.   Number of Child Welfare Centers and Sessions Held

Year	Number of Centers	Centers Per 10,000 Population	Number of Sessions Held
1951	5,030	1.15	262,392
1956	5,676	1.27	286,356
1961	5,985	1.30	307,548
1962	6,039	1.29	313,548
1963	6,263	1.33	329,435
1964	6,411	1.35	332,974
1965	6,376	1.34	342,820

Table 2-17.   Proportionate Attendance at Local Health Authority Child Welfare Clinics—1964

Number of Children	Children Under 2 Years 55	Children 2-4 Years 95
GP special clinic only	4%	8%
Local authority clinic only	74%	31%
Both GP and local authority	9%	4%
No clinics	13%	57%
Total	100%	100%

Source: Ministry of Health, *Child Welfare Centers* (London: HMSO, 1967).

The functions of the child welfare centers are routine medical examinations; detection of defects (physical and emotional); advice on infant nutrition and hygiene; parent counseling; health education; immunization; sale of welfare foods.

Some general practitioners hold child welfare clinics of their own. Attendance at these clinics is low.

Hospital Care of Children

The predominant pattern of care is to hospitalize children in pediatric departments of general hospitals. A survey done in England on one day in October 1970 revealed that of 15,591 children under fifteen years of age hospitalized in non-psychiatric hospitals, 27.1 percent were in children's hospitals, 55.4 percent were in children's wards of other hospitals, 10.5 percent were in adult wards with segregation, and 7.1 percent were in adult wards without segregation [11f]. In addition, there were 456 adolescents aged fifteen years and over cared for in children's wards. Currently, interest is being expressed about the lack of adequate hospital services for adolescents.

Table 2-18. Number of Children Attending Local Health Authority Child Welfare Centers

Year	Aged Under 1 Year #	Aged Under 1 Year %	Aged 1-2 Years #	Aged 1-2 Years %	Aged 2-5 Years #	Aged 2-5 Years %	Total	% of Population Under 5 Years
1951							1,369,043	36.8
1956	461,774	66.1	378,106	56.9	481,420	17.8	1,321,270	40.1
1961	568,565	70.7	485,373	62.1	564,142	19.4	1,618,080	44.1
1962	594,033	70.7	497,822	61.9	556,486	18.6	1,648,341	43.6
1963	622,352	72.7	527,721	62.8	560,344	18.2	1,710,417	43.9
1964	653,521	74.6	574,950	67.4	628,650	19.8	1,857,121	46.3
1965	660,346	76.7	609,417	69.6	678,468	20.7	1,948,231	47.4
1970	582,263	73.1	530,402		652,672		1,765,337	
1971	610,201	81.4	542,405		645,897		1,798,503	

Source: Ministry of Health, *Child Welfare Centers* (London:HMSO, 1967).

Table 2-19. Local Authority Child Health Services Clinical
Medical Staff—1967

Service	Full-time Local Authority	Part-time Local Authority	Part-time GP's
Mainly infant and preschool	734	774	1,198
Mainly school	865	526	491
Totals	1,599	975	1,689

Source: D. Court and A. Jackson, *Paediatrics in the Seventies* (London: Oxford University Press, 1972).

There has been interest in encouraging hospital visiting of children without restriction. Special facilities are provided to make it possible for a parent to stay in the hospital while the child is hospitalized.

Dental Health Service

The number of dentists providing general dental services in England in 1971 was 10,527. At present 3½ million people (5 percent of the population) have fluoridated water. There is little use of topical application of fluoride.

Throughout the general dental service, patients are provided with all forms of treatment which the dentist deems necessary. Dentists may take private patients as well as National Health Service patients. Dentists providing treatment in their office as part of the National Health Service are paid on a prescribed scale of fees, which are only partly covered by charges to patients. Unless they are exempt, the patient must pay half the cost of any treatment up to a maximum of £10 ($25) for a course of treatment. The following persons are entitled to exemptions from all charges: Expectant mothers or those who have had a child in the preceding twelve months; children under sixteen; youth under twenty-one and still in full-time schooling; others under twenty-one are exempt from all charges, except for the supply and modification of dentures or bridges. Most dental treatment may be given without further review; however, extensive and prolonged treatment of gums, some dentures, crowns, and inlays, and special appliances and oral surgery may be given only with the approval of the Dental Estimates Board.

The Dental Program In The School Health Service. There is a small dental staff (4) at the national level, and locally there are 1,500 school dentists. The school dental service is partly paid for by local funds, and partly by the central government.

Annually, of about eight million school children, 4½ million are inspected; 2½ million need dental treatment, and 1.3 million receive it. In addition, outside of the school dental service, children receive six million dental treatments from the general dental service of the National Health Service.

In 1965, a dental survey of a sample of 15,000 fifteen-year-old youth in England and Wales revealed the following:

	D1	*D2*	*M*	*F*	*DMF*
Boys	4.2	0.4	1.7	3.5	9.8
Girls	3.8	0.4	1.9	4.4	10.5
Boys and Girls	4.0	0.4	1.8	4.0	10.1

D1–Requiring filling   M–Missing
D2–Requiring extraction   F –Filled

Two-thirds of the youth had received treatment from the National Health Service, one-quarter from the school dental service. About 2 percent had received no previous treatment.

In 1970, 22,804 began orthodontia care and 18,790 completed it.

Battered Babies

This represents an increasing problem in the United Kingdom, and was the subject of a national report in 1970 [11d].

A study of seventy-eight battered children by the National Society of Prevention of Cruelty to Children in 1969 in the United Kingdom revealed that most incidents occurred at home, and involved parents or guardians. The younger the child, the more likely he is to be harmed, and the more severe the injury. More boys tend to be involved than girls. There was a higher than expected incidence in children who were of low birth weight. The adults were mostly between 20-30 years of age, married, more females than males, and in many instances the women were pregnant or recently confined at the time of infliction of the injuries. Many of the adults who injure children were found to have long standing emotional or social problems.

For 1967, a total of 71 cases were reported to the Registrar General. In addition, in a study of 679 postneonatal deaths, six infants died as a result of proven willful violence.

As a result, efforts have been made at the national level to stimulate the development of local committees (composed of representatives of the fields of health and social welfare) to review the situation in their local areas and to make plans. In most local areas, a case committee was set up to make contact with the child and his family, to coordinate the work of the various people involved, and to plan for long-term care. A second committee was set up to plan local policy and to cooperate with adjacent areas.

It is recognized that more preventive efforts are needed, on the part of local health and social welfare departments. This includes the provision of supportive services to the parents, the early identification of parents likely to experience unusual difficulties in child rearing, and more research in identification techniques. One important decision is the place of care of the child—whether he should be returned home, the timing of such return, alternate places of care. The need is recognized for diagnosis of the family situation and for mental health services. Some local communities have set up and use registers.

Day Care of Children

In 1948, legislation was enacted to make day care avilable for everyone. During World War II, there was considerable increase in day care of children. This declined subsequently, and is about to increase due to expansion of preschool education. It is estimated that 12 percent of preschool children receive some form of day care. Day care of children is the responsibility of the social service department of the local authority.

A new £34 million ($85 million) building program will provide at least 70,000 new places in nursery schools and classes attached to primary schools. This is the first step to provide part time nursery education for 35 percent of three-year olds, 75 percent of four-year olds, and full-time nursery education for 15 percent of both age groups. In general, the plan is for each local authority to concentrate the services in districts of special need.

Special Benefits [11g]

Family Allowances. These are cash payments, for the benefit of the family as a whole, to families with more than one child under sixteen years of age, and during any period up to nineteen years if a child is attending an educational institution fulltime. The family receives 90 pence a week (about $2.25) where there are two children, with a further £1 (100 pence or $2.50) a week for each additional child.

Family Income Supplement. This is payment of up to £5 a week ($12.50) to families whose normal gross weekly income is less than an amount prescribed by Parliament. Anyone can claim this, if he or she is in full-time work.

Welfare Milk and Vitamins. In families where there are two or more children under five years one month of age, one pint of milk a day is obtainable free of charge for expectant mothers and all but the first two children under school age. One pint of milk a day is also available free of charge for expectant mothers and all children under school age in families in special need, and for handicapped children 5-16 years of age. Children under five years one month attending an approval day nursery or play group are entitled to 1/3 of a pint free on each day they attend. Anyone whose family is entitled to free milk on the basis of income is also entitled to free vitamins; this applies to expectant and nursing mothers and children under school age.

Maternity Grant. There is a maternity grant of £25 ($62.50) provided. It may be paid on either the mother's own insurance or her husband's, but not on both.

Maternity Allowance. There is a maternity allowance of £6.75 ($16.87) a week for eighteen weeks, starting eleven weeks before the expected date of delivery. This is payable only to women who are or have been employed or self-employed and have been paying full flat-rate national insurance contributions.

Longitudinal Studies of Growth and Development

There have been two national longitudinal follow-up studies of maternity care and of growth and development of children and youth. In addition a third beginning study is under way.

Year Begun	Senior Investigator	Status
1946	J.W.B. Douglas	Continuing. Group is now 27 years old. Studying reproduction patterns of the adults, and their children.
1958	N. Butler	Completed the perinatal, 7-year-old, and 11-year-old groups.
	National Childrens Bureau	Planning for the 16-year-old group.
1970	Chamberlain	Study at 22 and 36 months of age.

The 1946 Douglas Study. This study began as a study of maternity care in the United Kingdom. Four major books have been published [12, 13, 14, 15]. This study has had considerable effect on maternity care in the United Kingdom and some effect on the care of children and youth. From the report "All Our Future" [14], significant findings at ages thirteen and fifteen years were as follows. (1) Teacher ratings of pupils for nervousness and aggression were found to be similar to parental ratings; those with high aggression ratings had a large number of accidents; (2) Those with high ratings for nervousness or aggression do less well on test scores for intelligence; (3) Those identified as nervous work hard and are well behaved; those as aggressive are more troublesome, neglect their studies, and are likely to be truant; (4) Those with stammering, nail biting, vomiting, abdominal pain, bed wetting, and thumb sucking are more likely to have negative attitudes towards school, be absent from school, have episodes of truancy, be reported as poor workers, and be less well behaved; (5) Delinquent boys were poor students, bored, inattentive, badly behaved, with a history of truancy, and more likely from manual working-class families, their parents take less interest in their school and are willing for them to leave school at the earliest opportunity; they are more likely to come from broken homes; the primary school records show that they were poor workers, lazy, had difficulty in concentration, or were difficult to discipline; (6) Those from larger families did less well on test scores; (7) Menarche was earlier among daughters of the well-to-do; (8) Absence from school is associated with poor performance; (9) Even severe illness had little effect on school progress.

This study is continuing. They are adding about 150 babies a year as offspring of the original study group. In this phase, they are collecting data on family size, unwanted pregnancy, family planning, premarital conception, birth spacing, childrearing and accidents.

The 1958 Butler-National Childrens Bureau Study. This study originally began as a study of perinatal mortality and morbidity. Four major books have been published [7, 8, 10, 17]. The perinatal phase has had considerable impact on maternity and perinatal care.

Among the major findings at seven years of age were: (1) There is a marked difference in the children from different social classes and circumstances; (2) There is need to enrich the preschool years and to continue this during the school years, for the culturally underprivileged or deprived child; (3) Children from unskilled working class families were least likely to use community health services; (4) These children are relatively poorly adjusted in school, their dental health is poor, and they show signs of delayed development (bladder control, speech, and physical coordination); their educational standard is low; their parents are not interested to seek a discussion with the teacher.

Plans are now under way for a study of the sixteen year olds. This will include: (1) A physical examination; (2) Psychological tests; (3) Personal questionnaire to be filled out by the youth; (4) Parent interview; (5) School questionnaire. Content areas are attitudes towards sex, drugs, alcohol, smoking, school, discipline; aspirations and expectations; interest in leisure time and marriage; relations with parents; housing; parental and home environment, education, and income.

Also included are special studies of certain groups; e.g., the adopted, the handicapped, the delinquents, the illegitimate, those in special care, the gifted, the socially mobile, the geographically mobile, those of one-parent families.

The 1970 Chamberlain Study. This is a study of children at twenty-two and thirty-six months of age. A 10 percent sample is being followed, which includes those small-for-dates, those below the 5th percentile, those over forty-two weeks gestation, and all twins. Among the questions to be answered are: (1) Did fetal malnutrition affect development? (2) Is there a relationship between head circumference and development?

SCHOOL HEALTH

Organization of Service

The Department of Education and Science has been responsible centrally for the school health service. Responsibility was transferred to the Department of Health and Social Security in April 1974, upon reorganization of the National Health Service.

Locally, the responsibility for school health services has been the responsibility of the local education authorities. This was transferred to the local health authorities in April 1974, upon reorganization of the National Health Service.

There are currently eight physicians employed full time centrally in the school health service, and in England approximately 2,300 physicians locally. In addition, in England there are approximately 800 general practitioners working part time in the school health services. There are over 6,000 health visitors, almost 3,000 nurses, almost 700 nurses' assistants, almost 600 speech therapists, 150 audiometricians, and 350 physical therapists employed in the local school health services. There are also 100 psychiatrists, almost 600 educational psychologists, almost 300 psychiatric social workers, 200 social workers, almost 600 remedial teachers, and about 100 psychotherapists employed in child guidance clinics and school psychological services.

Medical Examinations of Pupils

The Education Act of 1944 required the local education authorities to make arrangements for the compulsory medical inspection of pupils and for comprehensive free medical treatment under that Act or otherwise. With the enactment of the National Health Service in 1948 there has been increasing use of it for the treatment of school children.

The policy of routine or selective health examinations of pupils has undergone modification since 1944. Originally local education authorities had the policy of routine examination at specific times—after entry to school, in the last year of attendance at primary school, and during the last year in secondary school. Many authorities had arranged an additional examination on transfer to junior high school. By 1969, this original schedule had been modified by at least seventy-two local education authorities; they largely provide an examination on entrance to school; selective examinations upon referral during the school years; and frequently examination of school leavers (now sixteen years of age). Data on health problems found are shown in Tables 2-20 and 2-21.

Approximately 10 percent of pupils aged 14-16 plus years examined

Table 2-20. Prevalence of Certain Defects Requiring Treatment
Per 1,000 Pupils Examined, England and Wales—1968

	Entrance Exam	*Intermediate Exam*	*Leaver Exam*	*Special Exam*
Eyes	50.4	90.8	96.5	85.2
Nose and Throat	21.2	11.2	6.2	16.5
Orthopedic	17.8	18.3	14.3	18.4
Ears	19.4	14.1	7.7	34.4
Skin	12.4	18.2	21.9	96.8
Speech	9.7	4.6	1.1	8.5
Psychological	5.9	13.5	5.1	23.9
Sub-Total	136.8	170.7	152.8	283.7
Neurological	2.6	3.7	2.3	4.4
Developmental	6.0	7.1	3.8	5.6
Lungs	7.4	5.9	3.5	5.3
Heart	2.5	2.0	1.6	1.9
All other	10.8	13.6	9.1	79.3
Total defects per 1,000 children examined	166.1	203.0	173.1	380.2

Source: Report of the Chief Medical Officer of the Department of Education and Science, *The Health of the School Child* (London: HMSO, 1972).

by the school health service in 1968 were found to have health defects, using data from either routine or selective examinations (Table 2-22).

Findings recorded at various medical examinations show that the yield of defects (304 per 1,000 pupils) among pupils aged 7-13 years selected for examination is more than twice as great as that from routine examinations (143 per 1,000 pupils) (Tables 2-20 and 2-22).

More recent problems among school pupils—learning difficulties, psychiatric disorders, problems associated with puberty and adolescence (e.g. serious academic failure, behavior difficulties, pregnancy, delinquency, drug addiction, venereal disease) are reported to be largely missed by the school health service, until they reach crisis point.

The school health program is currently following a pattern of surveillance as follows:

1. Entrance medical examinations
2. Follow-up visits to the schools by the doctor
3. Subsequent medical examinations on request
4. Periodic parent questionnaire

Table 2-21.   Principal Disorders of Health and Development in School Children 1967-68—England and Wales

	Deaths (1968) Children		Hospital Admissions		Defects and Chronic Hand. Disorders (1968). Routine Med. Exams—Children	
	5-9 Years	10-14 Years	5-9 Years	10-14 Years	5-7 Years	8-14 Years
Percentage of Total Due to						
Accidents	37.0	36.2	12.9	18.5		
Malignant Diseases	19.2	18.7	0.8	1.9		
	56.2%	54.9%	13.7%	20.4%		
Infectious Diseases	3.5	2.9	4.4	4.3		
Bronchitis and Pneumonia	7.1	7.0	1.8	1.1		
Other Pulmonary Diseases	1.5	1.5	3.6	3.2	4.4	2.5
Asthma	1.3	3.7	1.2	1.9		
Diabetes	0.7	1.4	0.4	1.1		
Renal Disease	1.5	1.8	1.6	1.9		
Rheumatic Fever & Heart Dis.	1.1	2.7	0.2	0.7		
Congenital Heart Disease	7.3	4.5	0.6	0.6	1.5	1.0
Spina Bifida	1.2	0.7	0.1	0.1		
Other Congenital Anomalies	3.1	2.3	3.3	5.6	4.4	2.8
Musculo-Skeletal Disorders	0.4	0.5	1.8	4.8		
Cerebral Palsy	1.3	2.0	0.1	0.2	11.0	8.6
Epilepsy	1.5	2.1	0.5	0.9	0.6	0.8
Acute Upper Resp. Dis.	1.0	0.4	3.5	1.5		

	C1	C2	C3	C4	C5	C6
Hypertrophy T & A	0.2		32.9	12.6	12.6	4.5
Inf. of Ear & Mastoid	0.4	0.5	5.8	3.2	3.0	1.3
	89.3%	88.9%	75.5%	64.1%	37.5%	21.5%
Deafness			1.2	2.1	7.0	3.3
Squint			3.9	1.7	8.7	3.4
Refractive Errors					20.0	46.0
Speech Defect					5.7	1.4
Skin Disease			1.3	2.8	7.6	10.8
Nutritional Disorders			0.2	0.3	Data not available	Data not available
	89.4%	89.1%	82.1%	71.0%	86.5%	86.4%
Syphilis & Gonorrhea					Data not available	Data not available
Illegitimate Births & Abortions				43 girls		
Psychiatric Disorder		4 suicides	0.3	0.6		
Mental Retardation					3.4	4.8
Educational Retardation		0.3			Data not available	Data not available
	89.6%	89.6%	82.4%	71.9%	89.9%	91.2%
Miscellaneous	10.4	10.4	17.6	28.1	10.1	8.8
Total	100.0%	100.0%	100.0%	100.0%	100.0%	100.0%

Source: Report of the Chief Medical Officer of the Department of Education and Science, *The Health of the School Child* (London: HMSO, 1972).

**Table 2-22. Total Yield of Defects (Excluding Visual)
Requiring Treatment Per 1,000 Pupils Examined at Various Ages
England and Wales—1968—Leaver Examinations (14-16 plus years)**

	Per 1,000 Pupils Examined
1. In England and Wales	82
All LEA's, whether using routine or selective examinations	
2. In 35 LEA's applying selective examinations	102
3. In 6 LEA's applying selective examinations	
Newcastle	105
Plymouth	114
Stockport	87
West Bromwich	19
Hampshire	143
Northamptonshire	23

Source: Report of the Chief Medical Officer of the Department of Education and Science, *The Health of the School Child* (London: HMSO, 1972).
Note: LEA=Local education authority

5. Periodic screening procedures
    a. Vision—annually or every other year
    b. Hearing—at ages of 7, 10, and 13
    c. Measurement of height and weight
    d. Survey of feet and back, of skin and of hygiene—not less frequently than every three years (7, 10 and 13 years)
    e. Cleanliness survey
6. Advisory service for adolescents

Sex Education

The schools conduct an educational program for pupils, covering such topics as personal hygiene, personal responsibility, personal relationships, stability in marriage, menstruation, pregnancy, birth of the baby, baby care, venereal disease, smoking, drugs, and some information about contraception. This is done by health visitors. The whole question of sex education is interpreted as being difficult in the United Kingdom, and has encountered mixed parental reactions, including criticism. The present national government was described as being cautious in regard to the subject of sex education in the schools.

HANDICAPPED CHILDREN

Introduction
The care of handicapped children has received considerable emphasis in the United Kingdom by the national Department of Health and Social Security, and by the national Department of Education and Science. Among those areas receiving special emphasis recently are efforts to improve early case finding, the development of regional and district assessment centers, and studies of handicapped youth.

Case Finding of Handicapped Children
There have been specific planned efforts to identify handicapped children early. These have included the following.

Screening of the Total Infant Population. Included in this screening for phenylketonuria at the age of 6-14 days of age, through the home visit of a health visitor; about 80 percent of live births are covered by this. Another planned step consists of screening of response to sound of infants seen in child welfare centers at 8-12 months of age. In child welfare centers, children are screened for hearing and speech defects at 3-3½ years. In the year 1971, 81.4 percent of all infants under one year of age were seen in child welfare centers; the proportion of children aged 1-2 years seen in child welfare centers is 70 percent, and of children aged 2-5 years is approximately 21 percent.

Special Examination of the Total Infant Population. Included in this is an effort to carefully examine the newborn population. This examination pays special attention to the hip joint in an effort to identify congenital dislocation of the hip. Approximately 90 percent of all live births now occur in hospitals in the United Kingdom. There is an examination carried out at 4-12 weeks of age for instability of hip joints in infants seen in child welfare centers. Developmental assessment of children seen in child welfare centers is done at 8-12 months, 24-30 months, and 36-42 months. Examination is done on all children prior to entrance to school at 4-5 years of age.

General Observation and Examination of Selected Infants. This is planned to observe and examine more closely certain groups of infants of high risk, including those with a history of adverse factors during gestation or early life; those with suspected deprivation, illness, or maternal anxiety; and those of disadvantaged socioeconomic conditions.

Follow-up of Infants. This consists of a follow-up of those who have survived severe neonatal problems. Included in this is follow-up of infants weighing 1360 grams or less at birth.

Comprehensive Assessment and Reassessment. This includes infants with known defects in order to detect multiple abnormalities and secondary disabilities.

Notification of Congenital Malformations
There is a system of voluntary notification of congenital malformations. A special form is filled out at the time of birth and sent to the local medical officer of health. The infant is referred to an assessment center for a comprehensive assessment. The data are transmitted to the office of Population Censuses and Surveys for analysis and surveillance. In 1970, 14,019 babies had 17,293 malformations, a rate of 15.7 per 1,000 live births; 17 percent were reported to have more than one malformation (Tables 2-23 and 2-24).

Operation of Registers
Two types of registers have been in operation by local health authorities. One is a register of handicapped children; this is used as a method of follow-up of handicapped children. The second is a risk register; this latter was judged to be of less value, and it was recommended in 1970 for termination.

Assessment Centers
Seven regional assessment centers already exist for the evaluation, diagnosis, treatment, and rehabilitation of handicapped children. The British Paediatric Association has recently recommended the development of an additional thirteen regional assessment centers [18]. Each regional center would serve a population of about three million. The regional centers are located in connection with medical schools and their teaching hospitals. The regional centers have an interdisciplinary staff; in addition some of the staff of the local health authority attend and participate in the weekly staff conferences of the regional center, when individual children are presented and discussed. The British Paediatric Association has recommended that within each region there will be a number of district centers based in district general hospitals and serving a population of 200,000-400,000.

Development of Guides
Various guides have been developed, published, and distributed by the Department of Health and Social Security, with the assistance of experts in the respective field. The subjects have included Deafness in Early Childhood; Screening for the Detection of Congenital Dislocation of the Hip in Infants; Human Genetics; Care of the Child with Spina Bifida; Congenital Malformations [19a-19d].

Handicapped School Children
Local education authorities are responsible for finding children who

Table 2-23. Notified Congenital Malformations in Live and Stillborn Babies—1968-70—England and Wales

Year	Malform. Notified	Babies Involved	% With One or More Malform.				All babies with Malform. Rate Per 1,000 Total Births	Live Born With Malf.		Stillborn with Malformations #
			1	*2*	*3*	*4 or more*		*#*	*Rate per 1,000 Live Births*	
1968	16,613	13,954	86.7	9.7	2.4	1.2	16.8	12,071	14.7	1,883
1969	17,270	13,959	82.5	13.2	3.0	1.3	17.3	12,106	15.2	1,853
1970	17,293	14,019	82.9	13.2	2.8	1.1	17.6	12,285	15.7	1,734

Source: Department of Health and Social Security, *On the State of the Public Health* (London, HMSO, 1972).

Table 2-24.   Babies with Specific Malformations Notified in England and Wales—1967-1970 (Rate Per 10,000 Live and Stillbirths)

Malformation Group	1967	1968	1969	1970
Anencephalus	14.8	13.8	13.8	14.3
Spina bifida, hydrocephalus, or both	25.1	24.8	30.5	28.4
Cleft palate or lip, or both	13.9	14.1	14.0	13.9
Talipes	37.0	35.7	38.6	34.7
Congenital Dislocation of Hip	6.6	7.6	9.7	10.3
Exomphalos, omphalocele	2.9	2.8	2.2	2.7
Mongolism	7.3	7.8	6.7	7.3
Other malformations of the musculo-skeletal system			1.8	2.7
Pigmented Naevus			3.6	4.6
Other specified skin malformations			2.1	2.6
Multiple Congenital Malformations			1.7	1.9
Unspecified Congenital Malformations			1.9	3.0

Source: Department of Health and Social Security, On the State of the Public Health (London: HMSO, 1972).

require special education because of physical, emotional, or cognitive handicaps. These children are examined by the school health service.

Special education may be provided in ordinary schools, special schools, in hospitals, or at home. In 1971 there were 116,677 handicapped children receiving special education in a variety of settings [23] (Tables 2-25 and 2-26).

Services for the Mentally Retarded

During 1971, a report was published on Better Services for the Mentally Handicapped. This recommended a more rapid shift of care of the mentally retarded from hospitals to community centers. It recommended that mentally retarded individuals be cared for in residential homes, schools, and adult training centers. A new policy was recommended of limiting hospital facilities to 500 beds, and to locate them near the community to be served. Other recommendations include linking the facility for the mentally retarded with a district general hospital, and that it be part of a comprehensive district service [19f].

Studies of Handicapped Youth

The following two recent studies of handicapped 15-year olds have been made.

Table 2-25. Survey of Physically Handicapped Children in
Ordinary Schools, England—1969-70

Disability	Nursery	Primary School	Secondary Schools	Total
Limbs, including clubfoot and dislocation of hip	11	1,675	702	2,388
Heart defects—rheumatic or congenital	5	1,435	671	2,111
Cerebral palsy	15	1,005	442	1,462
Spina bifida	5	598	186	789
Post poliomyelitis		140	392	532
Perthes disease		344	112	456
Muscular dystrophy and atrophy	2	189	73	264
Achondroplasia and other forms of dwarfing	3	184	66	253
Hydrocephalus	2	210	34	246
Hemophilia		152	92	244
Scoliosis	3	126	97	226
Amputations		109	95	204
Rheumatoid arthritis		103	96	199
Osteomyelitis		52	41	93
Fragilitas ossium		44	22	66
Tuberculosis of bones and joints		11	15	26
Others	7	930	588	1,495
Total	53	7,307	3,694	11,054

Source: Report of the Chief Medical Officer of the Department of Education and Science, *The Health of the School Child 1969-1970* (London: HMSO, 1972).

Study of Handicapped School Leavers in Special Schools. There are about 220,000 children receiving special education in England and Wales (2½ percent of the total number of children of school age). There were 888 special schools known to the Department of Education and Science, of which 619 cooperated in a special study of 7,094 fifteen year olds about to leave school.

A sample of 1,700 was studied [24]. The study consisted of a questionnaire on each youth filled out by the teacher. An interview was held eighteen months later, with the handicapped youth, his parents, and his employer, where applicable; 788 were completed (at interview).

Half of the total group were rated by their teachers as severely or markedly handicapped. One-third were multiply handicapped. Mostly the handicapped began before the age of three years. Most of the blind, epileptic, and maladjusted were boarders; the other groups were day students.

Table 2-26.   Handicapped Pupils Requiring and Receiving Education in Special Schools, Independent Schools, in Special Classes and Units, and Boarded in Homes—January 1971

	Blind	Part. Sight.	Deaf	Part. Hear.	Phys. Handi.	Delicate	Maladjusted	Epileptic	Speech Defects	Educa. Sub-N.	Total
A. Requiring places in special schools											
DAY	5	76	56	131	425	254	242	6	30	8,235	9,460
BOARDING	86	142	65	73	316	425	1,623	47	63	1,879	4,719
B. On registers of maintained special schools											
DAY	21	1,232	1,552	1,036	6,350	4,246	2,243	171	128	47,677	64,656
BOARDING	220	393	541	392	1,217	1,931	2,337	101	35	7,888	15,055
C. On registers of non-maintained special schools											
DAY	30	33	206	63	386	1	5	–	3	306	933
BOARDING	847	422	1,271	494	1,199	695	981	472	90	1,186	7,657
D. On registers of independent schools	5	14	220	118	464	172	3,024	8	21	609	4,655
E. Boarded in homes	1	–	4	–	11	112	685	3	–	18	834
F. Being educated in											
HOSPITALS	1	1	1	3	284	177	266	4	1	31	769
OTHER GROUPS	3	4	11	11	355	40	605	10	2	82	1,123
HOMES	13	32	11	9	922	256	449	37	6	215	1,950
G. Being educated in special classes or units	–	73	–	2,324	288	167	2,074	–	–	–	4,866
H. TOTAL	1,232	2,422	3,938	4,654	12,057	8,476	14,534	859	379	68,126	116,677

Source: Report of the Chief Medical Officer of the Department of Education and Science, *The Health of the School Child 1969-1970* (London: HMSO, 1972).

Four-fifths were considered suitable for further education and for training; of this number, about one-third received it. Only 7 percent had attended industrial rehabilitation units or assessment centers. Seventy-six percent had ever worked; of those who had worked, over 20 percent had been unemployed for more than six months. Thirteen percent had been at home continuously since leaving school.

Recommendations were made concerning responsibility for their care, and the need for work experience courses closely identified with industry, need for further education and training, and need for improvement in transport and building design.

Survey of Fifteen-Year-Old Pupils in School for the Deaf–1969-1970. Thirty-five schools for the deaf were approached; five had no pupils aged fifteen years; of the other thirty schools, twenty were visited and 167 pupils were interviewed; of the 167, 62 were day pupils, and 105 were boarders. For the other ten schools, teachers provided information on 51 children, making a total of 218 youth in the age range surveyed [23].

Hearing Loss. All of the youth surveyed had a bilateral hearing loss. Twenty-four of the 167 youth had a hearing loss of less than 60 decibels.

Causes of Deafness. There was a marked increase in the causes due to perinatal conditions in youth in 1969-1970, compared with 1962-63 (16.2 percent compared with 1.4 percent), and a marked decrease due to infections (7.8 percent compared with 24.5 percent).

Additional Handicaps. In the survey, 59.3 percent of the youth had additional handicaps. Of this group, 15.0 percent were vision; 13.8 percent were social; and 13.2 percent were maladjustment.

Ability to Communicate Speech. In the survey, 38.9 percent had intelligible speech; 44.9 percent had partly intelligible speech; and 16.2 percent had no intelligible speech.

REFERENCES

Maternal Health, Family Planning, and Abortion

1. Cartwright, A. and Waite, M. "General Practitioners and Contraception in 1970-71." *Journal of the Royal College of General Practitioners.* Supplement Number 2, Vol. 22 (1972): 1-31.
2. Department of Health and Social Security
   a. *Report on Confidential Enquiries into Maternal Deaths in England and Wales 1967-1969.* London: HMSO, 1972.
   b. Standing Maternity and Midwifery Advisory Committee. *Domiciliary Midwifery and Maternity Bed Needs.* London: HMSO, 1970.
   c. *On the State of the Public Health.* The Annual Report of the Chief Medical Officer of the Department of Health and Social Security for the Year 1971. London: HMSO, 1972.

    d. *Annual Report.* 1971. London: HMSO, 1972.

    e. *Family Benefits and Pensions.* London: HMSO, 1972.

3. The Family Planning Association. 41st Report and Accounts 1972-73. Southwick Sussex: Grange Press.

4. Lambert, J. "Survey of 3,000 Unwanted Pregnancies." *British Medical Journal* 4 (Oct. 16, 1971): 156-160.

5. Milton, R. "Some Area Variations in Birth Control Services." *Community Medicine*, Dec. 8, 1972.

6. Waite, M. "Domiciliary Midwives and Birth Control Advice, 1970/71." *The Nursing Times*, Part 1—Dec. 7, 1972; Part 2—Dec. 14, 1972.

Child Health

7. Butler, N. and Alberman, E.D. *Perinatal Problems.* London: E & S Livingston Ltd., 1969.

8. Butler, N. and Bonham, D.G. *Perinatal Mortality.* London: E & S Livingstone Ltd., 1963.

9. Court, D. and Jackson, A. *Paediatrics in the Seventies.* London: Oxford University Press, 1972.

10. Davie, R.; Butler, N.; and Goldstein, H. *From Birth to Seven.* London: Longman, 1972.

11. Department of Health and Social Security. London: Her Majesty's Stationery Office.

    a. *Care of the Child With Spina Bifida.* 1973.

    b. *Screening for the Detection of Congenital Dislocation of the Hip in Infants.* 1969.

    c. *Human Genetics.* 1972.

    d. *The Battered Baby.* 1971.

    e. *Confidential Enquiry into Postneonatal Deaths. 1944-66.* 1970.

    f. *On the State of the Public Health.* The Annual Report of the Chief Medical Officer of the Department of Health and Social Security for the Year 1971. 1972.

    g. *Family Benefits and Pensions.* 1972.

    h. *Report of the Expert Group on Special Care for Babies.* 1971.

    i. *Report of the Working Group on Risk Registers.* July 1970. Mimeographed.

12. Douglas, J.W.B. *The Home and the School.* London: Panther Books Limited, 1967.

13. Douglas, J.W.B. and Bloomfield, J.M. *Children Under Five.* London: George Allen and Unwin Ltd., 1958.

14. Douglas, J.W.B.; Ross, J.M.; and Simpson, H.R. *All Our Future.* London: Panther Books Limited, 1968.

15. Douglas, J.W.B. and Rowntree, G. *Maternity in Great Britain.* London: Oxford University Press, 1948.

16. Ministry of Health. London: Her Majesty's Stationery Office.

    a. *Congenital Malformations.* 1963.

    b. *Haemolytic Disease of the Newborn.* 1962.

    c. *Child Welfare Centers.* 1967.

　　d. *Enquiry into Sudden Death in Infancy.* 1965.
17. Pringle, M.; Butler, N.; and Davie, R. *11,000 Seven Year Olds.* London: Longman, 1966.

Handicapped Children
18. Court, D. and Jackson, A. *Paediatrics in the Seventies.* London: Oxford University Press, 1972.
19. Department of Health and Social Security. London: HMSO.
　　a. *Care of the Child with Spina Bifida.* 1973.
　　b. *Screening for the Detection of Congenital Dislocation of the Hip in Infants.* 1969.
　　c. *Human Genetics.* 1972.
　　d. *Deafness in Early Childhood.* 1971.
　　e. *Better Services for the Mentally Handicapped.* 1971.
20. Department of Health and Social Security. *Report of the Working Group on Risk Registers.* London, July 1970. Mimeographed.
21. Kushlick, A. Personal conference. July 11, 973.
22. Ministry of Health. *Congenital Malformations.* London: Her Majesty's Stationery Office, 1963.
23. Report of the Chief Medical Office of the Department of Education and Science. *The Health of the School Child 1969-1970.* London: HMSO, 1972.
24. Tuckey, L.; Parfit, J.; and Tucket, B. *Handicapped School-Leavers.* London: NFER Publishing Company, Ltd., 1973.

Chapter 3

Child Health Services in the United Kingdom— Present and Future

Ross G. Mitchell

INTRODUCTION

The personal services in the United Kingdom have evolved gradually over many years, often in response to demand or the urgency of immediate events rather than as a planned development. This pattern of growth, almost haphazard at times, accounts for the complex and fragmented nature of the present services for children and for the pressures which have built up in recent years to reorganize them on a more rational basis. The outcome of the current ferment of thought and planning for the future will influence the lives of children and the work of doctors and other health workers for many years ahead. This chapter presents a brief account of the past and present services and the forces shaping those to come.

To understand what is happening it is necessary to know something of the way in which the United Kingdom is organized and governed. It consists of four countries—England, Scotland, and Wales (collectively known as Great Britain) and Northern Ireland. Despite the fact that the kingdom has been united under the monarchy for hundreds of years, each of its constituent parts retains its own historical and cultural identity, accentuated by differences of speech and in some cases language (as between Wales and England) and by ethnic differences, although intermarriage and migration have made race a less real basis for distinction than cultural variation. Scotland and England have separate legal systems, Scots law being based on Roman law and English on Anglo-Saxon common law, so that new developments often require different legal measures in the two countries.

Parliament in Westminster has responsibility for the whole United Kingdom, but there is some devolution of government to the four capitals—

London, Edinburgh, Cardiff, and Belfast—the pattern differing in each case. At present there is considerable pressure in Scotland and Wales to transfer more power from the Westminster parliament to Edinburgh and Cardiff, while the unsettled political situation in Northern Ireland is likely to result in a new relationship between Westminster and Belfast in the future.

While the pattern of central government is thus complex, there is a strong movement to disperse power still further to regions within the countries of the United Kingdom. Historically there has always been division of administration between local and central government, the general term "local government" including a wide variety of administrative authorities ranging from councils of large cities like Birmingham or Glasgow to those responsible for small towns or rural counties. The administrative structure is at present being reorganized on the basis of much bigger regional authorities, and in consequence many of the smaller units have disappeared. It is against this intricate and changing background of national and local government that the health services for children must be viewed.

DEVELOPMENT OF HEALTH SERVICES
FOR CHILDREN

Until the latter half of the nineteenth century, there was little organized provision for children and most of the services available depended on voluntary effort and religious and philanthropic institutions [4]. In 1870 public demand, stimulated by an awakening social conscience, led to the introduction of compulsory education for all children and this revealed the extent to which they were ill-nourished and diseased. The Infant Life Protection Act of 1872 was the first of a series of legislative measures designed to safeguard the lives and health of children, while in 1884 an association to promote school hygiene was founded. Despite these advances, there was little real progress towards the provision of child health services on a national scale until early in the present century.

It is a strange paradox that successive wars have been largely responsible for revealing deficiencies in child care and thus expediting the statutory provision of services. The poor physical state of recruits in the South African War (1899-1902) was a major factor in persuading the government to improve the quality of child life by a series of measures culminating in the so-called "Children's Charter" of 1907-08. This comprised a number of Acts of Parliament, which among other provisions authorized local authorities to provide meals for school children, created a school medical service, and set up juvenile courts.

The widespread employment of women in factories during the First World War exposed the inadequacy of arrangements for caring for pregnant women and young infants. At the end of the war, the Maternity and Child

Welfare Act (1918) gave local authorities power to organize schemes for the care of expectant mothers and of children under five years of age. The National Council for the Unmarried Mother and Her Child was also founded in 1918 and the first Act of Parliament regulating the adoption of infants and children was passed in 1926.

At the start of the Second World War in 1939, many children were evacuated from cities into the country to protect them from the air raids which were thought to be imminent. This mass exodus revealed the large numbers of children lacking proper care and the absence of any general responsibility for their welfare. The Children's Act of 1948 obliged local authorities to create Children's Committees with executive Children's Officers and laid on them a duty to exercise their powers in the interests of all children requiring care and protection in their areas. Although in some respects these Acts of Parliament have been superseded by subsequent legislation, they are important in that they created the basis of the child care services at present provided by local authorities throughout the United Kingdom.

While the foundations of statutory child care were being laid, health services for children were developing mainly as a result of voluntary endeavor. The medical care of children was, and indeed still is, largely in the hands of family practitioners, who before 1948 were enabled by the "panel system" to treat children of families unable to pay. Nevertheless, many children grew up without adequate health care, despite the employment by local health authorities of Health Visitors in increasing numbers from 1892 onward.

Most of the major children's hospitals were established by private effort between 1850 and 1900: during the first half of the twentieth century they continued to be supported by voluntary subscription. Other hospitals and wards for children were established by local authorities so that in 1948 a child requiring hospital care might go to a voluntary hospital (if there was room), a private nursing home (if his parents could afford it), or a local authority hospital.

In that year the climate of postwar opinion, the rising cost of medical care, and the policies of a socialist government together led to the introduction of the National Health Service. While this was too radical a change for some, and was opposed by many doctors, it did not go as far as to create a unified health service. The hospitals were indeed brought together under Regional Hospital Boards, but many health services for children were left in the hands of local authorities—especially the school medical service and the maternity and child welfare clinics—and family doctors continued to act as independent contractors. Thus the new National Health Service had the tripartite structure which has persisted until 1974. Its achievements in the sphere of child health have been considerable but the provision of pediatric care in three separate ways has been the source of much misunderstanding, duplication of effort, and deficient communication between health workers.

Children's nursing developed with children's hospitals and hospital wards and for years the letters R.S.C.N. (Registered Sick Children's Nurse) were the proudly borne hallmark of a nurse highly skilled in the nursing care of infants and children. The current trend toward a standard basic training for all nurses may be beneficial to the nursing profession as a whole, but it remains to be seen how many such generally trained nurses will later wish to specialize in children's nursing and to what extent young women anxious to nurse children will be diverted to other forms of service by the requirement to nurse adults during a large part of their training. Many who are concerned with the care of children fear that the very high standards achieved in children's hospital nursing in the middle of this century may never again be reached. The shortage of skilled nurses is accelerating the trend toward employing nursing aides, auxiliaries, nursery nurses, and other workers to help care for children under the supervision of registered children's nurses.

A brighter aspect of children's nursing is the growing importance of the Health Visitor, a trained nurse with post-registration qualifications which equip her to provide a continuing service to families in their own homes. The National Health Service Act (1948) made the provision of Health Visiting services obligatory on all local authorities. These services are at present mainly of a supervisory and educational nature, but in the future they may be complemented by practical help in time of need, now given by a separate corps of domiciliary nurses. A good Health Visitor can be very influential in establishing sound patterns of parentcraft and in helping mothers to bring up their children in the best health possible. Health Visitors are usually employed by local authorities but, as family doctors begin to form larger groups practicing from Health Centers, the attachment of Health Visitors to group practices is becoming common. The professional symbiosis of doctor and Health Visitor is helping to raise standards of child health by combining preventive and therapeutic pediatrics in the setting of home and Health Center. The present integration of health services affords the opportunity to create a single unified children's nursing service but whether this desirable development will happen depends on action by the nursing profession itself [5].

THE PATTERN OF MEDICAL CARE FOR CHILDREN 1949-74

During the twenty-five years since the introduction of the National Health Service, the health of children in the United Kingdom has steadily improved. They are now taller and heavier than their predecessors, their chances of dying in childhood have diminished dramatically, and many of the diseases which ravaged them have virtually disappeared. While these great advances are attributable mainly to better socioeconomic conditions and new knowledge about the prevention and control of diseases, the improved standard of care provided under the National Health Service undoubtedly made an important contribution. Because of these and other changes, the needs of 1974 are not those of 1948, and yet throughout this period of twenty-five years there has been little alteration in the pattern of medical services for children, a notable exception being the striking increase in the number of consultant pediatricians from a mere handful in 1948 to nearly 400 today.

The major reorganization which is currently taking place is primarily concerned with the changing roles of doctors in the Health Service and it is therefore necessary to consider how medical services have been provided for children since 1948.

Family Doctors

Family doctors in the United Kingdom provide primary care for people of all ages and there are no pediatric practitioners caring for children alone. While many family doctors are highly experienced in treating sick children, most have had little formal pediatric training and they tend to respond to requests for help, so that their role in preventive pediatrics has hitherto been limited. In the larger centers of population, the building of Health Centers to enable doctors to practice in groups with good facilities, as advocated in the Sheldon Report [1] is making it easier for at least one doctor in each group to concentrate on pediatrics and to maintain closer links with pediatricians than his colleagues are able to do. Such family doctors with a special pediatric interest help to maintain the standard of pediatric practice in the Health Centers, but they do not cease to look after adults as well nor do their colleagues cease to care for children. It is not the intention, therefore, to introduce the primary care pediatrician on the North American model into the National Health Service.

As practice from Health Centers becomes more common, some family doctors are participating to an increasing extent in preventive pediatrics, especially in developmental and other screening procedures for the children in their own practices. This trend is being accelerated by the attachment of Health Visitors and other supporting staff to Health Centers, and by postgraduate education in this field. Nevertheless, on the most optimistic estimate, it will be many years before even a large minority of family doctors assume responsibility for such work, since they are still too few in number and it takes time for established attitudes and practice to change.

Pediatricians

Pediatricians in the United Kingdom are usually consultants who spend most or all of their time in the hospital. To achieve consultant status, a young doctor must pass the examination to become a member of the Royal College of Physicians (M.R.C.P.), undergo a long and arduous program of postgraduate training, and compete for promotion at every level. In recent years there has been additional pressure to specialize within pediatrics, so that there are small but growing numbers of pediatric cardiologists, neurologists, gastro-enterologists and the like. Nevertheless the majority of the consultant pediatricians in this country are practicing general pediatrics in children's departments of district hospitals or in children's hospitals in the main teaching centers.

Local Authority Medical Officers

The former Local Authority Medical Officers, now employed by the new Health Authorities, are responsible for the great bulk of preventive pediatrics in the community, for the preschool and school health services, and for advising on appropriate arrangements for handicapped children. They see preschool children regularly in child health clinics, undertake developmental testing of all infants and young children at set intervals, conduct routine and special examinations of school children, and implement immunization programs. Many have other duties not related to child health and the amount of previous training they have had is very variable, some being very highly qualified and experienced while others have had little or no postgraduate pediatric education.

THE IMPETUS TO CHANGE

Recognition of the need for change in the health services for children and the stimulus to action derived from many sources—increasing professional awareness of the importance of preventive and social aspects of pediatrics; the realization that existing child health services are being used by those who need them least and are not reaching the most vulnerable families; dissatisfaction with the fragmentary nature of the services and the inappropriateness of their tripartite arrangement to present and future requirements for child health; and the growing numbers and professional standing of pediatricians, with consequent increase in their influence both on policymakers and on public opinion.

This tide of feeling has been welling up at a time of far-reaching changes in the structure of many British institutions. The devolution of power from central to regional government and the creation of strong Regional Authorities has already been mentioned. The National Health Service has now been integrated into one unified service, thus ending its inefficient tripartite structure. In the new organization, the hospital and general practitioners services and most of the health functions of the local authorities come together under Regional Health Authorities (Health Boards in Scotland). In general, the regions for which Health Authorities are responsible are virtually the same as those of the Regional Authorities for local government, so that local government and Health Authorities, though separate functional units, will work very closely on matters of mutual concern.

In the past five years, there have been major alterations in the social services [4], so that many of the responsibilities of local authorities for the care of children—residential care, fostering and adoption, support of families and so on–have been gathered together as the function of newly formed Social Service Departments, which have a general remit to provide necessary social support for all members of their community. In Scotland, there has been a bold and imaginative innovation in the approach to juvenile delinquency. Powers have been taken away from the courts, with their retributive and punitive connotations, and placed in the hands of carefully selected panels of ordinary citizens. A Children's Hearing, consisting of three panel members, decides what is best for a child and his family after hearing all about his behavior and background, and makes recommendations designed to help him rather than to punish him [2].

The educational system in Scotland differs from that in the rest of the United Kingdom, but in both systems changes are taking place, particularly in the field of special education. Mental handicap is increasingly being recognized as an educational and social problem and even severely mentally subnormal children, hitherto considered ineducable, are being brought within the educational system. Segregation of the handicapped in large isolated hospitals is giving way to a policy of support within their own community whenever possible, in their families or in small residential homes. Social, educational, and health agencies are working together to achieve these new objectives in a spirit of cooperation which has not always been conspicuous in the past.

In this propitious climate of change, the pressure to improve the child health services has been greatly reinforced. Following much discussion at professional meetings and among individual pediatricians, the British Paediatric Association undertook a detailed review of pediatric services in the United Kingdom and made comprehensive recommendations for future change and development. Their report, published in 1972 under the title "Paediatrics in the Seventies," is a landmark in the history of child health in this country and is already exerting an important influence on government planning for the future [3].

Wales and Northern Ireland, perhaps because they are smaller and more closely-knit than England and Scotland, were the first to redesign their health services. In Northern Ireland, the unified health service and the personal social services, including child care and adoption work, were joined together in 1973 under Health and Social Services Boards, one for each of four geographical areas.

A working party was set up in Scotland in 1971 and two years later produced its report "Towards an Integrated Child Health Service" [7]. While the working party was studying the needs of Scotland, the British Paediatric Association report on "Paediatrics in the Seventies" appeared and the Scottish plans incorporate many of its recommendations. In England, which is by far the largest country in the United Kingdom, a committee to consider the future of the child health services was appointed in 1973, under the chairmanship of Professor Donald Court, president of the British Paediatric Association. It may be expected that this committee will take careful note of "Paediatrics in the

Seventies" and of the Scottish proposals, especially since Professor Court was one of the editors of the former publication. While the eventual report of the Court Committee must not be anticipated, it will be surprising indeed if it differs in anything but detail from the general recommendations made by the British Paediatric Association and incorporated into the Scottish design. The outline of the new Child Health Service which follows is based on the Scottish report, but it is a fair assumption that, at least in principle, it is typical of the new pattern for the United Kingdom as a whole.

THE TASKS OF THE CHILD HEALTH SERVICE

From the outset it was believed essential to design a Child Health Service to meet future requirements without reference to existing resources and only thereafter to consider how the present system should be adapted so that it gradually assumes the new look. As a first step, therefore, an attempt was made to look into the future and define the tasks of the service, bearing in mind the great changes that have taken place in the health of British children in the past twenty-five years and the probability of further improvement. This expectation is based on anticipated advances in medical science, better technology, and a standard of living which is still rising, despite inflation and other ills that beset modern society. While such confidence may well prove unjustified, especially if war, pollution or other disasters should threaten our way of life, it was felt that optimism could be the only basis for designing a health service.

     The major tasks of the new Child Health Service are identified as the promotion of good health in a child population which is basically healthy, well nourished, and subject to comparatively few serious diseases, and the care of the minority of children who are abnormal from birth or early life. The treatment of disease in infancy and childhood will still be important and the aim will be to concentrate pediatric hospital facilities into larger and more efficient units, if possible of 100 or more beds and seldom less than 60, with supportive day care and outpatient services. The widespread establishment of special care units for newborn infants is already helping to raise the standard of neonatal pediatrics and this trend will be intensified. Despite these advances, acute hospital pediatrics will form a relatively small part of the total commitment of the Child Health Service, which will be based on prevention at least as much as on the treatment of disease. The essential unity of pediatrics is emphasized, school health and the care of the handicapped being integral components just as much as pediatric cardiology or neonatology and in no way to be regarded as lesser forms of practice. A necessary step in achieving such unity is to abolish the artificial division between hospital pediatrics, looked on as largely therapeutic, and local authority pediatrics, which has hitherto been almost entirely preventive.

SERVICES FOR HANDICAPPED CHILDREN

Integration of health services for children should make the care of chronically handicapped children easier and more effective. Screening programs for the early detection of disabilities of all kinds have been organized in most areas and are designed to cover the whole infant population. It is hoped that this work will increasingly be undertaken by family doctors and specially trained Health Visitors, but for some time it will be done largely by the former local authority doctors.

In the new Child Health Service, each region will have a major assessment center for handicapped children, fully equipped and staffed by a multi-professional team; less comprehensive centers will be provided at district level, usually based on district general hospitals. At present the health service is perhaps half way along the road to this goal, but the speed of advance is quickening as more assessment centers are established. Progress has often been slow because there is a shortage of pediatricians trained in this field and of other specialists, especially in physiotherapy and psychology.

Treatment recommended during the course of assessment will often be undertaken in the assessment center itself or its related departments. For less common or more complex disabilities, however, specialized treatment centers will be required, sometimes of a residential nature. While a few such centers already exist, most of them established by voluntary agencies, it is hoped that a national plan will be evolved so that all needs can eventually be provided for. At present, knowledge of total requirements and the facilities available is incomplete and there is urgent need for more information.

Children with mental subnormality, the largest group of handicapped children, are receiving increasing attention. Pediatricians now recognize mental handicap as their clinical responsibility and consultant pediatrician posts are being created in hospitals for mentally subnormal children. It is hoped that in the future many more of these children will be cared for at home. For those who must be in the hospital, small units closely associated with the general pediatric wards are considered preferable to large isolated mental subnormality hospitals. The change can only come slowly, as the capacity to provide social support for children and their families at home increases and as new hospital building is undertaken.

The importance of close liaison between health, educational, and social agencies in the management of handicapped children is fully recognized and future developments are planned to increase their integration. These include the setting up by Health Authorities and at national level of multidisciplinary Child Health Programme Committees, to advise on the coordination of health, educational, and social programs for children. The material needs which mean so much to the families of handicapped children can usually be met by social service departments of regional authorities, by government attendance allowances, and more recently through the Family Fund set up by the government to relieve stress on the families of children with severe disabilities of congenital origin. Although nothing can fully compensate parents for having a handicapped child, the new provisions will help to relieve them of at least some of the burden.

DOCTORS IN THE NEW CHILD HEALTH SERVICE

The quality of health care for children depends to a large extent on the abilities and attitudes of the doctors who provide it. Much thought was therefore given in the initial planning to the kinds of medical staff needed in the new Service. Three large groups were identified early—family doctors to undertake primary care, general pediatricians to provide a whole range of pediatric services at an advanced level, and pediatric specialists. These last will work mainly in hospitals, and include pediatricians who are highly skilled in a branch of medical pediatrics, such as cardiology or endocrinology, and also pediatric surgeons, child psychiatrists, otolaryngologists, and others who devote varying amounts of their time to children. In addition, specialists in community medicine will be required to contribute epidemiological skills, provide information and evaluate results, and help to administer the Service.

Adaptation to the new service will mean changes for all participating doctors, both in their attitudes and in the work they do. The transition will be gradual in the case of family doctors and will simply be an acceleration of a trend which has already started. There will be little change in the work of pediatric specialists in the large hospitals, though their numbers and expertise are likely to increase. The consultant general pediatrician will be expected to assume a wider role in pediatrics outside his hospital—undertaking some school and clinic work, providing a consulting service to Health Centers, and participating to a greater extent in the assessment and management of handicapped children. At the same time he will be required to maintain his skill in general hospital pediatrics. This should be less demanding in the future, however, for there will be a greater number of pediatric specialists to share responsibility for the complex case or the application of advanced diagnostic and therapeutic technology.

The greatest challenge is to the former local authority doctors. Initial plans for the reorganization of the health services "emphasized the coordinating and epidemiological responsibilities of specialists in community medicine, the primary care of the family doctor and the secondary and tertiary care of the consultant, but defined no clear role for those doctors previously working in the public health sector whose interests are mainly clinical. Their skill and experience are of the greatest importance in the unified child health service and they must be given a responsible role which gives full scope to their professional competence" [6]. As the new Health Authorities assume the functions previously carried out by local authority Health Departments, these doctors face a choice between specializing in community medicine and so giving up responsibility for individual children, and specializing in pediatrics within the Child Health Service. A large proportion, especially of the younger doctors, have already expressed or are likely to express, preference for the latter course. Because of their varied qualifications and experience, they cannot all become consultant pediatricians at the outset. It is expected that a few will be accorded consultant status on the basis of their considerable experience of preventive medicine and child health and that others will be able to qualify within a short period. Even these will require continuing in-service training in hospital pediatrics, just as the present hospital pediatricians will need further training in aspects of social and preventive pediatrics. Other former local authority doctors who opt for clinical pediatric work and have not the qualifications to become consultants will enter a new grade of appointment in the Child Health Service, which may be known as "Child Health Practitioner" or "Area Pediatrician" although the final title has not yet been approved. This will offer a career to doctors who do not wish to undergo the long training or assume the full responsibilities of the consultant, but who yet wish to practice pediatrics. It will be especially appropriate for part-time or married women doctors but should afford a satisfying whole-time career for both men and women. With further training and experience, it will be possible for these doctors to qualify for consultant status.

For some years at least, these doctors formerly employed by local authorities will continue to be responsible for the bulk of the work they have performed hitherto, viz. developmental screening, school health, and so on. Ultimately there may be enough consultant general pediatricians experienced in educational and preventive pediatrics and a sufficiently large increase in the number of family doctors practicing preventive pediatrics in Health Centers to render unnecessary the continuance of the Child Health Practitioner. That time is probably so far distant, however, that the pattern outlined above is likely to continue for the foreseeable future.

It will be clear then that for some time after the start of the new Child Health Service, many consultants will still work almost entirely in hospitals while others (those formerly in local authority service) will still be working in the schools and clinics. There will be increasing overlap between the two spheres, however, as existing staff work ever more closely together and as new general pediatricians trained in both preventive and therapeutic pediatrics enter the Service. Since the individual consultant will probably always have a greater interest in one aspect of pediatrics than in another, and may apportion his time accordingly, it may be expected that there will eventually be a spectrum of consultant general pediatricians, ranging from some based in hospital with only small outside commitments to others spending most of their time in the school health service and having but limited duties in hospital. It is hoped however that the majority will work in all parts of the community—hospital, clinic, Health Center and Assessment Center alike—and that in this way the goal of unity of pediatric practice will be achieved.

ADMINISTRATION AND THE TRAINING
OF MEDICAL STAFF

The integration of medical work in the reorganized Health Service is facilitated by the new administrative structure, in which all clinicians working in the same specialty are grouped in clinical divisions. Each division coordinates the work of its members, advises the specialist in community medicine who implements the agreed policy of the division, and sends representatives to the general and specialist committees which advise the Health Authority and its executive officers. Thus every doctor who devotes all or most of his time to the Child Health Service is a member of his pediatric division and each Health Authority has a pediatric committee to give advice on pediatric matters. In addition, some members of the pediatric division will be participating in the general medical advisory structure of the Health Service, at local and in some cases at national level. In this way, every doctor working in the Child Health Service has the opportunity of taking part in formulating policy and giving advice.

Those responsible for undergraduate and postgraduate medical education in the universities and colleges are already taking cognizance of the changing structure and roles in the integrated Child Health Service. The undergraduate curriculum is being adapted in most medical schools to lay the foundations for the new requirements: postgraduate programs in pediatrics are being widened to provide a common training in preventive pediatrics and school health as well as in the more traditional hospital practice; and courses have been organized to help existing pediatric and general practitioner staff to adapt to their new roles. In any event, however, the success of the reorganized Child Health Service will depend, in the words of the Scottish report, "on the willingness of doctors who are now employed in hospital and community to work together towards the common objectives" [7].

CONCLUSION

The changing pattern of health in infancy and childhood and the irrelevance of the existing services for children to the tasks that lie ahead constitute a challenge to the health service in the United Kingdom. The sweeping changes at present transforming the administrative structure of government and the health, educational, and social services provide the incentive to construct a new Child Health Service within the unified National Health Service. Such an integrated Service will remove the artificial barriers between preventive and therapeutic pediatrics and offer new opportunities to promote child health and to identify and help vulnerable groups of children as well as to satisfy overt need. With a unified approach it will be possible to determine objectives, plan and implement programs to achieve them and evaluate the results.

REFERENCES

1. *Child Welfare Centres.* London: Central Health Services Council, 1967 ("The Sheldon Report").
2. *Children's Hearings.* Edinburgh: Her Majesty's Staionery Office, 1970.
3. Court, D. and Jackson, A. (eds.). *Paediatrics in the Seventies.* London: Oxford University Press, 1972.
4. Mitchell, R.G. (ed.). *Child Life and Health.* Fifth Edition. London: Churchill, 1970.
5. *Nurses in an Integrated Health Service.* Edinburgh: Her Majesty's Stationery Office, 1972.
6. Report of a Joint Working Party set up by the British Paediatric Association and the Society of Community Medicine to consider the role of doctors in the Child Health Service, 1974.
7. *Towards an Integrated Child Health Service.* Edinburgh: Her Majesty's Stationery Office, 1973.

Chapter 4

Social Pediatrics: Aspect or Attitude?

Fred J.W. Miller

Definition constrains, paradoxically it does not necessarily clarify, and I have never found a definition which suffices to explain "Social Pediatrics." Indeed, in attempting to show what social pediatrics is, how it is provided, and how it is taught, I would rather call it an attitude toward the study of pediatrics when that subject is described as "that branch of medicine which treats of the child and *its development and care*, and of the diseases of children and their treatment," a statement chosen deliberately from an American medical dictionary. [1] For rather than being an aspect or segment of a subject, it is a way of thinking and an approach to a discipline; an approach which can be acquired and used by anyone working with children either as a clinical pediatrician in the community or hospital, as a specialist in preventive medicine, as a research worker or as a policymaker, organizer of medical care, or administrator. It can be applied to any type of activity at local, regional, national or international level.

Need for such an attitude is indeed implicit in the statement given above for it cannot be fulfilled without taking into account not only the biological but also the social, cultural, and economic factors influencing growth and development or therapy and treating the child in his total environment. Social pediatrics, in short, is the study and care of the child in his "ecosystem."[a]

We have four questions to answer: How does attitude affect study, how does it affect planning, how does it affect practice, and how does it affect teaching? These activities ordinarily happen simultaneously and are not necessarily closely interrelated, however much in logic this appears desirable. Events also occur in time and related to those which have gone before. Thus in considering our subject it would be artificial to describe the four processes as if

[a]Regarding human ecology i.e., man-environment relationships as a system.

they follow each other in local and regular sequence. I shall therefore attempt to bring out the principles which must be observed and are inherent in "Social Pediatrics" by describing the activities of a group of pediatricians in the North of England from the early 1930s to the present. We shall try to interweave activities concerned with study, practice, planning, and teaching in chronological order and demonstrate principles and the requirements of the social approach as the story unfolds. It is a story related to time, place, and population and this is the first of the two principles to emphasize—*that social pediatrics requires a sense of history relating to people in their community to locality and time* and *those undertaking the discipline must identify with the community in which they work.* The activities to be described should be seen as the outcome of the actions of a group of essentially like-minded pediatricians in a department founded by a man with outstanding powers of leadership who died in 1954.

NEWCASTLE UPON TYNE

To put the scene into perspective the relative sizes of the United States and the United Kingdom are shown in Figure 4-1 and the area in the North of England, which after 1948 became known as the Newcastle Hospital Region, in Figure 4-2. The whole region in 1973 has some 3.25 million people (800,000 children under fifteen years old) grouped into centers of heavy industry with intervening rich farmlands and hill grazing. At the center is Newcastle, some ten miles from

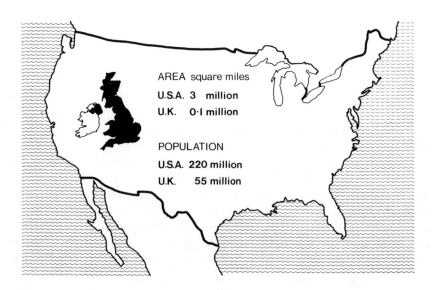

AREA square miles
U.S.A. 3 million
U.K.   0·1 million

POPULATION
U.S.A. 220 million
U.K.   55 million

Figure 4-1.

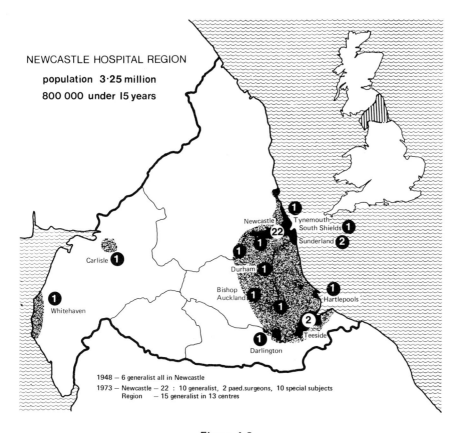

NEWCASTLE HOSPITAL REGION

population 3·25 million

800 000 under 15 years

Carlisle

Whitehaven

Newcastle

Tynemouth
South Shields
Sunderland

Durham

Bishop
Auckland

Hartlepools

Teeside

Darlington

1948 — 6 generalist all in Newcastle
1973 — Newcastle — 22 : 10 generalist, 2 paed.surgeons, 10 special subjects
Region   — 15 generalist in 13 centres

Figure 4-2.

the sea and settled for at least 2,000 years, in succession a Roman Bridgehead, a Saxon village, and a Norman fortress built in 1172 preceded the medieval town. Until 1750 or thereabouts the city remained largely within the thirteenth century walls but then expanded from 50,000 inhabitants in 1831 to 283,000 a century later, to become the commercial center of a highly industrialized riverside community. Even with a high birthrate such increase was possible only by large scale immigration from other parts of the country and from Ireland and Scotland. During these years prosperity was based on shipbuilding, coal exporting, chemical and glass manufacturing. Here the first railway locomotive, the first electric lamp, and the first marine steam turbine were made.

The city was overcrowded and ill housed. Disease, especially infective illnesses were epidemic, death rates high, as were the birthrates. In 1840 the expectation of life of a laborer was forty years. In 1865 there were 3,950 deaths in a population of 123,000 and 1,847 were in children under five years. This is the background [2, 3].

INQUIRIES INTO CHILD HEALTH AND THE ORIGINS
OF A DEPARTMENT OF CHILD HEALTH

In 1932, at a time of severe economic depression, the Medical Officer of a dispensary observed in his annual report that the mothers and children of the city were suffering from malnutrition. As a result a simple but telling study was organized which compared the physique and the clinical histories of children in professional families with those of the families of laborers or unemployed men. Naturally, the difference was marked and the report concludes:

> that at least 36.0 per cent of the children from the poor districts of the city were unhealthy or physically unfit and as a result they appeared malnourished—since this apparent malnutrition is not found in the children of better class families it is due to preventable causes—the main immediate cause of the apparent malnutrition of the city children is the physical damage occurring in young children at susceptible ages, and under conditions which prevent satisfactory recovery. [4, 5]

In the same years of industrial depression with high unemployment, the birthrate though falling was also high, while the maternal mortality rate, stillbirth rate, neonatal death rate were all above the national rates. Deaths and morbidity from bacterial infection continued high and tuberculosis was an important cause of death in children over the age of one year.

The first sulphonamides only became available in 1935. From 1935 the economy revived somewhat with the start of a rearmament program, but for the next two or three years no major change occurred in the death rates of infants or children.

At that time, although all families had access to family doctors, this was either by private arrangement, through "club" practice with regular small weekly deductions from the husband's pay or, for the very poor or unemployed and those in receipt of public relief, the services of the "parish" doctors. However devoted the general practitioner their resources were meager and their training in child health almost non-existent. Pediatrics as a specialty existed only in London and Birmingham. Doctors and health visitors in the Child Welfare were working hard in clinics and by home visiting to raise standards of infant care, but all too often they worked in isolation from family doctors and in families without sufficient resources.

The situation demanded inquiry: in 1938 the study of 1931 was repeated with almost the same result; [6] the children of the laborers and unemployed families were again shown to be shorter and lighter than those of professional families, they had more infective illnesses, active rickets could be found, and 10 percent of the children had a positive tuberculin reaction at five years of age.

In 1939 an inquiry was made into the circumstances of the death of every infant under the age of one year and was finished, despite the onset of war in September. The inquiry [7], a personal study, showed the importance of prematurity and infection as causes of deaths and also the significant fact that in as many as one-third of children the cause of death as given on the certificate was so inaccurate as to be meaningless [8]. *These various studies illustrate the need for local investigation and documentation.*

The next and the most important step forward came in 1943 when the Nuffield Foundation supported the creation of the first whole-time Chair of Child Health in the United Kingdom: Created in response to increasing concern for the well being of children and the need to teach students as well as study disease. The first professor was Dr. J.C. Spence.

PURPOSES OF A UNIVERSITY DEPARTMENT OF CHILD HEALTH

But it was not until 1946 that it was possible to begin to expand the department, to recommence local inquiries and pursue a conscious departmental philosophy. This ultimately, was based on four major tenets.

1. That the main concern of a university department is to profess its own subject—in our case child health and its determinants.
2. The second is to teach students, undergraduates and postgraduates, about the subject professed. Child health cannot be taught as an abstract exercise but must be related to a population and its needs.
3. The third is to care for sick children and their families and in doing so to provide a standard of excellence which might be an example to other groups.
4. The fourth is to have a sense of responsibility for the health of the children of the region and to possess data so that the department is able to advise official bodies. This declares that the university has its foundations in a community and acknowledges that child health, and not merely the treatment or prevention of disease, is the objective.

These tenets ensured that outlook went beyond the hospital into the community.

To practice such a philosophy with a limited staff and very limited budget demanded decisions about priorities of action. This was resolved by concentration upon common clinical problems and the study of the causes of illness in children in our local community.

THE ATMOSPHERE OF POSTWAR BRITAIN

Before examining the results of that decision the spirit of the times must be appreciated. The nation was at the end of six years of war, and had been sustained in hard and difficult times by the hope of greater opportunity and social change. War had brought hardships but also many other things, full employment and good wages, adequate although rationed food, much communal feeding. Although a considerable proportion of the doctors and nurses served in the armed forces, the preventive services at home continued and maternity services improved. The nutritional policy was excellent and provision for expectant and nursing mothers and all children under five included a pint of milk each day, protective vitamins, and special rations. The nation as a whole was better nourished than ever before. During the six years of war the national infant mortality and stillbirth rates fell by one-third: so did the mortality of children 1-4 years (Table 4-1), a marked contrast to the first war in which mortality rose. The falls in the local Newcastle rates were even more dramatic.

The physique of children, as judged by height and weight of London school children, had improved steadily throughout the century (Table 4-2) [9], despite the facts disclosed in the investigations of 1931 and 1938, and shows the differences revealed between looking at national averages and special groups.

Within five years of the end of the war five major Acts of Parliament all affecting children laid the foundation for great medical, educational and social improvements.

1. The Education Act, 1944
2. The Family Allowance Act, 1945
3. National Health Service Act, 1946
4. Children's Act, 1948
5. Adoption Act, 1950

THE NATIONAL HEALTH SERVICE

Titmuss, a discriminating and critical social observer, in writing of the National Health Service, says "The most unsordid act of British Social Policy in the twentieth century has allowed and encouraged sentiments of altruism, reci-

Table 4-1. Mortalities of Infants and Children, England and Wales—1929-1969

	Birthrate	Stillbirth	Infant Mortality	Death Rate 1-5 Years
1929	16.3	40	74	7.55 (1931)
1939	14.9	38	51	3.49
1946	20.2	27	43	2.08
1949	18.1	23	32	1.56
1959	16.5	21	22	0.91
1969	16.3	13	18	0.77

Table 4-2. Physique of Children as Judged by Height and Weight—London, England

Year	Average Height (Centimetres)				Average Weight (Kilogrammes)			
	5-5 years		13-5 years		5-5 years		13-5 years	
	Boys	*Girls*	*Boys*	*Girls*	*Boys*	*Girls*	*Boys*	*Girls*
1905-12	104.0	103.0	143.1	146.8	17.0	16.8	36.4	37.7
1938	109.1	108.4	149.0	152.2	19.4	18.9	41.1	43.8
1949	110.5	109.8	152.2	153.7	19.59	19.12	42.76	45.47
1954	111.1	110.2	154.0	155.4	19.90	19.38	44.32	46.21
1959	110.9	110.2	155.8	156.4	19.92	19.44	46.97	48.99

Source: Annual Report Chief Medical Officer, Ministry of Education, *Health of the School Child 1960 and 1961* (London: HMSO, 1962).

procity and social duty to express themselves; to be made explicit and identifiable in measurable patterns of behavior by all social groups and classes. In part this is attributable to the fact that, structurally and functionally, the Health Service is not socially divisive." [10]

For everyone who wished to partake, and 99 percent of the population did, it ensured a family doctor with free medicine, free hospital treatment and consultant services, and gave promise of the growth of an adequate hospital service. In administrative terms the service was composed of three parts: the general practitioner service, the hospital service, and the preventive and educational services of the public health departments. Each of these was administered separately but there were many ways in which the services met and interlocked so that, used responsibly by doctor and patient, excellent service was possible and adequate service general. Doctors retained and have continued to hold complete clinical independence and responsibility.

But an Act of Parliament does not of itself change men or produce overnight new systems of complex structures such as hospitals. The new relationships and provisions also revealed a mass of pent-up needs.

The old doctors continued to practice, their training and habits of practice had not changed, and many doctors mean many shades of outlook and opinion. Yet from that time family practice began to change and the build-up of hospital staffs and the formation of new clinical teams were initiated and still continue. But pediatrics was, in fact, a new discipline. Pediatricians were at first few in number, so few that they were, at first, confined to the larger cities and teaching centers. Here the difference between the practice of pediatricians in the United Kingdom and that in the United States must be noted, for the former pediatricians do not commonly give primary care to children. The difference, however, is a matter of organization and need not be one of attitude or approach to problems relating to child health. Since July 1948, when there were only six pediatricians, all in Newcastle, in the region, consultant pediatricians and clinical teams have been established in many other centers (see Fig. 4-2) and the number in Newcastle has grown so that in 1973 there are thirty-seven in the region working in about fifteen clinical teams. Many of the doctors having had their initial training in Newcastle, going away for further training in pediatrics, medicine and surgery, and other specialities, and returning for a consultant appointment or to work until a consultant appointment was ready. Today's widespread regional organization allows the referral to specialized units of children requiring special care of investigation in such matters as cardiology, neonatal surgery, some types of malignant disease, etc. All the consultants, whether holding university or health service appointments are engaged in clinical practice, but almost all this is within the National Health Service. Similarly, it has been our policy to endeavor to make our arrangements for hospital consultations and admissions of such a standard that all children are admitted to the National Health Service Hospital accommodation.

Practially all the departmental and regional pediatricians, in addition to their clinical work and teaching, have "community" interests in problems closely related to the social aspects of pediatrics; although there is naturally some overlap in interest and colleagues may unite and work together for specific problems, within the group individual members are recognized to have special interest outside strictly clinical work. Examples of these are found in the study of adoption, of illegitimacy, of children deprived of a "normal home life" by neglect or loss of parents [11], of morbidity and mortality [12], of accident and poisoning [13], of speech and speech development [14], and of the effects on family life of genetically determined illness such as hemophilia [15]. These interests naturally lead to the persons concerned becoming involved in advisory committees, in working parties which precede alteration in legislation or affect government policy and provision; and in this way attitudes of social pediatrics are carried from local and operational levels to national planning levels.

FOUR FIELDS OF DEPARTMENTAL ACTIVITIES

Within that necessarily brief indication of the service within which from 1948 most of the activities occurred, the department could be said to be engaged in four related fields of work.

1. Clinical practice and research
2. Teaching of child health to medical students and paramedical students, nurses, midwives, etc.
3. Social and operational research
4. Regional planning and national consultation.

All were directed towards increasing understanding of the child in his family and meeting the problems of delivery of health care to children in the context of home and hospital.

1. In the family at home, by family doctor, and by the maternity and child welfare services in the public health provision.
2. In the child in or at hospital still with the family in mind by members of the clinical hospital team.
3. Teaching which sought to impart a social attitude as well as technical skill and theoretical knowledge and which taught that the profession of medicine is fundamentally a social service.

These activities, though apparently separate, were in fact integrated and interrelated, each affecting the others, and as demonstrated below, clinical organization sometimes required a combination and integration of hospital and community services.

Clinical Practice and Research

Before 1950 the important and acute illnesses in children were respiratory bacterial infections, gastroenteritis, acute infectious fevers, acute rheumatic fever, acute intestinal emergencies (appendicitis, acute intussusception), acute staphylococcal illness, such as osteitis. The first problem was to achieve good technical care in situations which took cognizance of the care of the whole child, psychological as well as physical, and also his family [16]. "Rooming-in" for mothers with babies and young children had been part of our practice for many years, ward-schools were instituted and have continued, and the individual conditions were systematically tackled over years (Pyloric stenosis, appendicitis [17], osteitis [18], acute respiratory disease [19], acute intussusception [20], trauma and burns, tuberculosis [21]); various members of the department choosing different interests. Emphasis throughout was on the importance of clinical and social history, careful and repeated clinical examination, economy in treatment, and careful documentation and follow-up. But always with emphasis on the child in his social as well as clinical context.

Work in the maternity units took the same attitude; the hospital was seen as a brief and unnatural episode in the whole cycle of pregnancy, and as far as possible the conditions were created to help the mother to develop a relationship to her baby as much as she would have done if the baby had been born at home (as 50 percent of infants were in 1947). Thus again rooming-in was the accepted pattern and the infant went to his mother as soon as possible after birth, and, except in special circumstances, remained there in his crib beside the mother's bed.

The primary function of the pediatrician as a member of the staff of the maternity unit was (and still is) to ensure that healthy babies stay healthy; [22] secondarily he looked after low birth weight infants, babies with congenital abnormalities etc., but his role was primarily preventive and educative and this was also taught to students.

In those early days half the low-birth weight infants were born at home and half in the hospital: not all could be admitted, as suitable provision did not exist. With the university department and the local health authority working together, a home nursing service was instituted [23] and it was soon apparent that the results in infants of more than 1,500 grams birth weight were as good at home as in hospital.

Since then hospital provision has increased and the stillbirth rate and infant mortality rate have steadily declined (Table 4-1), but the incidence of low birth weight has not changed, and this group with its steep social gradient still contributes a very large proportion of stillbirths and first week deaths and a yearly toll of infants with respiratory distress syndrome, cerebral trauma, and other defects. This problem of the incidence of low birth weight remains unsolved and has not yet been studied systematically in our community. But now all such infants are born in hospitals, where 99.5 percent of all births take place. The organization of this service as in the case of the tuberculosis service described below makes the *point that university departments can be involved in community work through cooperation with local health authorities.* The result can then be ploughed back into teaching and into practice, not only of medical students and postgraduates but all categories of health workers dealing with children.

Regional Services for Hemolytic Disease
of the Newborn

A further and early application of the *principle of ascertainment and regional planning* came with the organization for the care of women with Rh-antibodies and the treatment of hemolytic disease of the newborn. The first step was the proof that exchange transfusion was better than simple transfusion, the second was to be able to predict from cord samples at birth which children were likely to need exchange transfusion either to counteract anemia or to avoid kernicterus.

Once that was done it was then possible, since all antenatal blood specimens were examined in the same laboratory and all expectant women had samples taken, to predict which women were at risk. Sufficient cooperation existed between family doctors, obstetricians, and pediatricians to enable all such women to be offered admission for delivery into one of five maternity units in the region where the infant could receive appropriate care. Immediately on delivery cord hemoglobin and bilirubin were measured and exchange transfusion given when necessary. The coverage was almost 100 percent and involved 5 in every 1,000 expectant mothers, giving some 250 affected children each year. [24 25]

This rationalization of treatment prevented the development of kernicterus due to hemolytic disease and reduced the death rate in our region to about one-quarter of that for the country as a whole. The lesson here is that *organization for the benefit of patients must come before the retention of any particular patient by any individual clinician*; this type of arrangement requires a certain outlook and considerable cooperation, but it is obviously easier when there is no financial contract between doctor and patient or patient and clinic or hospital. The welfare of the patient can be more easily the paramount consideration.

Children's Tuberculosis Service [26]

Another service in which clinical study and service were combined with hospital and community work and the university department was a partner of the City Health Department, was in the organization of a Children's Tuberculosis Service, providing for contact tracing; the control of BCG vaccination for children at risk or on leaving school; the treatment of children with asymptomatic primary tuberculosis; and the maintenance of a tuberculosis register for all tuberculin positive children. This service worked also with a long-stay children's hospital as well as with the hospitals of the city; at first merely epidemiological and advisory, but with the introduction of effective treatment in 1947, it became increasingly important to know which children had been infected; when BCG became available, it was offered first to children at risk and then to school leavers. Deaths of children from tuberculosis ceased and the occurrence of a positive tuberculin reaction became unusual (Table 4-3).

As time went on, standards of local and national nutrition also further improved and bacterial diseases became fewer. Acute rheumatism with carditis disappeared and children with old cardiac damage healed as they continued with penicillin for years without financial strain.

Table 4-3. Tuberculin Testing of Children—Newcastle 1955-1970

	1952	*1960*	*1965*	*1970*
Percentage tested Infants aged 5 and 6		75	66	90
Number tested	847	3,525	2,949	3,200
Had BCG		—	—	415
Percentage positive	7.2	1.8	0.3	0.1
	(1955)			
Percentage tested			74	91
Juniors aged 8+			2,693	
Number tested				3,077
Had BCG			—	677
Percentage unvaccinated			1.7*	0.2
Percentage tested Leavers aged 11+	1	70	73	77
Number tested	1,124	3,904	2,355	2,599
Had BCG	—	—	—	757
Percentage positive unv.	31	19	16	0.5

*Including BCG

Services for Handicapped Children

As this happened in the 1950s, other problems presented themselves. A new problem or a newly disclosed problem presented as the parents of children "spastic" from whatever cause sought medical and social help. The development of the regional service for such children illustrates well the *combination of voluntary and public funds and the cooperation of socially minded pediatricians with physiotherapists and teachers.* [27, 28] From 1949 there had been a local "spastic" society, a voluntary body largely composed of parents of handicapped children. This society with help from national funds enlisted the interest of the local education authorities who had a statutory obligation to provide education for handicapped children. At first, provision was made for the residential "school" care of 30 children, and a pediatrician undertook to make the selection of the most suitable 30 from a possible list of 300.

Obviously this was insufficient to meet the needs of the region and, following our first rule, a survey designed to ascertain the incidence of cerebral palsy was instituted taking as a sample for investigation 25 percent of the population of the region. As a result it was estimated that twenty places per million population were required for children aged 5-16 years and suitable for residential schooling, twelve places were provided for nursery children under five years of age so that eventually seventy-two were available for the region. A consultation center adjoined the residential school and to it children could come with their parents referred from family doctors, from hospital pediatricians, from doctors, from Child Welfare Centers. Consultations regarding handicap require considerable time and parents must feel not only at ease but also that they have been given full and careful consideration by doctors interested in them as people and appreciative of their situation. So mother and child came for about a week, were given a room together, and the initial steps in assessment began. This type of rooming-in was essentially an adaptation of that which for many years had been made available in the children's units in the city. In this work, health and educational enterprise combined and beneficially brought together pediatricians, physiotherapists, teachers, speech therapists, educational and clinical psychologists, and slowly a regional service developed with arrangements for physical, intellectual, and emotional assessment. Finally these were all brought together into a new regional assessment center with multidisciplinary staffs working as part of a child health service and therefore involved in the teaching of students and in the study of the subject. These activities all can be described as social pediatrics, insofar as they deal with the child in his family and give to each family the type of help and support which is needed—educational, social, and economic—either directly or indirectly. Yet assessment is not the objective, for after assessment comes treatment toward the development of each child's potential and toward helping the parents by their involvement in care and treatment to accept and to become adjusted to the sense of disappointment and guilt associated with children with handicap.

SOCIAL PEDIATRICS IN TEACHING AND
TRAINING OF UNDERGRADUATE AND
POSTGRADUATE STUDENTS

Medical education today generally tends to foster a technical and so-called scientific approach, which sees a patient as primarily a problem in pathology or physiology, in a hospital setting, not as a sick or potentially sick person with a family from a certain social milieu. Thus a disease diagnosis is thought insufficient, when a situational and social diagnosis is also required in order that needs might be met as fully as possible. Yet in every discipline in medicine the essential need is to train students and medical staff to see patients of any age as people influenced by previous experience, and their relationships with others in the home, in the school or neighborhood or workplace who can only be helped to the full if their situation is understood as completely as possible. This includes not only physical and psychological factors but also social, economic and cultural factors. [29, 30] Needed for the care of adults, this is quite vital for understanding of children.

This requirement should be laid down early in the medical course and certainly in the first two years. At the same time as he or she is studying biology, the medical student should be made aware of the broad evolution and development of human societies and the role of individuals and families. Behavioral studies must be combined with vital statistics and demography so that the student understands the dynamics of population structure and change, the causes and extent of mortality, and the social associations and consequences thereof. This type of study also makes the student aware of the professional and social roles of physicians and therefore of his or her own future responsibilities to society.

The particular occasions when the social aspects of pediatrics can be taught vary with the organization of teaching and learning and with the techniques used. But many are common to almost every teaching department.

Most students learn their skills and attitudes best by practical experience when working as members of a team engaged in clinical practice in the wards, in a consultative service or a patient's home, and thus the example of senior teachers is all important. The social history is as important in making the social diagnosis as the clinical history is in understanding the nature of the patient's symptoms or signs—and this is especially true of children. Details of family structure and size are required, together with a description of father's and mother's occupation and work record, some indication of income range—and if an adequate amount is available for family use, the feeding customs and type of food; later housing details, number of rooms and structure, washing and other facilities are noted and carefully recorded for ascertainment in the social diagnosis and the prescription of supportive therapy. Family relationships and stresses or tensions are important but more difficult to ascertain.

During ward work the student should be enabled and encouraged to make family visits insofar as this may be practically possible and in pediatrics these visits can arise spontaneously from the student's growing acquaintance with parents. Students and junior staff must be allowed to see home conditions other than those of their own social status, and how different families can appear at home and in hospital. In some situations students may give primary care to families.

The student needs also to see the operation and know the organization of social agencies and other organizations capable of giving patient-support in the community; especially with those who support by teaching families and parents to be more self-reliant and independent. Two of the best ways are to accompany workers from other agencies such as social workers or community nurses, or to attend and participate in working discussions between all involved.

Visits to well-baby clinics can be used to make students aware of social determinants of quality of infant and child care, for the whole impact of effective child welfare work depends upon the reality of social contact between parent and nurse and doctor. Social problems are never far from the surface and the influence of the concerned and informed doctor and health visitor can be considerable.

In lectures, discussion groups, and seminars, the social impacts of the subject under discussion must always be included, for whether the subject is low birth weight, child development, respiratory or other infective illnesses, rheumatism, trauma, poisoning, inborn errors of metabolism, or juvenile delinquency, there are always social causes or social consequences.

From discussions of this type the ideas of "at risk" situations or individuals, or vulnerable groups or "problem" families will arise, and the idea of social handicap as in illegitimacy, adoption, also arises and can be incorporated into a working conceptual framework.

During recent years courses for undergraduate students or for vocational training for family doctors have been started in many medical schools in both the United States and the United Kingdom. Inevitably such courses contain much that is essentially "child health," for the care of children and mothers is in fact at the heart of family medicine and family health.

The maternity hospital is another setting where social realities are part of everyday practice and inevitably present themselves to the student during teaching—social pediatrics and social obstetrics can here hardly be separated; the difference in the incidence of stillbirth and neonatal death in different socioeconomic groups, the effect of maternal age and parity on the risks to the baby. The social differences in the utilization of antenatal care, problems of illegitimacy, or of the child born in the hospital but without hope of a reasonable home life; the social and familial effects of congenital abnormalities. If neonatal teaching is well developed, the maternity hospital can be used as a major opportunity for social as well as purely clinical teaching.

Thus it can be seen that the whole of pediatric teaching can be permeated by a sense of social concern which will bring the staff of the department into close touch with the community in which it works and with the health services provided by the community. Yet formal or informal teaching must be supplemented and reinforced by the students' experience. And students must see the senior teachers display social concern. Only when they see teaching embodied in practice will they accept that the department believes what it teaches. Seven pillars of wisdom govern the teaching of social pediatrics. [31]

1. The medical staff must show social concern.
2. The senior staff must teach with a knowledge of social facts.
3. University Department must have roots in the community.
4. The teaching program must have relevance to community needs.
5. Teaching should occur outside as well as inside the hospital.
6. "Growth and Development" is the central theme.
7. Local inquiry must reveal local conditions and local data be used in teaching.

Social and Operational Research

The social studies and inquiries carried out before and indeed leading to the foundation of the department have been mentioned. At the end of the war we knew from our survey of infant deaths that acute infections formed the most important group of illnesses; we also suspected that official figures understated the frequency of this occurrence. But we had little idea of the frequency or the type of infections found in the population of the city or of the relationship to social conditions and we did not know how parents coped with illness in their families. We had students to teach and wished to teach them with relevance to the local population. We also knew that the practice of medicine is not confined to hospitals. In any case we felt a sense of responsibility to the local population which required that we should understand the origins of illness in children in order that we might perhaps prevent it. We therefore decided in the summer of 1946 that we would study the incidence and the types of acute infective illness in the first year of life in a representative group of infants in our own city. It would be an observer-recorder study without clinical responsibility. This was the origin of the 1,000 family study. Planned over the winter of 1946/47, it began in May 1947 and was successfully extended until in the end 750 of the original 1,142 children were followed in their families for fifteen years. The study which proved so rewarding in terms of understanding the needs of families and providing data for teaching has been described in three volumes. [32] *This study was again a joint project between the university and City Public Health Department exemplifying their common interest and responsibility, was freely entered by the families,* and the family doctors allowed us to record the course of illnesses under treatment. This necessitated a degree of cooperation which implies considerable understanding between colleagues.

The Department of Obstetrics began a Maternity Survey which

collected defined data for every birth in the city over a period of ten years. Although primarily an obstetrical activity, it also made available considerable detail relating to the infant and the factors associated with birth weight. Thus in 1963 it was shown that the excess of infant deaths in the City of Newcastle as against those in Aberdeen could be accounted for almost entirely by births to women of grand multiparity (four or more). [33] A drive for family planning in the group was then instituted and the infant mortality of the city further reduced.

From the Registers of the Maternity Survey, a further sample of infants was isolated, and followed with respect to certain criteria of development such as sitting up, walking, talking. The results of this study should establish norms, and any class or other differences should be apparent if they exist.

These studies illustrate a local approach to the need for local data, and are cooperative efforts between a *university department and a city health department, design and finding being cooperative and the collection of data being done partly by local and existing staff.* This is an important principle, for it is educational to both sides, utilizes existing local skills and relationships, and involves them in "research" which may contribute to policy-making and organization.

Ultimately, the possibility of such cooperation depends upon the relationship of the pediatricians with the senior public health officials and the *mutual possession of a similar approach to the problems of child health in the community.*

SOCIAL PEDIATRICS AT THE NATIONAL LEVEL

To this point I have illustrated what I understand to be a social approach to pediatrics by describing in a broad and brief outline the activities of a group of people working in their own region as members of a National Health Service but able and willing to use other available resources and to cooperate with many other disciplines and professions in furthering the level of health in the children of the community and in training family doctors and pediatricians.

Reference has been made to national policies such as the wartime rationing system and priority foods for expectant and nursing mothers and for young children, and programs of protective immunization which can certainly be included in that approach. Possibly the point has already been sufficiently made that the fundamental difference exists in the way problems can be tackled at national or at regional level.

Undoubtedly, after the war a series of studies [34-43] on a national scale beginning and continuing at intervals during the whole of the time between 1946 and the present have furnished a mass of data and have brought increasing understanding of the state of maternal and child health in the community. Space prevents anything other than a reference to them, but their cumulative results have been to demonstrate the independent effects of social, biological and geographical variables, the incidence of types of handicap, the existence of "at risk" factors, and the concept of "vulnerable" families. Together the results of these studies can be used to monitor the state of child health in the community. This indeed should be a built in and continuing process in any modern state. Thus researchers in social pediatrics at national and local regions usually complement each other, and both are required. The national studies can work with larger samples on wider issues, whereas local studies can answer more detailed and personal inquiries with smaller samples.

Local pediatricians from various parts of the country are frequently asked to serve on various types of national committees which consider the welfare of children. The mechanism is that a committee or working party is established at the request of a minister or member of the government, terms of reference are given, the committee then studies the subject, if necessary collecting its own data, reports with recommendations to the minister concerned. The report is then published and also may be used when new legislation is introduced. Service of this type is indeed both important and valuable and naturally the attitudes of the serving members influence the contents of the reports.

CONCLUSION

I have tried as briefly as possible to indicate that social pediatrics means a particular type of approach to the provision of services for the care of children; an approach which believes that medicine in all its branches—but in this case more particularly pediatrics—is ultimately a social service, provided or organized for the benefit of children and their families after needs have been ascertained and studied. Needs vary with locality and for many other reasons, and the basic problem is to meet needs in such a way that provision can be fitted to the particular family and that in doing so the family should be strengthened and educated so that the members become, not only physically well and free from disease, but socially mature and responsible citizens of their own countries. For this ultimately is what one means by family health and this in the last analysis is the objective of pediatrics. Such an objective will never be achieved without a philosophy which desires it and knowledge and understanding of the nature of children in their environments.

NOTES

1. Dorlands' Illustrated Medical Dictionary, 23rd edition (Philadelphia and London: W.B. Saunders Company, 1964).
2. Spence, James; W.S. Walton, F.J.W. Miller, S.D.M. Court, *A Thousand Families in Newcastle Upon Tyne* (Oxford University Press, 1954).

3. F.J.W. Miller, S.D.M. Court, W.S. Walton, E.G. Knox, *Growing Up in Newcastle Upon Tyne* (Oxford University Press, 1960).
4. J.C. Spence, *Investigation into the Health and Nutrition of Certain of the Children of Newcastle Upon Tyne between the Ages of One and Five Years* Report published by Newcastle Corporation Health Department, 1934.
5. J.C. Spence, "A Clinical Study of Nutritional Xerophthalmia and Night Blindness," *Arch. Dis. Childhood*, 6 (1931): 17.
6. E.G. Brewis, G. Davison, and F.J.W. Miller, *Investigation into the Health and Nutrition of Certain of the Children of Newcastle between the Ages of One and Five Years*, Newcastle Corporation Health Department, 1939.
7. J.C. Spence and F.J.W. Miller, *Investigation into Causes of Infantile Mortality in Newcastle during 1939*, Newcastle Corporation Health Department, 1941.
8. F.J.W. Miller, "Certification of Death in Infancy," *Lancet* 2 (1942): 269.
9. Annual Report Chief Medical Officer. Ministry of Education, *Health of the School Child. 1960 and 1961* (London: HMSO, 1962).
10. R.M. Titmus, *The Gift Relationship. From Human Blood to Social Policy.* Chapter 13. (London: George Allen & Unwin Ltd.), p. 255.
11. *Report of Care of Children Committee* (Curtis Committee) (London: HMSO, 1946).
12. Ruth Cammock and F.J.W. Miller, "Trend of Mortality in Childhood with Special Reference to Tuberculosis on Tyneside," *Lancet* 2 (1951): 764.
13. R.H. Jackson, J.H. Walker, and N.A. Wynne, "Circumstances of Accidental Poisoning in Childhood," *Brit. Med. J.* 4 (1968): 245.
14. S.D.M. Court, Muriel Morley, and H. Miller, "Delayed Speech and Developmental Aphasia," *Brit. Med. J.* (1947): 125.
15. P. Jones, "Answering the Needs of Haemophiliac Children and Their Families," *Community Medicine* 128 (1972): 351.
16. J.C. Spence, "The Care of Children in Hospitals," *Brit. Med. J.* (1947): 125.
17. R.H. Jackson, "Parents, Family Doctors and Acute Appendicitis in Childhood," *Brit. Med. J.* 2 (1963): 277.
18. A.E. Bremner and G.A. Neligan, "Pyogenic Osteitis," Chapter 13 in *Recent Advances in Paediatrics*, 2nd Edition (London: Churchills, 1958).
19. S.D.M. Court, J.P. Stanfield, A.E. Wright, P.S. Gardner, and C.A. Green, "Viruses, Bacteria and Respiratory Disease in Children," *Brit. Med. J.* (1960): 1, 1,077.
20. James Spence and S.D.M. Court, "Acute Intussusception in Childhood," *Brit. Med. J.* (1950): 11, 920.
21. F.J.W. Miller, R.M.E. Seal, and M.D. Taylor, *Tuberculosis in Children* (London: Churchill, 1963).
22. W.D. Bowman and J.G.P. Hutchison, "Staphylococcal Epidemiology in a Maternity Hospital," *Acta Paediatrica* 46 (1957): 125.
23. F.J.W. Miller, "The Home Nursing of Premature Babies in Newcastle," *Lancet* 2 (1948): 703.

24. P.L. Mollison and W. Walker, "Controlled Trials of the Treatment of Haemolytic Disease of the Newborn," *Lancet* 2 (1952): 429.
25. W. Walker, "Haemolytic Disease of the Newborn," *Brit. Med. J.* 2 (1951): 1142.
26. Miller, Seal, and Taylor, "Tuberculosis in Children."
27. E. Ellis, "Responsibilities in Cerebral Palsy," *Lancet* 1 (1958): 784.
28. E. Ellis, "Cerebral Palsy in the North of England," *Newcastle Med. Journ.* (1958): 25, 251.
29. F.J.W. Miller, "The Place of 'Social Paediatrics' in Undergraduate Teaching," *Acta. Paed. Scand.* 58 (1969): 125.
30. S.D.M. Court, "Knowledge, Skills and Professional Attitudes Required of the Community Paediatrician," *Brit. J. Med. Ed.* 3 (1969): 332.
31. Miller, "Place of 'Social Paediatrics.' "
32. Spence et al., *A Thousand Families in Newcastle Upon Tyne* Miller et al., *Growing Up in Newcastle Upon Tyne*; F.J.W. Miller, S.D.M. Court, E.G. Knox, and S. Brandon, *School Years in Newcastle Upon Tyne* (London: Oxford University Press, 1974, in press).
33. J.K. Russell, D.V.F. Fairweather, D.G. Miller, A.M. Brown, R.C.M. Pearson, G.A. Neligan, and G.S. Anderson, "Maternity in Newcastle Upon Tyne. A Community Study," *Lancet* 1 (1963): 711.
34. J.W.B. Douglas, *Maternity in Great Britain* (London: Oxford University Press, 1948).
35. J.N. Morris and J.A. Heady, "Social and Biological Factors in Infant Mortality," *Lancet* 1 (1955): 343, 395, 445, 499, 554.
36. J.W.B. Douglas and J.H. Blomfield, *Children Under Five* (London: George Allen & Unwin Ltd., 1958).
37. N.R. Butler and Eva D. Alberman, *Perinatal Mortality: First Report of 1958 British Perinatal Mortality Survey* (Edinburgh: Livingston, 1969).
38. N.R. Butler and Eva D. Alberman, *Perinatal Problems: Second Report of 1958 British Perinatal Survey* (Edinburgh: Livingston, 1969).
39. J.W.B. Douglas, J.M. Ross, H.R. Simpson, and Peter Davies, *All Our Future* (London, 1968).
40. Jessie Parfitt, *The Community's Children* (London: Longmans, 1967).
41. *11,000 Seven Year Olds.* National Child Development Study. First Report. (London: Longmans, 1966).
42. Eileen Crellin, M.L. Kellmer Pringle, and P. West, *Born Illegitimate. Social and Educational Implications*, National Foundation for Educational Research in England and Wales, 1971.
43. Jane Rowe and Lydia Lambert, *Children Who Wait. A Study of Children Needing Substitute Families* (London: Association of British Adoption Agencies, 1973).

Chapter 5

Family Planning and Abortion in the United Kingdom

Michael Victor Smith

In 1967 the National Health Service (Family Planning) Act gave local health authorities permissive powers to provide free contraceptive advice; seven years later, on April 1, 1974, the National Health Service Reorganization Bill became law, and the existing local health authorities were replaced by area health authorities who are obliged, rather than permitted, to provide a free service.

This change has, in great part, been due to the constant work and example, over many years, by the Family Planning Association and other voluntary bodies in providing a service to meet the increasing demand. A brief review of the progress of events following the founding of the first birth control clinic in London in 1921, by Marie Stopes, is therefore relevant.

In the ten years following Marie Stopes' action, five separate birth control societies were founded and opened clinics in various parts of the country. Under the slogan "Children by choice, not chance," their aims were the improvement of maternal and child health and the increase of marital happiness.

In 1930 these separate organizations were united to become the National Birth Control Council; and in the same year the Ministry of Health issued a circular to the local health authorities conferring on them permissive powers to provide birth control advice to women "for whom a further pregnancy would be detrimental to health."

The National Birth Control Council decided to press Local Health Authorities to implement the Ministry's circular. Progress was slow, however, and most local authorities, through timidity or hostility, ignored the circular and even two years later (with one notable exception), no local authority clinics had been opened. The exception was in Plymouth, on the South Coast, where the Pilgrim Fathers set sail for the New World nearly 300 years earlier. The Medical Officer of Health in Plymouth offered the National Council the use of the

Maternity and Child Welfare Clinic and by doing so, set the future pattern, since nine out of ten family planning clinics now occupy local authority premises.

By 1939, sixty-five Family Planning Association clinics were operating and the Association was concerned with the whole problem of fertility; including sub-fertility. This was reflected in the aims of the Association, which are now:

> To preserve and protect the good health, both mental and physical, of parents, young people and children; and to prevent the poverty, hardship and distress caused by unwanted conception.
>
> To educate the public in the field of procreation, contraception and health, with particular reference to personal responsibility in sexual relationships.
>
> To give medical advice and assistance in cases of involuntary sterility or of difficulties connected with the marriage relationship or sexual problems for which medical advice or treatment is appropriate.

In 1946, although the number of clinics had not increased, the first Marital Difficulties sessions were started and formal training in contraceptive techniques for doctors and nurses was established, to take place in designated training clinics.

Two years later, in 1948, the National Health Service Bill was passed by Parliament and free medical care for all became a reality. Regrettably, the bill made no reference to family planning since for both social and moral reasons neither the public nor the medical profession saw the necessity or indeed even the desirability for a free birth control service. Nearly twenty years were to elapse before local health authorities were allowed to provide free contraceptive advice, though not until April 1, 1974 were they obliged to do so.

During the next ten years many more clinics were opened until in 1958 nearly 300 were operating, and significantly the Lambeth Conference of the Church of England accepted the statement that birth control is a "right and important factor in Christian family life."

From then on progress became much more rapid and, on average, sixty new clinics opened each year; until, in 1971, over 1,000 Family Planning Association clinics had been established.

Some important landmarks during the sixties and early seventies were:

1961 Oral contraceptive approved for use in Family Planning Association Clinics.

1965 Intrauterine devices accepted for use in Family Planning Association Clinics.

1967 The National Health Service (Family Planning) Act became law on June

25. The Act conferred permissive powers on local authorities to provide birth control advice, without regard to marital status, to social as well as medical cases, using voluntary organizations such as the Family Planning Association as their agents if they so wished.

1967 On October 27, the Abortion Act, which legalized the termination of pregnancy under certain conditions, was passed.

1970 The Family Planning Association negotiated a National Family Planning Agency Scheme under which it provided a family planning service as agents for public authorities.

1972 An amendment to the National Health Service (Family Planning) Act 1967, empowered local authorities to provide vasectomies free.

1973 The National Health Service Reorganisation Bill was passed, under which family planning became part of the National Health Service from April 1974. From this time on, it is mandatory, and not permissive as previously, for free contraceptive advice, and supplies on payment of a nominal prescription charge, to be provided at public expense.

Following this brief historical review, the situation as it exists today will be outlined—with particular reference to the resources available, the training of personnel and the financial aspects.

CLINIC SERVICES

In Britain there are:

3,144,000 single women between the ages of 15 and 44
72,000 widows between the ages of 15 and 44
147,000 divorced women between the ages of 15 and 44

This gives a total of 3,363,500 unmarried women in the fertile age range. There are 7,019,100 married women in Britain. This gives a total of 10,382,600 women in the fertile age range in Britain.

To cater for the above there are just over 1,000 Family Planning Association clinics in the United Kingdom and about a further 500 clinics operated by local government authorities. In 1972, 805,642 patients were seen in Family Planning Association clinics and of these 284,207 were new patients. The methods used by the Family Planning Association's new patients were:

Oral Contraceptives	164,122
Diaphragm	25,828
Intrauterine Device	36,605
Sheath	6,692
Vasectomies	8,898
Other	20,458 (includes vasectomy counseling)

The Family Planning Association's clinics are staffed by 2,025 doctors and 2,439 nurses employed on a sessional basis and they provide expert medical advice on all modern methods of contraception. This includes examination, consultation, prescription, teaching the use of the individual method and regular medical supervision. As an adjunct to the clinic service a home visiting scheme has been organized in some areas for women who are unable or unlikely to visit an FPA clinic. Often a car ferrying service to and from the clinic is provided for such patients.

Couples trying to have a child without success are also investigated and treated, but artificial insemination by donor is not practiced and is as yet only available through a small number of doctors in private practice and a few National Health Service Hospitals.

Special sessions for helping couples with difficulties in their sexual relationships are held in some clinics and in others, vasectomy sessions for male sterilization are provided.

Two other important services are available in the clinics, namely a pregnancy testing service and a cervical smear (cyto test) service for women for the early detection of cancer of the cervix.

Finally, since April 1, 1974, contraceptives are provided free (not even a prescription charge is made by retail pharmacists). Free literature and leaflets on methods of birth control are distributed by the clinics.

TRAINING

Separate three-day basic courses of lectures and discussions are held for doctors and nurses and cover such subjects as contraception, sub-fertility and the psychological aspects of birth control. Following attendance at a lecture course trainees must successfully complete eight or more practical sessions at a clinic in their own area. About 900 doctors and the same number of nurses undertook this training in 1974. A similar course but with special emphasis on underdeveloped countries for nurses from overseas (or proceeding abroad) is also organized in conjunction with the Overseas Development Administration.

There are courses for instructing doctors and nurses as well as courses in more specialized aspects of family planning. These include a two-day sub-fertility course for doctors of appropriate gynecological or obstetric experience who wish to train in sub-fertility techniques, and a one-day course for doctors appropriately qualified who wish to undertake vasectomy counseling and surgery or counseling only. Both types of courses are followed by practical training, when necessary, at one of the Association's clinics.

Psychosexual training for doctors has been organized by the FPA for a number of years and takes the form of attendance at seminars led by accredited leader doctors in London and the provinces on a sessional basis over a period of two to three years. At present five seminars are being held, each attended by up to twelve doctors. The primary object of training doctors in the management of psychosexual problems is to enable them to give greater help to patients in their ordinary clinics. For those doctors who wish to work in special Family Planning Association psychosexual problem clinics, however, the full three-years seminar training is necessary. There are two parts to this training: two years attendance at ordinary seminars and a further year's attendance at an advanced seminar. Doctors wishing to proceed to the advanced seminar must be recommended as suitable by their leader doctor.

Three experimental one-year seminars for training nurses in this field were started in January 1974 but indications now are that a further year's attendance will be necessary if the nurses are to obtain the maximum benefit from this training. The aim is to make members of the nursing profession who have a special interest, aptitude, and motivation for psychosexual work aware and sensitive to the problems presented by individuals seeking contraceptive advice and which require the development of appropriate skills.

Family planning appreciation courses for midwives and health visitors sponsored by the Department of Health and Social Security are run at the request of area health authorities in places of their choosing. The course is designed to extend knowledge of birth control by providing details of all methods and their availability and to give practical advice in meeting the needs of the patients with whom trainees normally deal.

The FPA is also heavily involved in sex education as distinct from medical and nursing training. Sex education courses for teachers, youth workers, and health educators are designed to help those working in the field of sex education and personal relationships to examine the needs of young people and to attain the necessary confidence and sensitivity to meet those needs. The syllabus for these courses includes physiology and psychology of sex, puberty and adolescence, socioeconomic effects of unwanted births, contraception, personal relationships, moral education, venereal diseases, abortion, teaching methods and resources.

Finally, a number of hospitals in London and the provinces run basic family planning courses for doctors and nurses in their gynecology department. The syllabuses are similar to the Family Planning Association's and in a number of cases arrangements exist for the successful trainees to be given the Association's certificate. In addition the medical profession has advanced plans for taking over the training responsibility which the Family Planning Association, a voluntary body, has largely born until now. A Joint Committee of the Royal College of Obstetricians and Gynaecologists and the Royal College of General Practitioners will approve courses, trainers, and centers and issue a certificate of competence to the successful trainees. The Family Planning Association's basic syllabus, trainers, and centers are being recognized by the Royal Colleges and the holders of its certificate are likewise regarded as of equal merit.

FINANCIAL ASPECTS

Clinic Services

The Family Planning Association's income is derived from three sources:

Patients' fees and sales of supplies and literature	94% in 1972
Donations	3% in 1972
Government grants	3% in 1972

In years past the vast majority of the Family Planning Association's patients were private patients who paid their own fees. Recently, as more and more local authorities have appointed the Family Planning Association as their agents, fees have increasingly been recovered from these local authorities and not taken directly from the patients. Some already provide a direct service, and starting in April 1975 (i.e., a year after the National Health Service Reorganization Bill becomes law) the Family Planning Association gradually handed over its 1,000 clinics progressively to Area Health Authorities (the successors to existing Local Health Authorities).

During 1974, therefore, the area health authorities who do not provide a direct service continued to use the Family Planning Association as their agents and, indeed, after 1975 some (though how many is not yet known) may continue to do so. Many general practitioners will also provide (as at present) a family planning service and will probably receive a National Health Service payment for this in the future although this has yet to be decided.

In addition, a private service will be provided for a small number of patients by the Family Planning Association in the centers owned by them, of which there are about thirty. The annual patient's fee will be £6.40 (excluding supplies, which they will purchase privately at retail prices), some examples of which are:

Oral Contraceptives

Gynovlar 21	43p for one month's supply
Ovulen	37p for one month's supply

Intra-Uterine Devices

Lippes Loop	£1.45 each
Gravigard	£2.70 each

Sheaths

Durex Gossamer	63p per dozen

Patients attending publicly financed clinics or general practitioner's surgeries will pay nothing for contraceptive advice and supplies and for such patients, the Family Planning Association (where it acts as an agent) receives £6.40 per year from public funds for each patient seen.

Doctors, nurses, and lay workers staffing the Family Planning Association's clinics are paid sessionally; for doctors the basic rate is £8.11 for a 2½ hour birth control session and the rate increases to £9.83 for IUD, sub-fertility or psychosexual problem sessions, and £9.65 per session for surgeons carrying out vasectomies. The basic nurses' rate is £3.70 (£3.95 for instructing nurses) for a 3½ hour session and clinic secretaries are paid between £1.30 and £2.90 per session dependent on the number of weekly sessions worked.

Cost of Training

For 1974 nearly £200,000 was required to implement the program of training outlined above. The hope was that the bulk of this money would be made available from National Health Service funds.

Long-Term Intentions of Her Majesty's Government

Sir Keith Joseph, Secretary of State for Social Services, when introducing the National Health Service (Reorganization) Bill in Parliament on December 12, 1972, said: "We expect that in response to this demand the total cost for England, Wales and Scotland will build up to about £12 million per year over the next four years compared with current annual expenditure of about £4 million. This represents total additional expenditure of £20 million over the four year period."

ABORTION

Although abortion was legalized in the United Kingdom in 1967, the Family Planning Association does not have a policy on abortion. The operation is not carried out in Family Planning Association clinics, although patients making inquiries are referred either to National Health Service hospitals through their general practitioners or to one of two charitable organizations: British Pregnancy Advisory Service, which has a nationwide service and Pregnancy Advisory Service, the smaller organization centered in London.

In addition there are a number of other charitable organizations and private abortion clinics in London and the provinces licensed by the Secretary of State for Social Services.

In all cases the opinion of two medical practitioners is necessary; thus to quote from the Abortion Act of 1967:

> ... a person shall not be guilty of an offence under the law relating to abortion when a pregnancy is terminated by a registered medical practitioner if two registered medical practitioners are of the opinion, formed in good faith:
> a. that the continuance of the pregnancy would involve risk to the life of the pregnant woman or any existing children of her family, greater than if the pregnancy were terminated:

or

b. that there is substantial risk that if the child were born it would suffer from such physical or mental abnormalities as to be seriously handicapped.

In 1972 a total of 156,174 abortions were carried out in the United Kingdom as follows:

Age	Single	Married	Widowed Divorced Separated	Not Stated	Total
Under 16	3,098	1	0	0	3,099
16-19	27,013	904	259	0	28,176
20-34	43,095	43,741	9,625	0	96,461
35-44	1,534	21,519	2,709	0	25,762
45+	28	581	63	0	672
Not Stated	1,090	1,094	233	127	2,544
TOTAL	75,859	67,840	12,889	127	156,714

The cost to the patient can vary from nothing to as much as £250. In a National Health Service Hospital the operation is, of course, carried out free of charge.

The two charitable organizations to whom Family Planning Association patients are referred operate a remission scheme and in certain circumstances terminations are carried out free, but more often patients are charged between £60 and £100. Private abortion clinics are unlikely to charge less than £100.

It is difficult if not impossible to obtain termination of pregnancy under the National Health Service in some parts of the country and in 1972, 100,666 (64.2 percent) were paid for privately.

CONCLUSION

In just over fifty years the cause of family planning has advanced to the stage where advice and supplies are freely available, where abortion is legal, and where vasectomies can be obtained at public expense.

Whether or not these measures will stabilize the population in the United Kingdom remains to be seen, since accurate population forecasting depends upon variables which are inherently unpredictable, for example, political and economic factors, and also fashion.

Nevertheless, it has been predicted that by the end of this century the population of the United Kingdom will increase from the present figure of 56 million to 62.1 million. This additional 6.1 million people would require eight new cities as large as Fort Worth, Texas, to accommodate them, which allied to the fact that there are now 839 people per square mile in England and Wales (a density only exceeded in Bangladesh and Formosa) is a grim reminder of the problem facing this country.

SOURCES

The Registrar General's Quarterly Review of England and Wales
The Registrar General's Statistical Review, Supplement on Abortion
The Registrar General's Statistical Review of England and Wales
Social Trends
Population Projections 1972-2012
Health and Personal Social Services Statistics
Annual Report of the Department of Health and Social Security
On the State of Public Health
Birth, Deaths, and Marriages, Quarterly Return of the Registrar General for Scotland
Annual Report of the Registrar General for Scotland
     (All of the above are published by Her Majesty's Stationery Office)
The Family Planning Association, *41st Report and Accounts 1972-1973*

Chapter 6

Perinatal Care in the United Kingdom

Beryl D. Corner

INTRODUCTION

Planning and provision for perinatal care in Britain have followed a long process of evolution extending over more than a hundred years as an integral part of the development of maternity services, with the emphasis shifting to much greater concern for the fetus and newborn child in the last two decades.

Prior to the introduction of the National Health Service in July 1948 there was no uniformly applied national planning for perinatal care. As a result of pressures by voluntary societies and statutory bodies at local and national levels, there had been considerable legislation which enabled some medical services for care of mothers and young children to be developed by local government.

The Ministry of Health was established in 1919 to act largely as an advisory body with control of central exchequer funds, from which grants were made to local welfare authorities for schemes approved by the Ministry.

Services provided by local authorities which were available to all mothers and children without restriction included:

1. Midwifery service. State certified midwives provided a domiciliary confinement service for the majority of women with prompt emergency medical aid from general practitioners for their patients and babies. In Scotland joint care by midwife and medical practitioner could be arranged and, if needed, the services of a specialist obstetrician were called upon.
2. A home visiting service by registered health visitors (Equivalent to Public Health Nurses).
3. Hospital accommodation for acute disorders of pregnancy, confinement and

illness of early infancy. Maternity homes for mothers with social needs, e.g. illegitimacy.

These services became so popular that by 1944 in England and Wales local authority clinics provided antenatal care for 77 percent of the total registered births, and 96.8 percent received an early home visit by a health visitor. A total of 3,825 infant welfare centers had been established with regular consultations given by local authority medical officers and health visitors.

A small number of consultant obstetricians and gynecologists provided specialist services in voluntary and local authority hospitals and private maternity homes in the larger cities.

Pediatricians were little involved in routine care of newborn infants until the British Paediatric Association defined and strongly advocated the role of pediatricians in newborn care (British Paediatric Association Memorandum 1943) which resulted in the appointment of a few consultant pediatricians to teaching hospital maternity departments. Outside the large teaching centers there was very little consultant pediatric service.

CARE OF THE PREMATURE BABY, 1930-48

The high neonatal and infant mortality rates associated with prematurity and immaturity were identified in 1930 by the Birmingham Local Welfare Authority, which made the first planned attempt to remedy this in 1931, when Dr. Mary Crosse organized a ward for premature babies at Sorrento Municipal Maternity Hospital with associated transport and home care nursing services. Great benefit came from the "Sorrento" training courses for nurses and midwives, which provided skilled personnel for premature baby care to meet national and also to some extent international needs. This pioneer work identified many of the problems of the low birth weight infant and proved that skilled nursing care and simple measures to control the environment could halve the mortality rate (Crosse 1945).

The successful Birmingham experiment influenced the Ministry of Health to advocate the extension of this type of scheme. To identify the need, local welfare authorities were advised to include weight at birth on birth notification certificates which are returned to them by the birth attendants within forty-eight hours of the birth, and were recommended to develop comprehensive schemes for care of premature babies in their own areas both at home and in hospitals (Circular 20/44, Ministry of Health 1944). Thus from 1945-48 experimental schemes for domiciliary and hospital premature baby care were begun by some local welfare authorities in collaboration with a few consultant pediatricians.

Vital statistics for England and Wales for the first year after notification of birth weight had been introduced, 1945, showed that of 674,780 notified live births 4.5 percent weighed 5 lb. 8 oz. or less at birth, 86.8 percent of these being born at home and 13.2 percent in hospital (Report of the Ministry of Health). The mortality rates for premature births (i.e., deaths of infants with birth weight of 5½ lbs. or less per 1,000 total live births) varied considerably according to locality; low birth weight was associated with approximately 50 percent of all stillbirths.

THE NATIONAL HEALTH SERVICE, 1948-74

Since 1948 comprehensive maternity care has been available for all women within the National Health Service. Although there are limited facilities for private care in National Health Service Hospitals and private maternity homes, the demand is small owing to the very high cost. Whenever necessary infants born to private patients are transferred to the most appropriate National Health Service special care baby unit.

The National Health Service Act (1946) made provision for comprehensive health care for all citizens without direct charge, financed from national taxation and to a small extent from compulsory national insurance. Until April 1974 services were administered according to the traditional tripartite divisions of medical practice with overall responsibility by the Department of Health and Social Security (DHSS, formerly Ministry of Health), with the Secretary of State for the department being responsible to Parliament. The DHSS formulated policies with the assistance of a Central Health Services Council, representative of the health professions, and Standing Advisory Committees for specified sections of the Service, including a Standing Advisory Committee for Maternity and Midwifery. Policy advice and allocation of funds were given to regional and local administrative bodies, which were then responsible for local planning and provision of services. Advice from the medical profession has been available at every level of administration through medical advisory committees and representation on policy-making bodies.

Changes in policy have been initiated in a variety of ways. Among the most frequent are identification of trends and needs by the Department of Health from statistical studies and research projects; pressure from professional and other organizations; experimental schemes organized locally by individuals and groups.

The tripartite administration of the services from 1948-74 was as follows:

1. *Local Health Authority Services* expanded from those provided by the former local welfare authorities with responsibility to provide arrangements for prevention of illness, care, and after-care of sick persons. The principal services included: buildings and staff for health centers (including antenatal and postnatal clinics); community nursing, midwifery and health visiting; ambulance transport service for sick patients and maternity cases to and from hospitals.

2. *General Medical Practice* and pharmaceutical services have been administered by local executive councils serving the same population as local health authorities. Every citizen is entitled to register with a general practitioner (known as the family doctor) who contracts to give primary medical care, with referral to consultants (specialists) including request for domiciliary consultations for any patients unable to travel to hospital, and referral for hospital services as required. General practitioners temporarily relinquish care of patients admitted to hospital to consultants. Remuneration is on a per capita basis, but many services attract extra payments. There is freedom of choice for patient and physician within geographical limits, and complete choice for referral to hospital and specialist services.

3. *Hospital and Specialist Services.* The country has been divided into administrative regions with populations varying approximately from one to five million people, and with at least one University medical school in each region. Regional Hospital Boards (appointed by the Secretary of State, DHSS) provided and controlled hospital and specialist services according to policy advice from the DHSS; day-to-day management with financial allocation was delegated to Hospital Management Committees. Boards of Governors had similar functions in regard to teaching hospitals.

The Boards appointed Consultants to Hospital Groups to give specialist medical services, supported by medical staff in training grades.

PERINATAL CARE, 1948-74

Provision for perinatal care has developed in phases which have been marked at approximately ten-year intervals by important policy changes which have resulted from reviews of various aspects of the service. The rapid advances in scientific technology as applied to the newborn infant have also created demands for changes in the pattern of care particularly during the last decade.

Phase I: 1948-1958. Assessment of the position of maternity care in Britain (Maternity in Great Britain 1948) just prior to the National Health Service revealed extremely uneven distribution and overall great shortage of skilled obstetric care with a large amount of domiciliary midwifery. The first objective therefore was the prevention of maternal and perinatal loss and morbidity by improved distribution and an increase in skilled medical personnel for obstetrics and more hospital facilities for antenatal care and confinement.

Consultant obstetricians were appointed to major centers of population which necessitated a considerable expansion in postgraduate training. These obstetricians then became responsible for improving the standards of obstetric service in their areas in cooperation with general practitioners and the local authority midwifery service. The concentration of effort was at first largely on antenatal care. Criteria were established to identify those patients who were in need of consultant obstetric care throughout pregnancy and required to be booked for confinement in a hospital bed (see Appendix A).

"The Obstetric List" of general practitioners with experience or postgraduate training in obstetrics (usually a six-months approved hospital resident appointment and the Diploma of the Royal College of Obstetricians and Gynaecologists by examination) was created to give obstetric care to mother and child at home or in maternity homes, and emergency medical aid to domiciliary midwives. Any general practitioner may undertake maternity care, but maximum extra payment can only be claimed by those on the obstetric list. Some general practitioner obstetricians participate in local authority antenatal clinics, and some have clinical attachments to consultant obstetricians for sessional work in hospitals.

Distribution of hospital beds for obstetrics was also very uneven and shortage of building, labor and materials permitted very little new construction. The policy was followed that hospital obstetric departments should be established in association with major general hospitals which could provide the full range of diagnostic and supporting services. Where existing local authority maternity homes and maternity beds in small general practitioner hospitals were considered suitable, these were grouped with major hospitals for administrative purposes and upgraded both in standard of accommodation and provision of midwifery nursing staff. This facilitated ease of transfer of mothers and babies to consultant units in emergency. (In official statistics, beds in general practitioner maternity homes are regarded as equivalent to domiciliary care. "Hospital beds" are designated as such only if the patients are under the direct control of a consultant.)

By the end of this decade there was a consultant obstetric service with availability of hospital beds for patients selected on recognized criteria in all cities and within a radius of twenty to thirty miles of most women living in rural areas. As there was still variation in available facilities, selection criteria were adjusted accordingly in each center (see Appendix B).

Pediatric care for newborn infants progressed more slowly as there were still few consultant pediatricians, most of whom were working in teaching centers. The need for special provision for care of the premature baby however was emphasized by the WHO Report on Prematurity (1950). This resulted in a joint memorandum on the care of premature babies from the British Paediatric Association and the Royal College of Obstetricians and Gynaecologists, which recommended a program for care and prevention and advised the following: (1) assessment of requirements; (2) hospital care; (3) home care; (4) transport; (5) follow-up care; (6) integration with other services; and (7) regular appraisal of results (British Paediatric Association 1951). Although implementation of these recommendations was difficult due to lack of resources, there were some notable experimental schemes.

In Bristol a comprehensive service for premature babies was established by mutual agreement and cooperation of hospital pediatric and obstetric consultants with local authority medical and midwifery staff and general practitioners (*The Care of the Premature Baby in the Bristol Area* 1951). The scheme included two hospital premature baby units with specially trained nurses sited in two hospital obstetric departments; attendance of a unit nurse and a pediatric resident (registrar) at premature births in the hospital; a mobile infant resuscitation team for the Bristol area; an emergency ambulance transport service to bring very small premature infants to the units from the South Western Region; a domiciliary midwifery team linked with the hospital units using equipment on loan; a specialist health visitor for follow-up clinics for detection of handicaps and general advice; a human milk bureau sited at one hospital with milk collection and distribution for the locality and the region; a cubicled mother and baby ward for infected infants, and neonatal surgery in the same hospital as the larger premature baby unit. Regular perinatal conferences for obstetricians and pediatricians were instituted and a very high rate of postmortems (90 percent) was achieved.

An important feature of the scheme was that with cooperation of general practitioners and consultant obstetricians, most mothers who started premature labor before thirty-seven weeks gestation were automatically admitted for delivery to either of the two hospitals with premature infant units, so that gradually premature births elsewhere became unusual in this area. Similar schemes were later established in other centers.

In Newcastle on Tyne, Miller (1951) found that 41.6 percent of premature infants (636 infants) were born at home from 1945-49, so that in cooperation with the local health authority a home nursing service with nurses specially trained and suitable equipment loaned for home use was organized and survival rates for larger premature babies improved. This was a relatively inexpensive scheme which obviated the need for scarce resources of hospital buildings and medical staff, and proved suitable for healthy babies of birth weight at least 1800 gm, provided the home environment fulfilled certain criteria, notably freedom from infection in the household and adequate room heating. Similar schemes were also organized by some local health authorities for rural areas.

To assess the achievements of perinatal care in this first decade, improved survival of premature infants was used as the indicator. Vital statistics had shown that for each year prematurity was the outstanding cause of perinatal death, and approximately 7 percent of babies weighed 2,500 gm or less. In 1956 prematurity or immaturity was associated with 57 percent of first week deaths and more than 50 percent of stillbirths. The Ministry of Health instituted an inquiry from hospital boards and local health authorities into the organization for hospital and home care of premature infants in 1956 in England and Wales. Information was requested concerning medical and nursing staff, equipment, transport provision, follow-up and after-care schemes, and nurse training programs.

This review covered 30,582 premature infants cared for in the National Health Service schemes. There were 71 specially staffed hospital premature units, which catered to 38 percent of all premature infants. In 148 other obstetric departments or hospitals premature babies were nursed in nurseries with normal newborn babies or in a separate room in the obstetric department, but without specially trained or separate nursing staff. In each of 158 hospitals a very small number of premature babies (less than 50 in a year) were nursed without any special facilities. Fifteen percent of all premature babies weighed 1500 gm or less but only 45 percent of these were in separately staffed units for premature infants.

This inquiry also revealed that consultant pediatricians were primarily responsible for medical care of 61 percent of premature infants and consultant obstetricians for 16 percent. The remainder were under the care of midwives and general practitioners.

A wide diversity of arrangements for care was revealed and a great variation in provision of equipment both for home and hospital use. As examples, only six hospitals operated emergency transport arrangements for premature babies; in one region there were four specialist premature baby centers to which all low birth weight babies from other maternity hospitals and domiciliary births were transferred.

Phase II: 1959-1969. Three important reports initiated changes in policy. In 1959, a Report of the Maternity Services committee of the Ministry of Health (The Cranbrook Report) reviewed the state of the maternity services. The tripartite administration was considered to hamper the coordination needed to develop a comprehensive service. The most important recommendation was that provision should be made over the country as a whole for sufficient maternity beds to allow of an average of 70 percent institutional confinements. This also implied a considerable increase in skilled obstetric and midwifery personnel.

In 1961, a report of the Central Health Services Council to the Ministry of Health on "The Prevention of Prematurity and the Care of Premature Infants" emphasized the need of "Special Baby Care" facilities not only for premature but for other categories of sick and abnormal newborn infants, including "Haemolytic Disease of the newborn" for which an organized service had already been recommended (Central Health Services Council 1958). It was advised that the term "Special Care Baby Unit" should replace "Premature Baby Unit." Among categories to be included were: low birth weight; severe asphyxia neonatorum; hemolytic disease of the newborn; difficult and complicated births; some congenital malformations. The principal recommendations made were:

1. "Special Care Baby Units" should be provided only in large and medium-sized maternity departments which cater mainly to abnormal obstetrics. Babies born at home or in other hospitals should be transferred to these units soon after birth.

2. Optimally these units should contain not less than 20 cribs for a population of 200,000 approximately, and provide one crib for every ten consultant-staffed obstetric beds.
3. The units should be staffed by pediatricians and suitably trained nurses.
4. Suitable transport should be organized from place of birth to the unit.
5. Midwives should receive special training for domiciliary care of premature babies and equipment should be loaned for home use.
6. Frequent home visiting should be carried out for the early weeks after discharge from hospital by health visitors with special experience of premature babies.
7. Consultant pediatricians should conduct follow-up clinics at hospitals.
8. Training schemes for special care baby nursing should be established in association with these units as all these recommendations were very widely applied.

To meet these recommendations regional boards gradually established district general hospitals with obstetric and pediatric departments often in close physical proximity and staffed by consultants. Supervision of the care of all newborn babies in hospital obstetric departments including medical examination of healthy babies gradually became a routine responsibility of pediatric teams in addition to responsibility for premature and sick infants.

As policy, Special Care Baby Units have usually been sited either as an integral part of obstetric departments or immediately adjacent rather than in the pediatric department in order to maintain contact between mother and baby. Nursing establishment and training for units has been decided by hospital boards with great emphasis on the quality of practical nursing care.

Experience is regarded as the most important qualification for these nurses. Many training courses of varying lengths from three to six months are available, and it is recognized policy that a registered nurse or midwife with this training should have overall responsibility, but at all times there should be at least one nurse and usually two on duty who are experienced in neonatal special care. The usual staffing ratio is one nurse per crib. (Three experienced: five others is the minimum number for any unit. "Nurse" includes state registered and enrolled nurses, state certified midwife, certified nursery nurse, student nurse and midwife.) This staffing establishment has been achieved in the larger nurseries, but in small units it is difficult so that some of these do not provide sufficient expertise to care for some babies.

In 1958 The National Birthday Trust undertook a unique nationwide survey which covered 17,000 births as well as a detailed analysis of 7,000 stillbirths and neonatal deaths. The inquiry included relevant sociological, administrative, obstetric, and pediatric data. The first report, *Perinatal Mortality*, (Butler and Bonham 1963) has had a great influence on planning and the subsequent pattern of maternity and perinatal care in Britain.

Avoidable factors in perinatal mortality were identified in each category. The outstanding fact that emerged was that by reason of a combination of adverse factors including biological and sociological, the degree of "risk" of perinatal mortality could be predicted for the individual woman. Women could be identified as being in "high-risk" or "low-risk" groups in terms of: (1) overall perinatal mortality risk; and (2) intrapartum fetal death risk. The following factors were found to determine high overall risk:

1. Low socioeconomic status (husband unskilled worker).
2. High maternal age—35 years and over.
3. High parity (fifth or subsequent delivery).
4. Heavy smoking category (10+ cigarettes daily).
5. Height of mother under 5 ft. 2 ins. (155 cms.).
6. Poor past obstetric history.
   One or more previous stillbirth(s) and neonatal death(s).
   One or more previous premature livebirth(s).
7. Toxemia of pregnancy.
   Moderate (diastolic blood pressure over 100 mm.)
   Severe (Proteinuria with diastolic blood pressure over 90; or diastolic blood pressure over 110 mm.).
8. Antepartum hemorrhage.
   Accidental APH.
   Placenta praevia.
   Unspecified APH.

The following additional maternal factors were found to increase "risk in labor":

1. Primiparity.
2. Maternal age over thirty in both primiparae and multiparae.
3. Previous live birth weighing less than 2.5 kg or an antepartum hemorrhage in a previous pregnancy.
4. Delivery before thirty-seven weeks and after forty-two weeks' gestation, especially in the presence of hypertension.
5. Hemoglobin less than 60% during pregnancy.
6. Babies weighing less than 3 kg. and more than 4.5 kg.
7. Babies which are substantially overweight or underweight for their gestational age, especially if delivery occurs after forty-one weeks' gestation.
8. Labor complicated by antepartum hemorrhage, prolapse of the cord or breech presentation. These abnormalities were present in 57% of all intrapartum deaths in the survey.
9. First stage of labor longer than 24 hours and the second stage longer than 150 minutes. Mortality increases when the interval between rupture of the membranes and delivery is greater than 24 hours.

The other important observation concerned the size of the fetus in relation to gestational age. A group of very vulnerable babies was identified, in whom the birth weight was less than two standard deviations below the mean for gestational age, to which the term "small-for-dates baby" was given. In the survey one-third of those born at thirty-eight weeks or later could be classified as "premature" by weight definition, but the perinatal risk for them was eight times greater than for babies weighing more than 2500 gms. born at term. The findings strongly supported the World Health Organization recommendation (1961) that the description "low birth weight" should replace "prematurity."

The interaction between length of gestation, birth weight, and necropsy findings proved important. The major causes of death of infants of short gestation were respiratory distress syndrome, intraventricular hemorrhage, and extreme immaturity; whereas the incidence of intrauterine anoxia and massive pulmonary hemorrhage was high in the low birth weight infants born after thirty-eight weeks. The "risk" of perinatal death associated with short gestation and reduced birth weight was identified and the influence of cigarette smoking on birth weight and mortality was established (Butler and Alberman 1969).

Planning based on predictable risk of perinatal loss and morbidity implies the principle of selection for optimum care on agreed criteria. This report in conjunction with the recommendations of the "Cranbrook Report" determined the need for a great expansion of hospital facilities. The "Cranbrook Report" set the target for hospital births at 70 percent, but through this decade a greater decrease in domiciliary births has occurred with a trend to selection of "low risk" patients for general practitioner maternity homes with easy facilities for transfer to hospital if complications occur.

Resources did not immediately allow sufficient expansion of specialist hospital care but experiments in various centers to increase patient coverage by early discharge home at forty-eight hours began (Ministry of Health 1965). The popularity of this scheme has increased the hospital delivery rate of "high risk" patients very significantly; subsequent domiciliary care is undertaken by the general practitioner and the local authority midwife for fifteen to twenty-eight days after delivery.

As even forty-eight-hour hospital admission may be refused by the "high risk" group of older multigravida of low socioeconomic status, "hospital delivery units" have been opened comprising a separate delivery and recovery suite in a consultant-staffed hospital. Labor is managed by an "obstetric list" general practitioner and a domiciliary midwife who gives all nursing care and accompanies the patient home by ambulance from two to six hours after delivery. This enables the general practitioner to maintain his skill and interest in midwifery, but hospital resources are immediately available in emergency, e.g., blood transfusion, or pediatric care for infant resuscitation and ventilation. As a result of all these schemes an overall hospital delivery rate of 90 percent has been achieved, with 98 percent in many areas.

During this decade a worldwide interest in fetal development and physiology arose so that university neonatal research units have been established, notably at the London Hospital (Kenneth Cross), at Hammersmith Postgraduate Institute (Peter Tizard), and at Oxford University (Geoffrey Dawes). Monitoring and diagnostic techniques for detection and management of disorders became available and new treatments for serious and often lethal disorders of the newborn. To meet this new challenge neonatology has been established as a pediatric sub-specialty.

As perinatal mortality steadily declines, concern has arisen for the quality of survival, which demands more critical assessment and more elaborate investigation and treatment. Improved obstetric monitoring of pregnancy and labor has accentuated the need for close cooperation of obstetricians and pediatricians. Infant resuscitation has become an important feature of perinatal care so that the presence of a pediatrician at the delivery of all "high risk" mothers has been organized in some of the large hospitals, but as it is essential that skilled neonatal resuscitation should invariably be available in delivery rooms and special care nurseries, others who frequently undertake this task include anesthetists, obstetricians, and nursing officers after appropriate training. Since 1963, the Central Midwives Board has required all student midwives to receive instruction in neonatal intubation and use of intermittent positive pressure respiration.

Phase III: 1969-74. In 1968 an Expert Group on Special Care for Babies was appointed by the Ministry of Health to review progress and make recommendations for future developments. The Report (Dept. of Health and Social Security 1971) indicated that big changes had taken place in the previous decade. Perhaps the most significant had been the increasing provision and changed attitudes to "special care."

In 1969, 184,000 babies were estimated to require special care which could be classified under four broad categories:

1. Babies born after difficult deliveries.
2. Low birth weight babies (2,500 gram or less).
3. Sick newborn infants, including many with congenital malformations, an increasing number of whom required surgery.
4. Perinatal deaths. Sixty-six percent of these occurred in low birth weight babies and it was considered that some stillbirths should be included in estimating special care cribs needs as with improved obstetric management and resuscitation service they might be expected to survive.

The statistics indicated that there had been a steady increase in the number of babies treated in special care cribs. The provision by Regional Board Areas averaged 4.4 cribs per 1,000 live births (range 3.6 to 6.5 cribs); 257 nurseries had been established representing 3,369 cribs; 47 nurseries (1,253 cribs) contained twenty or more cribs.

Ninety percent of these babies were born in specialist maternity departments. The overall average length of stay was 8.5 days but the average length of stay for low birth weight babies was 19.1 days, and babies after difficult delivery but with no obvious illness or defect, 3 days.

From 1948-1969 the stillbirth rate fell from 23.2 (per 1,000 live births) to 10.2; and late neonatal deaths (one week and under four weeks) from 4.9 to 1.8. The fall in first week deaths was less, from 16.2 to 10.2 (1969) and indicated the need for further effort to reduce early mortality (see Tables 6-1 and 6-2).

The Expert Group recommended that the aims of a special care service for babies should be to anticipate and prevent damage before and during birth, and to provide special treatment, staff training, follow-up, research. Area planning should include close obstetric-pediatric cooperation and liaison committees to prevent or anticipate antenatal complications.

Two types of special nursery provision had already begun to emerge

Table 6-1.

Period	Stillbirths per 1,000 Live and Stillbirths	1st-week Deaths per 1,000 Live Births	Perinatal Deaths per 1,000 Live and Stillbirths	Late Neonatal Mortality 1 week and under 4 weeks
1946-50				4.9
1948	23.2	15.6	38.5	
1958	21.5	13.8	35.0	2.4
1964	16.3	12.0	28.2	1.8
1969	13.2	10.2	23.4	1.8

Source: Office of Population Censuses and Surveys.

Table 6-2.   Percentage Fall of Mortality Rate Between 1953 and 1971

Birth Weight Group	Mortality rate		Stillbirth rate 1955-71
	Day 0	Days 1-28	
≤ 1500G	9.9	37.0	12.2
1501-2000G	12.4	48.3	30.2
2001-2250G	18.7	52.2	38.3
2251-2500G	23.8	50.6	46.7
>2500G	15.0	43.3	54.5
All	18.9	44.7	46.1

Source: E. Alberman, "Stillbirths and Neonatal Mortality in England and Wales by Birth Weight, 1953-1971," *Health Trends* 6 (1974): 14-17.

as the pattern best suited to the existing organization of obstetric and pediatric resources and it is recommended that this should be extended.

The Special Care Nursery

These nurseries have been developed in association with the majority of specialist obstetric and children's departments of district general hospitals. They provide a level of care for newborn babies that is not available elsewhere. Most of these babies need special investigation or treatment, controlled temperature, and suitable feeding techniques, and should invariably be under direct clinical control of consultant pediatricians. Some special care nurseries are too small to staff adequately and provide insufficient experience for staff; these will be phased out as new building allows reorganization of obstetric and pediatric beds. Normally one nursery with 24 cribs should serve 250,000 population, but population density, birthrate, social class distribution, and incidence of low birth weight may necessitate variation. From statistics it is estimated that six special care cribs per 1,000 live births should suffice to meet the need for some years to come.

Intensive Care for the Newborn

"Intensive care" with the use of highly specialized techniques for monitoring and mechanical ventilation has been introduced for management of a small number of babies with a high early neonatal mortality rate. These include: babies of very low birth weight; severe hemolytic disease; respiratory distress syndrome and other respiratory problems. This type of intensive care needs considerable expertise and a high ratio of medical and nursing staff to patients so that these units have been developed in hospitals which have large resources of staff and usually research facilities (see also Appendix B).

The trend has arisen for intensive care areas to be set up in a few existing special care nurseries where very sick or very small infants can be concentrated to benefit from specialized equipment and highly experienced staff. The report recommended that in England and Wales, 320 intensive care cribs are needed for the following categories: (1) 50 percent of live born babies of less than 1500 gm., and (2) An equal number of very sick babies of larger birth weights. Close obstetric-pediatric collaboration in antenatal care often makes it possible to plan for the delivery of "high-risk" women in a hospital where neonatal intensive care is available, as for example in severe hemolytic disease; otherwise transportation of these very sick babies from the place of birth is made by special ambulance equipped with incubators and mechanical ventilation so that a nurse and a doctor accompany the infant during the journey.

The medical staffing needs to be generous for infant intensive care. The recommended establishment is two part-time consultant pediatricians, a registrar assigned to the special care nursery, and three resident pediatric staff engaged solely in neonatal work with an extra resident available if needed. These nurseries provide a very valuable clinical situation for perinatal research units which have been developed in several centers.

The nursing allocation for "intensive care areas" in special care units is three nurses to one crib. To increase the supply of well-trained nurses which have always been essential to special and intensive care for babies, the Joint Board of Clinical Nursing Studies (1973) in collaboration with the Ministry of Health established a first level post-basic nursing course of four months duration in special and intensive baby care, and a higher level course of six months duration for those with experience in preparation for posts of responsibility in these departments. These courses are undertaken in approved hospitals and qualify for national certification.

REORGANIZATION OF THE NATIONAL HEALTH SERVICE, 1974

The tripartite administration was replaced in April 1974 by a unified system which is aimed to promote more efficiency in the use of resources by defining priorities over the whole field of medical care with more emphasis on preventive and community care and better assessment of needs and results. (*Reorganisation of the National Health Service*, England, 1972.)

The Department of Health and Social Services is responsible for national planning, allocation of finance and monitoring of performance. New regional health authorities are responsible for all services, including the teaching hospitals, in similar geographical areas to the former hospital boards.

Ninety Area Health Authorities (England) corresponding to local government boundaries within regions, assess needs, plan and operate services within their areas in accordance with regional and national policies. Areas containing medical schools are designated "teaching" areas and have special responsibilities for appointment of medical staff and provision of facilities for undergraduate medical teaching activities. Areas are divided into health districts (approximately 200 districts) as the natural level for delivery of comprehensive health care for populations of 200,000 to 1,000,000 people. The Area Health Authority coordinates district plans and provides finance.

District Management Teams organize the District Health Services and are advised by specialist professional planning committees which must include an advisory committee for child health services. The District General Hospital provides for major specialties, but some specialties will not be represented in every hospital. In urban communities which are divided into several health districts it is probable that the past trends will continue whereby large obstetric and pediatric departments situated together in one or two district hospitals will serve a whole area and thus enable large special care nurseries to be developed with one neonatal intensive care unit for the area.

Nursing services are managed by a district nursing officer which has already shown the advantage of improved communication and greater flexibility as between the hospital and community services, which particularly assists organization of antenatal care and follow-up for the maternity and perinatal services.

The main benefits that are expected are that cooperation between all professional personnel at the district level will improve standards and facilitate new developments in patient care.

COST OF SPECIAL AND INTENSIVE CARE BABY UNITS

The National Health Service method of budgeting and accounting does not normally allow for costing of beds in a particular department separately from the average cost for the whole hospital of that type, which in this case is usually a maternity hospital.

However the approximate cost for 1973 of one modern purpose-built air-conditioned special care baby unit with an area for six intensive care cribs, which is well equipped and fully staffed according to the recommendations (DHSS 1971) with an average thirty crib occupancy, has been estimated at £5683 (U.S. $13,616) per crib per annum. Average cost per baby treated (786 annual admissions) was £211 (U.S. $496). This does not include transportation costs for 102 babies brought to the hospital after birth, of after-care by specialist health visitors, but includes an appropriate portion of salaries of pediatric medical staff.

THE FUTURE

The Health Service has promoted a wide distribution of skills and facilities so that the overall standard of perinatal care has improved immeasurably in twenty-six years. Resources have been made available so that research methods have in many instances been applied to clinical care without delay. The future lies in expansion of services on the present pattern but with better organization to meet the total need for close cooperation with obstetricians for antenatal and perinatal care; planned detailed studies of individual perinatal deaths and morbidity on a national as well as local scale to delineate the problems more precisely and define avoidable factors; research into still obscure areas of fetal and neonatal physiology, the prevention and treatment of serious disorders of the newborn, and methods of support for babies of low birth weight and short gestation.

APPENDIX A

The following list is an example of criteria for the admission of women to a Consultant Maternity Unit in 1967. Women with one or more of the following indications should be confined in a Major Maternity Unit.

1. *Primigravidae*

    30 years of age and over or *17 years of age and under*
    Below 5 feet in height
    With abnormal obesity (over 13 stone if average height)
    Essential hypertension
    History of infertility + investigation
    Deformities of the bony pelvis
    Preexisting medical diseases, e.g.
        heart disease, chronic nephritis, diabetes, tuberculosis, puerperal psychosis.

2. *Multigravidae*

    35 years of age and over
    Parity Four and over (fifth or subsequent pregnancy of 28 weeks or over)
    Pre-eclampsia and/or eclampsia
    Previous *abortions*
    Previous *antepartum hemorrhage*
    Previous *difficult labor*
    Previous *caesarean section, hysterotomy, myomectomy or operation on the Fallopian tubes or ovaries, pelvic floor repair or third degree tear*
    Previous *Perinatal fetal loss*
    Previous *premature labor at less than 37 weeks*
    Previous *low weight babies* (less than 5 lbs.)
    Preexisting medical diseases (see under "primigravidae" above).

3. *All Women Who During Pregnancy Develop Complications Such as:*

    Pre-eclampsia and/or *eclampsia*
    Essential hypertension
    Persistent malpresentations, including *breech* and *instable lie*
    Multiple pregnancy
    Antepartum hemorrhage or *threatened abortion*
    Medical disorders of pregnancy, e.g. severe anemia (70% or less) not responding to treatment, recurrent urinary infections.
    Hydramnios
    Rhesus negative with antibodies
    Non-engaged head at term in a primigravida
    Post-maturity of more than seven days
    Premature labor at less than 37 weeks

APPENDIX B

**Notes on Design and Equipment of
Nurseries for Intensive Care[a]**

Intensive Care Within a Special Care Nursery. The intensive care area

---

[a]Compiled from the Report of the Expert Group 1971.

comprises one room with space for six to eight babies to allow for economy in nursing and for continuous observation. Another room should be available to allow for closure for cleaning and two isolation single rooms. Fifty square feet per crib is desirable, especially if mothers participate in nursing care.

There should be unimpeded vision of all working areas with glazed panelling to within 76.2 cms (2 ft. 6 inches) from the floor. Heat regulation should provide for room temperatures of 24°C to 27°C. (Higher temperatures are only required if open crib nursing of very small babies, 1500 gm or less, is used.) The intensity of lighting should be high with supplementary lighting to assist observation of seriously ill babies. Lighting and decoration should not distort important clinical signs, such as cyanosis and jaundice.

Piped oxygen, compressed air, and piped suction are desirable. Each crib station should be provided with ample power outlets. An emergency call system should be provided wherever babies are nursed.

The following basic equipment is required: Monitors for heart rate and ECG; respiration and apnoea, temperature, blood pressure; equipment for phototherapy, mechanical ventilation, oxygen analyzers, pressure transducers, infant warming tables.

Facilities for X-rays should be available in the unit. A small laboratory should be provided for blood gas analysis, and other simple biochemical measurements.

REFERENCES

Alberman, E. "Stillbirths and Neonatal Mortality in England and Wales by Birth Weight. 1953-1971." *Health Trends* 6 (1974): 14-17.
British Paediatric Association Report. "Arrangements for Newly Born Babies in Maternity Hospitals." *Arch.Dis.Child.* 18 (1943): 157-158.
British Paediatric Association. "Memorandum on the Care of Premature Babies in Urban and Rural Areas." *Arch.Dis.Child.* 26 (1951): 276-278.
Butler, N.R. and Bonham, D.G. *Perinatal Mortality.* London: Livingstone, 1963.
Butler, N.R. and Alberman, E.D. *Perinatal Problems.* London: Livingstone, 1969.
The Care of the Premature Baby in the Bristol Area. A symposium. Southmead Hospital Group Management Committee. Bristol, 1951.
Central Health Services Council. *Haemolytic Disease of the Newborn.* London: HMSO, 1958.
Central Health Services Council. *Prevention of Prematurity and the Care of Premature Infants.* London: HMSO, 1961.
Crosse, V.M. *The Premature Baby.* London: Churchill, 1945.
Department of Health and Social Security. *Report of the Expert Group on Special Care for Babies.* Reports on Public Health and Medical Subjects, No. 127. London: HMSO, 1971.
Maternity in Great Britain. A Survey. London: Oxford University Press, 1948.
Miller, F.J.W. *Medical Officer* 86 (1951): 13.
Ministry of Health. *Care of Premature Infants.* Circular 20/44. London: HMSO, 1944.

Ministry of Health. *Report of the Maternity Services Committee.* (Chairman: The Earl of Cranbrook). London: HMSO, 1959.

Ministry of Health. *Early Discharge of Maternity Patients.* Circular 6/65. London: HMSO, 1965.

World Health Organization. *Expert Group on Prematurity.* Technical Report Series No. 27. Geneva: WHO, 1950.

World Health Organization. *Public Health Aspects of Low Birth Weight.* Technical Report Series No. 217. Geneva: WHO, 1961.

Chapter 7

Longitudinal Studies in the United Kingdom

J.W.B. Douglas

I have defined a cohort here as a nationally representative group of persons who are all of the same age and whose illness or other experience approximates to that of their own generation. The cohort studies described are longitudinal. In each instance a complete week's births was taken initially and some or all have been followed in succeeding years. The two studies are the 1946 National Survey of Health and Development and the 1958 National Child Development Study. Mention is made of a further cohort born in 1970 which may form the basis of a further longitudinal study.

THE 1946 COHORT—NATIONAL SURVEY OF HEALTH AND DEVELOPMENT

The 1946 cohort was the first and has to some extent formed a template for the two subsequent studies. It is therefore relevant to discuss its origins in some detail. In 1945 the Royal Commission on Population needed information about the maternity services to answer questions on "how well they were meeting the needs of those who use them," the "extent to which they varied from one part of the country to another," the "proportion of women offered and accepting analgesia," and "the costs of having a baby." At the instigation of the Royal Commission, a joint committee of the Royal College of Obstetricians and Gynaecologists and the Population Investigation Committee was set up to seek the answers. Professor David Glass, who was the secretary of this committee, has been deeply involved with this study from its beginning and without his help and advice we would undoubtedly have foundered many years ago.

    It was clear at the outset that the best way to answer the questions put by the Royal Commission was to study the experience of women who had recently had a baby. It was therefore decided to take a week's births in England, Wales, and Scotland, and ask health visitors to conduct a special interview, some two months after the birth, in which detailed questions would be asked about the services used as well as about home conditions and expenditure on maternity care and layette. In choosing a week's sample we were governed by limitations of funds and time. An answer was needed within two years and the total money available was only sufficient to cover this period. The data had therefore to be collected quickly as well as analyzed quickly. The health visitors had many strong recommendations as interviewers. They were on the spot and could combine this study with their normal work, and they knew the maternity and child welfare services well and had access to records. Moreover no payment was required—or indeed would have been allowed—for their participation.

This plan was welcomed by the local maternity and child welfare authorities and out of 458 in the whole country only 34 were unable to help, the majority having good reasons for refusing based on shortage of staff. A total of 15,130 births were notified in the cooperating authorities during the week chosen, which was the first in March 1946, and 90.5 percent of the mothers were successfully interviewed; the main loss was failure to trace unmarried mothers who had moved away from their homes to have their babies and then moved on before the health visitors called to interview them two months later.

The interviewing was completed by September 1946 and the final report, "Maternity in Great Britain," was published in 1948. In the meantime the unexpected success of the venture made us feel that a long term follow-up would be possible. This would be likely to yield valuable information on the relation of home circumstances to infant and child morbidity and mortality. Moreover cohort studies such as this, if repeated at regular intervals, would provide a means for monitoring the effects of changes in the medical and social services on the welfare of those who should have benefited from them.

While we were anxious to follow up this group, the total number was too large for our resources and we therefore took all births to non-manual workers' families and the families of agricultural workers, but only a quarter of the rest. The reason for sampling in this way was that it left sufficient numbers in the more prosperous groups for useful comparisons to be made with the disadvantaged. Illegitimate children and twins were excluded as being likely to provide problems that we could not afford to deal with. The first follow-up survey was done when the children were two years old and subsequent contacts have been at intervals of never more than two years.

This extension of the 1946 study was made possible by the generous help of health visitors, school doctors, school nurses, teachers, and youth employment officers who interviewed the young people on our behalf. Owing to the wide scatter of the sample members, there were few in any one area or any one school, which meant that we could ask for special school medical examinations, for teachers to keep running records of absence checked with the parents, and for the regular tests of pupils for ability and attainment without feeling that we were putting a heavy burden on the teachers or schools. The disadvantage of this method was that we were unable to brief the interviewers and had to rely on printed instructions on the questionnaire forms. We therefore concentrated mainly on factual questions which could be checked either with records or by comparing the answers given on one questionnaire with those to similar questions given on the next. All hospital admissions have been checked with the institutions concerned and so have all educational courses and qualifications.

A major change in the way information was collected was introduced in 1965 when mail questionnaires were used to obtain relatively simple information on accidents, hospital admissions, contacts with family doctors or outpatients departments, marital status, children, and employment. Those who were known to be of poor literacy were not sent forms but were interviewed by health visitors who also followed up those who did not reply to our mail questionnaires. In this way contact was maintained with more than 80 percent of the sample.

In 1972 for the first time trained interviewers who had been well briefed were used to interview all members of the sample. The interview, which lasted between 70 and 90 minutes, covered among other aspects, marriage, children, housing conditions, employment, training, earnings, the educational origins of the spouse, religious beliefs, leisure interests, voting behavior, and perception of society. The survey members were also given the same test of reading that they had completed eleven years earlier at school and also repeated the short form of the Maudsley personality inventory they had previously filled in at the age of sixteen. These interviews at twenty-six are seen as the last major contact with the original sample and are designed to provide accurate dependent variables against which the earlier data can be compared. At the present moment interviews have been successfully completed with 86 percent of the sample members still living in Great Britain and it is likely that a further 2 to 3 percent will be contacted during the next few months. A substantial proportion of those that were unwilling to be interviewed have filled in a short form giving basic information which will give us a rather better estimate of bias and loss than we have at present.

Losses have been low throughout this inquiry. They vary, of course, between the different types of interview. Medical examinations, for example, are associated with relatively high losses, 12 percent, whereas with home interviews they are approximately 10 percent. The success in retaining the sample stems partly from the fact that the study is nationwide so that we are not plagued by losses from internal migration. Moreover the interviews were in general done by people known to the parents as working with the health authority or the schools. Initially, losses were rather higher in the non-manual than in the mainly working class group but in recent years this has been reversed partly owing to the higher proportion of manual working class youths who have entered the services and the merchant navy. While we have not attempted to get further information about those who went abroad, we are able to describe the characteristics of families who have done so. Unfortunately, we were not able to include in this sample the corresponding group of immigrant children who have moved to Britain in succeeding years.

The state of retention of the sample may be summarized by saying that at each interview between 86 and 90 percent of the sample members living in the country have been seen, though, of course, the same young people were not necessarily contacted on each occasion. Complete information on measurements or education tests is likely to be available for between 60 and 80 percent of the sample depending on the number of individual contacts involved. On the other hand for hospital admissions, accidents, educational qualification, etc., we have always asked questions in the form: "The last accident you had was when you were 16-1/2 and broke your wrist playing soccer. What accidents have you had since then?"—so that gaps were likely to be filled in even if they were of several years duration. Information of this type may therefore be regarded as relatively complete even if there have been occasional lapses from the study.

A further extension of this study was initiated in 1969—when Mr. Wadsworth started following up the first born children of survey members. The aim was to obtain information when they reached the age of four years that would allow us to compare care and health over two generations. This has now been extended to an additional interview at eight years when we propose to test the children using the same tests as were given to one of their parents some twenty years earlier. At the same time we hope to test the other parent. This study, of course, is on a very much smaller scale than the original and in each year only some 200 to 250 children come up for study. A report on the first 800 is now being prepared.

THE 1958 COHORT—NATIONAL CHILD DEVELOPMENT STUDY

The stimulus for the 1958 cohort study came from the National Birthday Trust Fund and the Royal College of Obstetricians and Gynaecologists. Whereas the initial aim of the 1946 study was to describe the nature and function of maternity services, the 1958 study was concerned with answering questions on perinatal mortality, i.e., stillbirths plus first week deaths. In the twelve years that had elapsed since the 1946 survey there had been substantial changes in the maternity services and little evidence of any fall in stillbirths or first week deaths. This, it seemed, was an area where more knowledge was urgently needed. The plan was to collect information on one week's births and also to study all stillbirths and early and late neonatal deaths during a period of three months. By coincidence, the birth week chosen was the first week in March 1958. The midwife in attendance at delivery was asked to complete a schedule covering the main details of pregnancy and labor and giving a relatively brief account of home circumstances, employment of father, smoking, etc.

This time it was the midwives who were asked to complete the initial form and 98 percent of the total of the mothers of the 17,205 infants born were successfully interviewed.

In addition to the one week interviews, a special study was made of stillbirths and neonatal deaths during the months of March, April, and May 1958. In addition to collecting information on pregnancy and labor, an attempt was made to secure a pathological examination. This was highly successful in March when 91 percent of deaths came to necropsy but less successful in the subsequent two months when necropsies were secured for 55 percent and 68 percent respectively.

The results of the perinatal study were published in 1963 and 1969 and represent a major contribution to our understanding of stillbirths and early infant deaths as well as presenting a picture of maternity care after ten years of the National Health Service. It was not, however, until 1965 that these children were contacted again. As with the 1946 study there had initially been no firm intention to follow the children up and the problems of analysis were so formidable that it was five years or so before any decision could be taken. Even so it is doubtful whether the money for a follow-up would have been forthcoming if it had not been for the need of the Plowden Committee on primary education for information about the relation between home circumstances and school achievement. This, while it made the financing of this longitudinal study possible, meant that the children were seen and tested at seven rather than at eight, which would have been more suitable because, on the one hand, a direct comparison with the earlier study could be made and, on the other, more reliable and valid tests of attainment could have been used.

The perinatal study entered its longitudinal stage as the National Child Development Study with Professor Neville Butler and Dr. Kelmer Pringle as co-directors and the National Childrens Bureau as its home.

The 1958 cohort has been followed up *in toto*. After the first midwives' interview the same sources of data were used as in the earlier study, namely, head teachers, class teachers, the school medical service, and health visitors. Subsequent contacts were made at eleven when the children were about to change from primary to their secondary schools, and sixteen, which was the final year of compulsory education.

THE 1970 COHORT—BRITISH BIRTHS STUDY

This study covered the births in one week, the first in April 1970. It was under the joint auspices of the National Birthday Trust Fund, who had been concerned with the previous studies, and the Royal College of Obstetricians and Gynaecologists, and was mainly directed towards obtaining details of pregnancy, labor and the puerperium. Two limited follow-ups have been in progress: one where the particular focus is on the problems of light-for-date babies, and the other a regional study in the west of England, which so far has been mainly concerned with describing the family environment and verbal communication. The reports from this cohort study are still to come.

THE VALUE OF COHORT STUDIES

The three studies mentioned here had their origin with concern about the maternity services and indeed provide bench marks to chart their development from 1946, two years before the introduction of the National Health Service, to the present day. In this they have served a valuable purpose and it might be suggested a sufficient one. There are, however, substantial reasons for wishing to follow up birth cohorts into adult life. The medical, social, and educational services are changing rapidly and it is important that we should know how these changes affect different groups in the population and whether the new services are fulfilling the policies that engendered them. The three cohort studies, for example, are well placed to assess the impact of educational changes in both the preschool and the secondary school period. For the 1946 group, preschool education was rare whereas for those born in 1970 it was substantial. By comparing the progress of children in these three cohorts we would see changes in the uptake of preschool educational provision by different sections of the population and the extent to which the behavior and progress of children when they reach school reflects the preschool education they have received. The sorts of questions that might be answered are: How far are the new services reaching the families for whom they were intended? If they are failing to reach some of these families, what are the reasons? How far are they achieving the aims for which they were designed? What is the evidence that they are reducing social inequalities in educational opportunities?

At a later stage of the educational process the three cohorts span years of important change. The 1946 group went through a system that was almost wholly selective with a division into grammar, technical and secondary modern schools being made at 11+. By the time the 1958 group reached their secondary schools the system was largely comprehensive, and it is likely that with the 1970 group it will be almost wholly comprehensive. There is here a unique opportunity to see whether and in what ways the change from a selective to a comprehensive type of educational system has altered the social, sexual, and geographical inequalities in educational achievement which were so marked in the 1946 study.

A third example of the value of comparisons between cohorts lies in the hospital care of children. In 1946 there was little recognition of the needs of infants and children in hospital; in more than a thousand admissions only three mothers came into hospital with the child and only 16 percent of children were admitted to hospitals where visiting was "unrestricted" in the sense that it was not limited to parents and relations. Since then, and particularly after the publication of the Platt report in 1959, there have been great improvements aimed at reducing the distress of children in hospital. While the median length of stay has been halved and the facilities for visiting and for mothers being admitted with their children greatly improved, the proportion of children going to hospital has increased as has also the proportion of children who are readmitted. There is strong evidence from the 1946 study that some children admitted to hospital in the first five years of life have persisting disturbances of behavior and learning, detectable in adolescence, that seem to stem from their hospital stay; for example, there is a quantitative relationship between adolescent disturbance and both length of stay and number of readmissions. It is important for admission policy that this analysis should be repeated on one of the later cohorts to see whether the improvements in care have been accompanied by a reduction or elimination of persistent disturbances of behavior and learning or whether they have been offset by the increasing proportion of children admitted on several occasions. The 1958 and 1970 cohorts could provide the answers.

While it is in the process of monitoring the effects of new policies that I see cohort studies as making a uniquely valuable contribution, they offer, as the lists of papers below show, many other research opportunities. What stands out from these lists of papers is that returns are immediate and it is not a matter of waiting till the end of the study before the harvesting begins. Of course the focus of interest changes as the studies progress. For example, now that the 1946 group have reached adult life my interest is concentrated on analyzing the circumstances and decisions that have contributed to their present state. In our twenty-eight-year olds, for example, can I predict from what I know of their early life who will end up in the most deprived 10 percent and, apart from their home environments, what decisions and what illnesses or disturbances of behavior have contributed to this outcome?

The studies I have described suffer from a lack of consistent planning. They started as one type of study and ended up as another. From being limited to the maternity and child welfare services they have been extended through the preschool years, into adolescence or adult life. This has imposed severe limitations and what is now needed is a careful assessment of the functions of any further studies of this type that may be projected and the sampling and organization that are needed for them.

THE NATIONAL SURVEY OF HEALTH AND DEVELOPMENT PAPERS GIVING THE RESULTS OF THE SURVEY

I. *The Maternity and Child Welfare Services*
II. *The Premature Child*

III. *Morbidity*
IV. *Education*
 V. *Behavior Problems*
VI. *Miscellaneous*

I. The Maternity and Child Welfare Services

*1. "A Survey of Childbearing in Britain." *Population Studies* 1 (1947): 99.
*2. *Maternity in Great Britain*, Oxford University Press, 1948.
*3. Douglas, J.W.B., and Rowntree, G. "Supplementary Maternal and Child Health Services, Part I, Postnatal Care—Part II, Nurseries." *Population Studies* 3 (1949): 205.
*4. Rowntree, G. "Supplementary Child Health Services, Part III, Infant Welfare Centres." *Population Studies* 3 (1950): 375.
*5. Rowntree, G. "Diphtheria Immunization in a National Sample of Children Aged Two Years in March 1948." *Monthly Bulletin of the Ministry of Health* 9 (1950): 134.
*6. Douglas, J.W.B. "Deux Enquetes Nationales sur la Maternite et la Sante de l'Enfant en Grande Bretagne." *Population* 5 (1950): 625.
*7. Douglas, J.W.B. "The Environmental Challenge in Early Childhood." *Public Health* 78 (1964): 195-202.

II. The Premature Child

*1. Douglas, J.W.B. "Some Factors Associated with Prematurity." *Journal of Obstetrics and Gynaecology of the British Empire* 57 (1950): 625.
 2. Douglas, J.W.B. "Birthweight and the History of Breastfeeding." *Lancet* (1954): ii, 685.
*3. Douglas, J.W.B. and Mogford, C. "The Health of Premature Children during the First Four Years of Life." *British Medical Journal* (1953): i, 748.
 4. Douglas, J.W.B. and Mogford, C. "The Growth of Premature Children." *Archives of Disease in Childhood* 28 (1953): 436.
 5. Douglas, J.W.B. "The Age at which Premature Children Walk." *Medical Officer* 95 (1956): 33.
 6. Douglas, J.W.B. "The Mental Ability of Premature Children." *British Medical Journal* (1956): i, 1210.
*7. Douglas, J.W.B. "Premature Children at Primary Schools." *British Medical Journal* (1960): i, 1008.
 8. Douglas, J.W.B. "Effects of Early Environment on Later Development." *J. Roy. Coll. Phycns.*, London, 3 (1969): 359-364.

---

*Reprints are no longer available

III. Morbidity

1. Douglas, J.W.B. "Social Class Differences in Health and Survival during the First Two Years of Life. The results of a National Survey." *Population Studies* 5 (1951): 35.
*2. Douglas, J.W.B. "The Health and Survival of Children in Different Social Classes. The Results of a National Survey." *Lancet* (1951): ii, 440.
3. Rowntree, G. "Accidents among Children under Two Years of Age in Great Britain." *Journal of Hygiene* 48 (1950): 323.
4. Rowntree, G. "Accidents among Children." *Monthly Bulletin of the Ministry of Health* 10 (1951): 150.
5. Blomfield, J.M. "An Account of Hospital Admissions in the Preschool Period." Mimeographed. (Copies available on application to the Joint Committee.)
*6. Douglas, J.W.B. "Reproductive Loss," in *Society: Problems and Methods of Study.* Edited by A.T. Welford, Michael Argyle, D.V. Glass, and J.N. Morris (Routledge & Kegan Paul Ltd., 1962).
7. Douglas, J.W.B. "Ability and Adjustment of Children Who Have Had Measles." *British Medical Journal* 2 (1964): 1301.
8. Cooper, J.E. "Epilepsy and a Longitudinal Survey of 5,000 Children." *British Medical Journal* (1965): i, 1020-1022.
9. Douglas, J.W.B. and Waller, R.E. "Air Pollution and Respiratory Infection in Children." *British Journal of Preventive and Social Medicine* 20 (1966): 1-8.
10. Pless, I.B. and Douglas, J.W.B. "Chronic Illness in Childhood, Part 1, Epidemiological and Clinical Characteristics." *Pediatrics* 47 (1971): 405-414.
11. Douglas, J.W.B. "Prospective Study of Effectiveness of Tonsillectomy in Children." *International Epidemiology Association*, 941-950. Proceedings of 6th International Scientific Meeting, Primosten, Yugoslavia. Savremena Administracija, Belgrade, January 1973.
12. Colley, J.R.T.; Douglas, J.W.B.; and Reid, D.D. "Respiratory Disease in Young Adults; Influence of Early Childhood Lower Respiratory Tract Illness, Social Class, Air Pollution, and Smoking." *British Medical Journal* (July 1973): 195-198.

IV. Education

*1. Douglas, J.W.B. "Waste of Talent." *Advancement of Science* (1963): 564.
2. Douglas, J.W.B. *The Home and the School* (MacGibbon and Kee, 1964).
*3. Douglas, J.W.B. and Ross, J.M. "The Effects of Absence on Primary

School Performance." *The British Journal of Educational Psychology* 35 (1965): 28-40.

*4. Douglas, J.W.B. and Ross, J.M. "The Later Educational Progress and Emotional Adjustment of Children Who Went to Nursery Schools or Classes." *Educational Research* 7 (1964): 73.

*5. Douglas, J.W.B. and Ross, J.M. "Age of Puberty Related to Educational Ability Attainment and School Leaving Age." *Journal of Child Psychology and Psychiatry* 5 (1964): 185.

*6. Douglas, J.W.B. "Education and Social Movement." In *Biological Aspects of Social Problems*, edited by Meade and Parks. (Oliver and Boyd, 1965), pp. 81-91.

*7. Douglas, J.W.B.; Ross, J.M.; and Simpson, H.R. "Some Observations on the Relationship Between Heights and Measured Ability among School Children." *Human Biology* 37 (1965): 178-186.

8. Douglas, J.W.B.; Ross, J.M.; Walker, D.A.; and Maxwell, S.M. "Differences in Test Score and in the Gaining of Selective Places for Scottish Children and those in England and Wales." *British Journal of Educational Psychology* 36 (1966): 150-157.

*9. Ross, J.M. and Case, P. "Why Do Children Leave Grammar School Early?" *New Society* 11-13 (November 1965).

*10. Douglas, J.W.B. "The Age of Reaching Puberty. Some Associated Factors and Some Educational Implications." *The Scientific Basis of Medicine Annual Reviews* (1966): 91-105.

*11. Ross, J.M. and Case, P. "Who Goes to Oxbridge." *New Society* 11-13 (May 1966).

*12. Douglas, J.W.B. and Ross, J.M. "Single Sex or Co-ed? The Academic Consequences." *Where* 5-8 (May 1966).

*13. Douglas, J.W.B. "The School Progress of Nervous and Troublesome Children." (Abstract) *British Journal of Psychiatry* 112 (1966): 1115-1116.

*14. Ross, J.M. "Should More Grammar School Boys Apply to Oxbridge." *Where* 10-11 (March 1967).

*15. Douglas, J.W.B.; Ross, J.M.; and Cooper, J.E. "The Relationship Between Handedness, Attainment and Adjustment in a National Sample of School Children." *Educational Research* 9 (1967): 223-232.

16. Douglas, J.W.B.; Ross, J.M.; and Simpson, H.R. "The Ability and Attainment of Short-Sighted Pupils." *The Journal of the Royal Statistical Society, Series A (General)* 130 (   ): 479-503.

17. Douglas, J.W.B.; Ross, J.M.; and Simpson, H.R. *All Our Future.* Peter Davies Ltd., 1968.

*18. Douglas, J.W.B.; Ross, J.M.; and Simpson, H.R. "The Myopic Elite." *New Society* (October 1968).

*19. Douglas, J.W.B. and Ross, J.M. "Do Independent Schools Deserve Their Reputation for Academic Success." *Where* 5-7 (November 1968).

*20. Douglas, J.W.B. and Ross, J.M. "How Are Girls Affected by Coeducation." *Where* 10-11 (Supplement 16), 1968.

*21. Ross, J.M. "Short-Sighted Children and Their Progress at School." *Mother and Child* (December 1968).

*22. Douglas, J.W.B. "The Child at Home and School." In King (ed.), *The Teacher and the Needs of Society, in Evolution.* Pergamon Press, 1970.

*23. Douglas, J.W.B. "Parental Encouragement." In M. Craft, *Family Class and Education.* Longman, 1970.

*24. Armitage, P.; Phillips, Celia; and Davies, Judith. "Towards a Model of the Upper Secondary School System." Higher Education Research Unit, London School of Economics, *J. R. Statist. Soc.,* Series A. (1970): 166-205.

25. Ross, J.M. and Simpson, H.R. "Educational Attainment." *British Journal of Educational Psychology* 41 (1971): 49-61.

*26. Ross, J.M. "The Able Misfits." *Where* (May 1971).

27. Ross, J.M. and Simpson, H.R. "The Rate of School Progress Between 8 and 15 Years and Between 15 and 18 Years." *British Journal of Educational Psychology* 41 (1971): 125-135.

*28. Orr, Lea. "The Dependence of Transition Proportions in the Education System on Observed Social Factors and School Characteristics." Higher Education Research Unit, London School of Economics, *J. R. Statist. Soc.,* Series A., 135 Part I (1972): 74.

V. Behavior Problems

*1. Bransby, E.R.; Blomfield, J.M.; and Douglas, J.W.B. "The Prevalence of Bed-Wetting." *Medical Officer* 94 (1955): 5.

2. Blomfield, J.M. and Douglas, J.W.B. "Bed-Wetting: Prevalence among Children Aged 4-7 Years." *Lancet* No. 1 (1956): 850.

*3. Douglas, J.W.B. and Mulligan, D.G. "Emotional Adjustment and Educational Achievement—the Preliminary Results of a Longitudinal Study of a National Sample of Children." *Proceedings of the Royal Society of Medicine* 54 (1961): 885-891.

*4. Mulligan, D.G.; Douglas, J.W.B.; Hammond, W.A.; and Tizard, J. "Delinquency and Symptoms of Maladjustment—the Findings of a Longitudinal Study." *Proceedings of the Royal Society of Medicine* 56 (1963): 1083-1086.

5. Douglas, J.W.B.; Ross, J.M.; Hammond, W.A.; and Mulligan, D.G. "Delinquency and Social Class." *The British Journal of Criminology* (1966): 294-302.

6. Douglas, J.W.B. and Ross, J.M. "Adjustment and Educational Progress." *British Journal of Educational Psychology* 38 (1968): 2-4.

*7. Douglas, J.W.B. and Ross, J.M. "Characteristics of Delinquent Boys and

Their Homes." *Genetic and Environmental Influences on Behaviour*, edited by Meade and Parkes. Oliver and Boyd, 1968.

8. Douglas, J.W.B. "Broken Families and Child Behaviour." *J. Roy. Coll. Phycns.*, London 4 (1970): 203.

9. Douglas, J.W.B. "Early Disturbing Events and Later Enuresis." In *Bladder Control and Enuresis*, I. Kolvin, R.C. MacKeith, and S.R. Meadow, Spastics. International Medical Publishers, 1973, pp. 109-117.

VI. Miscellaneous

*1. Douglas, J.W.B. "The Extent of Breastfeeding in Great Britain in 1946, with Special Reference to the Health and Survival of Children." *Journal of Obstetrics and Gynaecology of the British Empire* 57 (1950): 336.

*2. MacCarthy, D.; Douglas, J.W.B.; and Mogford, C. "Circumcision in a National Sample of Four-Year-Old Children." *British Medical Journal* 2 (1952): 755.

*3. Rowntree, G. "Early Childhood in Broken Families." *Population Studies* 8 (1955): 247.

*4. Douglas, J.W.B. and Blomfield, J.M. "Maternal Employment and the Welfare of Children—an Account of a Survey in Progress." *Eugenics Review* 49 (1957): 69.

5. Douglas, J.W.B. and Blomfield, J.M. *Children Under Five*. Allen and Unwin Ltd., 1958.

*6. Douglas, J.W.B. "The Height of Boys and Girls and Their Home Environment." Printed in Switzerland, Separatum, S. Kargar Gasel, New York. In *Modern Problems in Paediatrics*.

*7. Douglas, J.W.B. and Simpson, H.R. "Height in Relation to Puberty, Family Size and Social Class, A Longitudinal Study." *Milbank Memorial Fund Quarterly* 42 (1964): 20-32.

*8. Nelson, D.M. "Studying the Employment and Training of a National Sample of 17-year-olds." *Occupational Psychology* (1964).

9. Douglas, J.W.B. and Blomfield, J.M. "The Reliability of Longitudinal Surveys." *Milbank Memorial Fund Quarterly* 34 (1956): 3.

10. Nelson, D.M. "The Predictive Value of the Rothwell-Miller Interest Blank." *Occupational Psychology* 42 (1968): 123-131.

*11. Douglas, J.W.B. "The 1946 National Survey of Health and Development in Britain. Some Early Findings and Later Developments." *Sociological Microjournal* microfiche, 7 (1973): 35-36.

12. Douglas, J.W.B. and Lowe, M. "Longitudinal Surveys and the Study of Social Mobility." Part I, *Soc. Sci. Inform.* 12, 4 (1973): 67-88.

National Child Development Study (1958 Cohort): Publications

Books

Books	Author(s)	Publisher(s)
Perinatal Mortality (1963)	Butler, N.R. and Bonham, D.G.	E. & S. Livingstone, Edinburgh
11,000 Seven-Year-Olds (1966)	Pringle, M.L. Kellmer; Butler, N.R.; and Davie, R.	Longman in association with National Children's Bureau
Perinatal Problems (1969)	Butler, N.R. and Alberman, E.D.	E. & S. Livingstone, Edinburgh
Born Illegitimate (1971)	Crellin, E.; Pringle, M.L. Kellmer; and West, P.	National Foundation for Educational Research
Growing Up Adopted (1972)	Seglow, J.; Pringle, M.L. Kellmer; and Wedge, P.	National Foundation for Educational Research
From Birth to Seven (1972)	Davie, R.; Butler, N.R.; and Goldstein, H.	Longman in association with National Children's Bureau
A Pattern of Disadvantage (1972)	Donnison, D. (Ed.)	National Foundation for Educational Research
Born to Fail? (1973)	Wedge, P.J. and Prosser, H.	Arrow Books, London

Chapters in Books

Chapter Heading	Book Title	Chapter by	Publisher(s)
"Complications of Birth Asphyxia with Special Reference to Resuscitation"	*The Obstetrician, Anaesthetist and the Paediatrician* (1963)	Butler, N.R.	Pergamon Press
"The First Follow Up of the Children Born in the Control Week"	*Perinatal Problems*	Davie, R.	E. & S. Livingstone
"Planning and Programming for Child Care"	*Selected Papers on Learning Disabilities* (1969)	Pringle, M.L. Kellmer	Academic Therapy Publications, San Rafael, Calif., USA.

"Reading at the Infant Stage: Some Results from the National Child Development Study" (1958 Cohort)	*Reading: Problems and Perspectives* (1970)	Davie, R.	United Kingdom Reading Association
"Appendix VII: Likely Outcomes of Longitudinal Studies. Section: National Child Development Study" (1958 Cohort)	*Longitudinal Studies and the Social Sciences* (1970)	Davie, R.	Heineman for the Social Science Research Council

Papers in Journals and Other Publications

Paper entitled	*Author(s)*	*Journal/Publication*
"National Survey of Perinatal Mortality: First Results"	Butler, N.R.	*Brit. Med. J.* 1 (May 6, 1961): 1313-1315.
Perinatal Mortality Survey under auspices of the National Birthday Trust Fund	Butler, N.R.	*Proc. Roy. Soc. Med.* 54, 12 (Dec. 1961):1089-1092 (Section of Paediatrics, pp. 39-42).
"Congenital Diaphragmatic Hernia as a Cause of Perinatal Mortality"	Butler, N.R. and Claireaux, A.E.	*Lancet,* March 31, 1962, pp. 659-663
Perinatal Mortality Survey	Butler, N.R.	*Brit. Med. J.* 2 (Nov. 3, 1962): 1187.
"Fatal Coxsackie B Myocarditis in a Newborn Infant"	Butler, N.R.	*Brit. Med. J.* 2 (Dec. 1962): 1463-1465.
Perinatal Mortality Survey	Butler, N.R.	*Brit. Med. J.* 2 (Dec. 1962): 1463-1465.
"An Analysis of Data on 'High Risk' Mothers in Relation to Perinatal Mortality"	Butler, N.R.	*Report on Symposium on the Role of Obstetricians in Maternal and Child Health Programmes.* World Health Organisation. Copenhagen, 1965, pp. 69-72.
"Gestational Age, Size, and Maturity: Perinatal Death"	Butler, N.R.	*Clinics in Developmental Medicine,* No. 19, 1965.

"The Problems of Low Birth-Weight and Early Delivery"	Butler, N.R.	*J. Obstet. & Gynaec. of the Brit. Comm.* 72, 6 (Dec. 1965).
"Prevention of Handicaps in Children"	Butler, N.R. and Pringle, M.L. Kellmer	*Maternal and Child Care* II, 17 (1966): 237-242.
"Seven-Year-Olds in England"	Davie, R.	*Special Education*, III, vol. 55 (1966): 9-11.
"The Hypoplastic Left Heart Complex"	Alberman, E.D. (et al.)	*J. Med. Genet.* 4 (1967): 83-87.
"National Child Development Study" (1958 Cohort)	Butler, N.R. and Pringle, M.L. Kellmer	*What is Special Education?* Assoc. for Special Education, London (1967).
"Summary of the First Report of the National Child Development Study"	Davie, R.	*Forward Trends* 2, 1 (1967): 5-13.
"Follow-Up of Adopted Children"	Pringle, M.L. Kellmer	*J. of Medical Women's Federation* 49, 3 (1967): 146-148.
"National Child Development Study" (1958 Cohort)	Davie, R.	*Research Relevant to the Education of Children with Learning Handicaps*, pp. 18-21. The College of Special Education (1968).
"The Behaviour and Adjustment of Seven-Year-Old Children: Some Results from the National Child Development Study" (1958 Cohort)	Davie, R.	*Brit. J. Ed. Psych.* 38, part 1 (1968).
"Longitudinal Studies and the Measurement of Change"	Goldstein, H.	*The Statistician* 18, 2 (1968): 93-117.
"National Child Development Study" (1958 Cohort)	Pringle, M.L. Kellmer	*Research Relevant to the Education of Children with Learning Handicaps*, pp. 12-17. The College of Special Education (1968).

"The Prevalence of Congenital Defects in the Children of the 1958 Cohort"	Alberman, E.D.	Concern No. 3, pp. 29-33, National Children's Bureau (1969).
"Children at Risk"	Butler, N.R.	Concern No. 3, pp. 8-16 (1969).
"Local Authority at Services"	Davie, R.	Concern No. 3, pp. 17-22 (1969).
"Children in Care"	Mapstone, E.	Concern No. 3, pp. 23-28 (1969).
"Policy Implications of Child Development Studies"	Pringle, M.L. Kellmer	Concern No. 3, pp. 40-48 (1969).
"16,000 Home Visits"	Ross, E.	*Nursing Times* (Nov. 27, 1969): 1511-1513.
"Regional Differences in Child Behaviour"	Pringle, M.L. Kellmer	*Eugenic Society Bulletin* 1, 4 (1969).
"The Second Follow-Up of the National Child Development Study"	Wedge, P.J.	Concern No. 3, pp. 34-39 (1969).
"Comparison of Birth Weight/Gestation Distribution in Cases of Stillbirth and Neonatal Death According to Lesions Found at Necropsy"	Fedrick, J.	*Brit. Med. J.* 3 (1969): 745-748.
"Scotland for Good Parents and Happy Children"	Pringle, M.L. Kellmer	*Times Educational Supplement*, Jan. 9, 1970.
"The Bevaviour and Adjustment of 7-Year Olds in England, Scotland, and Wales; some Comparative Results from the National Child Development Study" (1958 Cohort)	Pringle, M.L. Kellmer	*Scottish Educational Studies, Edinburgh* 2 (1970): 3-10.
"Children at Risk"	Davie, R.	*Froebal Journal*, No. 16 (1970).

"The 'At Risk' Register. A Statistical Evaluation"	Alberman, E.D. and Goldstein, H.	*Brit. J. of Prev. & Soc. Med.* 24, 3 (1970).
"Homes Fit for Children?"	Petzing, J. and Wedge, P.J.	*New Society*, Sept. 10, 1970.
"Why are the Most Stable Pupils Found in Scotland?"	Pringle, M.L. Kellmer	*Education* 136, 14 (1970).
"Housing for Children"	Wedge, P.J. and Petzing, J.	*Housing Review* 19, 6 (1970).
"Health and Height in Children"	Wedge, P.J., Alberman, E.D. and Goldstein, H.	*New Society*, Dec. 10, 1970.
"Certain Causes of Neonatal Death, I: Hyaline Membranes"	Fedrick, J. and Butler, N.R.	*Biol. Nenonate* 15, 3-4 (1970): 229-255.
"Certain Causes of Neonatal Death, II: Intraventricular Haemorrhage"	Fedrick, J. and Butler, N.R.	*Biol. Nenonate* 15, 5-6 (1970): 257-290.
"Factors Influencing the Height of Seven-Year-Old Children. Results of the National Child Development Study" (1958 Cohort)	Goldstein, H.	*Human Biology* 43 (1971): 92-111.
"Visual Acuity of a National Sample (1958 Cohort) at 7 Years"	Alberman, E.D.; Butler, N.R.; and Sheridan, M.D.	*Dev. Med. & Child Neurology* 13, 1 (Feb. 1971): 9-14.
"Children with Squints at Seven Years—A Disadvantaged Group? An Enquiry from the National Child Development Study" (1958 Cohort)	Alberman, E.D.; Butler, N.R.; and Gardiner, P.A.	*The Practitioner* 206 (Apr. 1971): 501-506.
"Size of Class, Educational Attainment and Adjustment"	Davie, R.	Concern, No. 7, pp. 8-14 (1971).
"Possible Teratogenic Effects of Cigarette Smoking"	Fedrick, J.; Alberman, E.D.; and Goldstein, H.	*Nature* (June 1971): 529-530.

"Certain Causes of Neo-natal Death, III: Pulmonary Infection (a) Clinical Factors"	Fedrick, J. and Butler, N.R.	*Biol. Neonate* 17, 5-6 (1971): 458-471.
Certain Causes of Neo-natal Death, III: Pulmonary Infection (b) Pregnancy and Delivery"	Fedrick, J. and Butler, N.R.	*Biol. Neonate* 18, 1-2 (1971): 45-57.
"Certain Causes of Neo-natal Death, IV: Massive Pulmonary Haemorrhage"	Fedrick, J. and Butler, N.R.	*Biol. Neonate* 18 (1971): 243-262.
"Certain Causes of Neo-natal Death, V: Cerebral Birth Trauma"	Fedrick, J. and Butler, N.R.	*Biol. Neonate* 18 (1971): 321-329.
"Neonatal Deaths—Time of Death, Maturity and Lesion"	Fedrick, J.	*Biol. Neonate* 18 (1971): 369-378.
"The Right to a 'Full Life' "	Wedge, P.J.	Paper read at the conference, The 'poor' of the 1970s held at Shotton Hall, Shropshire. Published in the proceedings (1971).
"Socio-Biological Influ-ences on Children's Development"	Davie, R.	In *Determinants of Behaviour and Development*, Ed. F.J. Monks, W.W. Hartup, and J. De Wit. Academic Press (1972).
"Height, Weight and the Assessment of Obesity in Children"	Newens, M. and Goldstein, H.	*Brit. J. of Prev. & Soc. Med.* 26, 1 (1972): 33-39.
"Preliminary Findings at the Age of 11 Years on Children in the National Child Development Study" (1958 Cohort)	Pearson, R.C.M. and Peckham, C.S.	*Community Medicine*, No. 3318, 127, 9 (1972): 113-116.
"Smoking in Pregnancy and the Health of the Baby"	Goldstein, H.	*Mother and Child* (March-April 1972): 10-11.
"Adoption and After"	Adams, B.D.	*New Society* (March 23, 1972): 590-592.

"Born Illegitimate" (Research feedback)	Pringle, M.L. Kellmer	Concern, No. 8, pp. 7-13, Winter 1971/2.
"Birthweight and the Displacement Hypothesis"	Goldstein, H.	*Am. J. Epidem.* 95, 1 (1972): 1.
"Cigarette Smoking in Pregnancy: Its Influence on Birth and Perinatal Mortality"	Butler, N.R.; Goldstein, H.; and Ross, E.	*Brit. Med. J.* 1 (1972): 127-130.
"Reported Influenza in Pregnancy and Subsequent Cancer in the Child"	Fedrick, J. and Alberman, E.D.	*Brit. Med. J.* 2 (1972): 485-488.
"Housing for Children: A Second Look"	Parrinder, D.	*Housing Review* 21, 3 (May/June 1971): 85-86.
"Accuracy of Registered Causes of Neonatal Deaths in 1958"	Fedrick, J. and Butler, N.R.	*Brit. J. of Prev. & Soc. Med.* 26, 2 (1971): 101-105
"Houses Before Schools"	Davie, R.	*Times Educational Sup.,* No. 2977, June 9, 1972, p. 4.
"Weighing Children"	Wedge, P.J.; Newens, M.; and Goldstein, H.	*New Society* (June 1, 1972): 467-468.
"The Unequal Start"	Davie, R.	*Sunday Times Colour Sup.* (June 4, 1972): 25-31.
"Reported Incidence of Hearing Loss in Children of 7 Years"	Sheridan, M.D.	*Dev. Med. & Child Neur.* 14, 3 (June 1972): 296-303.
"The Missing Year"	Davie, R.	*Guardian* (Dec. 9, 1972): 16.
"From Birth to Seven"	Goldstein, H.	Concern, No. 10, pp. 6-12, Summer 1972.
"Preliminary Findings"	Pearson, R.C.M. and Peckham, C.S.	Concern, No. 10, pp. 16-20, Summer 1972.
"The Prevalence of Mental Retardation in Children"	Frew, R.	Concern, No. 10, pp. 27-31, Summer 1972.
"Mental Retardation: A National Study"	Frew, R. and Peckham, C.S.	*Brit. Hosp. J. & Soc. Serv. Rev.* (Sept. 16, 1972): 2070-2072.

"School Attainment of Seven-Year-Old Children with Hearing Difficulties" — Peckham, C.S.; Sheridan, M.D.; and Butler, N.R. — *Dev. Med. & Child Neur.* 14, 3 (October 1972): 592-602.

"The Longitudinal Approach" — Davie, R. — *Trends in Education*, H.M.S.O., No. 28, October 1972, pp. 8-13.

The 2nd Kenneth Gibson Memorial Lecture — Butler, N.R. — *J. of Brit. Epilepsy Assoc.*, Autumn 1972.

"The Behaviour and Adjustment in School of Seven-Year-Olds: Sex and Social Class Differences" — Davie, R. — *Early Child Dev. & Care* 2 (1972): 39-47.

"Children in One-Parent Families" — Ferri, E. — NCB Conf. 1972, *The Parental Role*, pp. 18-21.

"The Allocation of Resources in Population Screening. A Decision Theory Model" — Goldstein, H. — *Biometrics* 28 (1972): 499-518.

"Speech Defects in Children Aged 7 Years" — Butler, N.R.; Peckham, C.S.; and Sheridan, M.D. — *B.M.J.* (Feb. 3, 1973): 253-257.

"Convulsive Disorders in British Children" — Ross, E. — *Proc. of the RSM* 66, 7 (1973): 703-704.

"Children of 7 Years with Marked Speech Defects" — Sheridan, M.D. — *Brit. J. of Disorders of Communication* 8, 1 (1973): 9-16.

"Speech Defects in a National Sample of Children Aged 7 Years" — Peckham, C.S. — *Brit. J. of Disorders of Communication* 8, 1 (1973): 1-8.

"Characteristics of Motherless Families" — Ferri, E. — *B. J. Soc. Work* 3, 1, pp. 91-100.

"Children and the Cycle of Deprivation" — Wedge, P.J. — *F.S.U. Quarterly* 4 (Spring 1973).

"Hearing and Speech at Seven" — Sheridan, M.D. and Peckham, C.S. — *J. of Spec. Ed.* 62, 2 (June 1973).

"A National Study of Child Development" (MCDS Cohort) (Abridged)		*Proc. of the RSM* 66, 7 (July 1973): 701-704.
(a) Preliminary Findings in a National Sample of 11-Year-Old Children	Peckham, C.S.	
(b) Convulsive Disorders in British Children	Ross, E.	
"The Single Parent Family: Aspects of Children's Welfare"	Ferri, E.	*Royal Soc. of Health*, 80th Congress, 1973 (publ. in the proceedings), pp. 168-170.
"Family Size and Children's Development"	Prosser, H.	*Health and Soc. Serv. J.* (March 10, 1973).
"Eleven Years of Childhood"	Davie, R.	*Statistical News*, No. 22, August 1973.
"Aspects of Children's Welfare"	Ferri, E.	Paper read before the Health Congress of the Royal Society of Health at Eastbourne, May 1973.

Chapter 8

Services for the Adolescent in the United Kingdom

S.T. Morton and I. Kolvin

INTRODUCTION—DEFINITIONS

Adolescence may be defined as the period of development between childhood and adult maturity. It is difficult to be more precise about this period in terms of chronological age as it consists of naturally phased periods of further growth and development following on those of childhood which have an intrinsic variability. The onset and course of adolescence are influenced by constitutional and a variety of environmental factors such as nutritional, social, cultural, climatic, and psychological. Onset, i.e., the lower limit, is marked by the appearance of puberty which is initiated by complex hormonal factors which, in turn, are influenced by external environmental factors. Although there is remarkable sequential uniformity in the appearance of physical changes at puberty there is considerable variation in the chronological onset. Detailed study of adolescence, therefore, requires the concept of developmental age which is based on skeletal age, dental age, secondary sexual characteristics, etc. These factors, together with the rate of change and their emotional accompaniments, constitute the legendary adjustment processes which characterize this life epoch.

It is noteworthy that researchers have often utilized chronological age as a simple, convenient criterion of adolescence. For instance, some have used the operational criterion of the second decade of life (i.e., eleven to twenty inclusive) while others the teenage period (thirteen to nineteen inclusive).

We are indebted to our colleagues in collating statistics for this chapter, especially Dr. G. Blessed, Dr. L. Mills, and Mr. W. Walton. Dr. Ian Berg kindly made available some invaluable administrative documents.

We would like to thank Mrs. M. Blackburn and Miss D. Gething for their diligent secretarial help.

However, in view of the variability in onset and course there must be questions about the validity of comparisons, especially cross-cultural ones, which are undertaken without consideration of developmental age.

Turning to definitions of psychiatric disorder in adolescence, the clinician or research worker is confronted with problems which are probably greater than at any other period of life. As Henderson et al. (1971) point out, different observers "will perceive the same behavioral phenomena in different ways." Broad definitions with loose criteria lead to high prevalence rates, narrow definitions with strict criteria to low prevalence rates. At no stage of life are such rates more sensitive to differing concepts of illness, the politico-socio cultural frameworks of the illness (Kolvin 1974) (highly abnormal neurotic behavior or rebellion and dissident behavior can all too easily be labeled psychotic) and the importance of the distinction between "normal adolescent turmoil" and true psychiatric disturbance.

Indeed, while some assert that adolescent turmoil and crises are normal, others deny this (Masterson 1967; Offer 1969; and Offer and Offer 1969). Furthermore, not only do some think that adolescents do not spontaneously grow out of these states (Masterson 1967) but others have gone on to speculate whether they are precursors of schizophrenia (Rinsley 1972). On the other hand, Rutter and Graham (1973) deny the extent and significance of the *proverbial* family conflicts and communicational difficulties of adolescence, asserting that clinic experience has tended to give a generally misleading picture of adolescent difficulties.

CONTRIBUTION OF UNITED KINGDOM RESEARCH

The Size of the Problem

Point prevalence rates of psychiatric disorder in adolescence are difficult to achieve mainly on account of differences of definition of adolescence and acceptance of what constitutes illness, not only between cultures but often within cultures as well. Such factors may account, in part, for the rarity of scientifically rigorous prevalence studies at this age range. In the face of such difficulties some research workers have resorted to studying the use made of psychiatric services for adolescents to reach an estimated rate of disturbance. Other ways of overcoming such problems are to use standardized interview schedules (Masterson 1967; Offer 1969), Teacher and Parent Inventories (Rutter and Graham 1973) or Self-Rating Inventories such as the Cornell Medical Index (1949) or the General Health Questionnaire (Goldberg 1969).

Various methods, such as screen parent and teacher questionnaires (Rutter et al. 1970) and evidence gathered in a systematic fashion by community nurses (Brandon 1960) have shown that in the United Kingdom the percentage of children alleged to be suffering from psychiatric disorder to cover a range from 6.8 percent (Rutter 1970) to 17.9 percent (Brandon 1960). A recent review (Garside et al. 1973) suggests a fair overall estimate of psychiatric disturbance consists of at least one child in ten. Studies of the referral rates of psychiatric disorders in adolescence have tended to use two main criteria, firstly at least one consultation with a psychiatrist and secondly that the incident occurred during the second decade of life (and most have excluded patients with I.Q. below 70). Results in the Aberdeen City Study (Kidd and Dixon 1968) showed an annual rate of referral to specialists' services of 6.6 per thousand at risk in the teenage population. Less than half of the patients were referred by their general practitioners. Half of the girls referred were seen at the request of the hospital service, the remainder being referred by their family doctor. On the other hand, the proportion of boys not referred by the family doctor was divided between those sent by the hospital agencies and by statutory authorities. These findings suggest that for young people social as much as clinical factors act as the primary determinants of referral (Kidd and Dixon 1968). Studies in Edinburgh (McCulloch et al. 1966; Henderson et al. 1967) show a referral rate of 5.6 per thousand at risk. In this series 30 percent of the boys and 37 percent of the girls poisoned or injured themselves before being examined by a psychiatrist. In contrast only 6 percent of the boys and 29 percent of the girls in the Aberdeen series were seen because of self-poisoning. This suggests that factors operating locally affect the rate of referral.

In the city of Newcastle Upon Tyne the hospital and community services are staffed by the same psychiatric personnel. Using information deriving from records we have calculated new case referral rates. The findings (Table 8-1) were that in 1973 there were few referrals up to the age of five.

Table 8-1. Referral Rates by Age and Sex

Age Range	Male	Female	Total	
Up to 5 years	17	14	31	(4.75%)
6 to 10 years	125	51	176	(26.9%)
11 years	29	13	42	(6.4%)
12 years	39	20	59	(9.05%)
13 years	37	18	55	(8.44%)
14 years	30	26	56	(8.59%)
15 years	27	24	51	(7.82%)
16 years	16	21	37	(5.67%)
17 years	14	25	39	(5.9%)
18 years	11	22	33	(5.06%)
19 years	16	20	36	(5.5%)
20 years	14	23	37	(5.67%)
			652	

Thereafter there was a slow increase in numbers of referrals with a plateau in the low 40s at nine, ten, and eleven years. There is then approximately a 40 percent increase in younger adolescents, i.e., twelve, thirteen, fourteen, and fifteen, followed by the expected drop (see later discussion) for older adolescents. The other main finding is that the high male/female ratio for childhood begins to even out in mid-adolescence and then inverts in older adolescents. It is of significance that in spite of a comprehensive child and adolescence outpatient psychiatric service some 57 percent of the adolescents were initially referred to general hospital outpatient clinics (Table 8-2). Finally, there were some 36,000 school children in Newcastle in 1973 with approximately 3,000 in each age range. From census figures we calculate there were another 19,000 between sixteen and twenty years inclusive, i.e., about 3,800 at each age range. The overall consultation rate per 1,000 population at risk over the age of five was 12.6; at ten years 14.00; at thirteen years 18.3, but at eighteen years it drops to 8.7. An estimated mean rate for adolescence is 13.5 per 1,000, which is almost double the rates reported in Edinburgh (Henderson et al. 1967) and Aberdeen (Kidd and Dixon 1968).

Evans and Acton (1972) demonstrated an increasing referral to the adolescent psychiatric service in Edinburgh from 1966 to 1970. This showed an increase of rate of referral by 50 percent annually during the earlier years following the opening of an adolescent service to 20 percent increase annually after five years. Thus the later Edinburgh and the current Newcastle research underlines the dangers inherent in the administrative use of referral rates as indices of incidence. They can only provide a rough guide and closer estimates depend on ratios of referral rates to prevalence rates, but true incidence can only be determined from general practice or other epidemiological surveys. From general practice surveys and from an epidemiological study (Rutter et al. 1970) there is an indication that only about one in five children with disorders come for help. If such a factor of one in five is valid in adolescence then one can prorate and obtain a prevalence rate of about 3 percent to 6 percent. We will later present evidence that this is far too low, which suggests that a much higher ratio and hence multiplication factor is necessary in adolescence as compared to younger children.

Table 8-2.

Source	Total	Age 11 — Children	Age 12 + Adolescents
1. Hospital and Community Clinics specifically for children and adolescents	418	245	173
2. General Hospital Psychiatric Outpatient Clinics	234	4	230

Standardized interview schedules have been developed for adult research (Wing et al. 1967) and for selected adolescent groups in the United States only (Masterson 1967; Offer 1969). So far the General Health Questionnaire has not been used in the United Kingdom but Davies et al. (1968) have used the Cornell Medical Index in Australia and report that 11.4 percent of males and 23.8 percent of female medical students have significant psychiatric symptomotology. On the other hand, surveys of students in Belfast and Edinburgh (Caldbeck-Meenan 1966; and Kidd and Caldbeck-Meenan 1966) reveal rates of 9 percent for males and 13 percent to 14 percent for females. A more detailed analysis is provided by Ryle (1971), who estimates that serious psychiatric disorder affects 1-2 percent of university students in the United Kingdom during their undergraduate career, with a further 10-15 percent having emotional disorder of a level sufficient to require treatment.

In our opinion the most reliable and valid prevalence study of psychiatric disorder in the adolescent community in the United Kingdom is that of Rutter and Graham (1973) and this only refers to 14/15 year olds on the Isle of Wight. They report a corrected prevalence rate of 21 percent. However, as the rates at 10/11 years on the Isle of Wight, which is a stable and more affluent area of the country, proved low compared to those in London (Rutter et al. 1973) and Newcastle (Brandon 1960) we would suspect that this is a minimal rate, and that a fairer and probably more accurate overall rate would be in the region of 25-30 percent. It is interesting to note that, while the rate for conduct disorders was similar at 10/11 and 14/15 (and more common in boys at both ages), the rate of emotional disorders was much higher at 14/15, consisting mainly of anxiety states, phobic disorders, and also some depressive conditions. These disorders were more common in girls. They also report that psychosis was rare, which supports the Kolvin (1971) impression from his hospital survey.

To summarize there has been little in the way of specific studies of prevalence rates of psychiatric disorder at different age ranges of adolescents in the United Kingdom conducted with scientific rigor. It is not clear whether this is due to simple neglect or whether the subject of definition and classification in adolescence is so daunting as to deter even the most rash researchers from dabbling in this area.

Surveys and Follow-up Studies

Surveys of adolescent populations are particularly helpful for answering questions about:

1. the legendary rebelliousness and crisis phenomena of adolescence
2. the transience of adolescent psychiatric disorders
3. the efficacy of treatment.

It merits reiterating (Capes 1973) that the so-called "crazy mixed-up kid" adolescent type of crisis which was previously thought to be characteristic of adolescence has been questioned both in the United States by Offer and Offer

(1969) and in the United Kingdom by Rutter and Graham (1973). The latter researchers conclude that such generalizations appear to be based on findings with selected clinic populations.

In his five year follow-up of seventy-two disturbed adolescents, Masterson (1967) reports that three-quarters were at least moderately impaired at the age of twenty-one. A more elegant study was conducted by Rutter and Graham (1973), who report on the carry over of disturbance from pre- to mid-adolescence. Of those with conduct disorders at 10/11 years, 75 percent showed handicapping disorders in adolescence; while those with neurotic disorders at the earlier age, 50 percent were free of those with disorders at 14/15, one-third had previously had disorders at 10/11. However, about 50 percent developed their disorders for the first time at this age and were mostly emotional in type, mainly affecting girls.

Coming to treatment, so far no one has tried to emulate the Buckingham Child Guidance evaluative follow-up (Mitchell and Shepherd 1966) with an adolescent population. They compared fifty non-delinquent and non-psychotic children attending child guidance clinics with a non-treated, non-referred control group who were said to be comparably disturbed. Two-thirds of each group improved significantly. While the methodology of this research has been extensively questioned, (Rutter et al. 1970; Garside et al. 1973), one inescapable conclusion is that less severe degrees of psychiatric disorder in childhood often remit spontaneously. However, there is insufficient evidence to indicate that such improvement occurs with the more severe degrees of disorder.

In the light of the latter conclusion, it is interesting to note the findings of two follow-up studies of adolescents severe enough to be admitted to in-patient units (Annesley 1961; and Warren 1965). Annesley followed up adolescent patients some two years after discharge and Warren some five years after. Nevertheless, their findings are broadly similar with an encouraging prognosis in two-thirds to three-quarters of the group with neurotic type disorders, a moderate prognosis of 50 to 60 percent in the conduct or behavior disorder group, but a poorer prognosis in those with psychosis and brain damage. These are complemented by Capes' Study (Capes et al. 1971; Capes 1973), which emphasize the severity, the long duration, the unsatisfactory preschool home environment and type of disorder (all but two antisocial) of the nineteen adolescents with extremely poor prognosis of the 150 studied. She reports (1973) "one of the most significant facts to emerge from this survey was the very long history of disturbance in many of the cases . . . over half of the 88 psychiatric referrals had been a cause of worry to their parents before they were 6, etc." This again underlines the refractory nature of the more severe chronic disorders of childhood.

PLANNING HEALTH CARE FACILITIES
FOR ADOLESCENTS

In any attempt to plan health care facilities for adolescents one needs not only reasonably precise information about the size of the problem but also the potential use of the available services by the community. It is worthwhile examining the situation in child psychiatry where the above themes have been the subject of more intensive study. In 1955 a Ministry of Education Committee (The Underwood Committee) based its recommendations on evidence that 0.5 percent of the child population would actually be referred if adequate clinical facilities were available. In a later evaluation of services Garside et al. (1973) pointed out that in the 1970s at least 1 percent of the school population were attending either child psychiatry units or child guidance clinics and further argued that if such services were built up to more even levels throughout the country then closer to 2 percent than 1 percent of children would attend for treatment.

If we accept their estimate, i.e., that an overall prevalence rate of disturbance of children in the U.K. population is about 10 percent and if 2 percent of these attended psychiatric clinics, we can derive a prevalence attendance ratio of 5 to 1. We have also estimated that 20 to 30 percent of adolescents suffer psychiatric disorder.

If, as has been shown, that about 6.6 per 1,000 (approximately 0.7 percent) (Aberdeen 1968) to 13 per 1,000 (Newcastle 1973) of the adolescent population with disturbance attend for help, the question arises why 1 in 5 of children with psychiatric disorder attend clinics and why, at the most, 1 in about 20 of adolescents. There are a number of possible explanations, some of which we will develop at greater length. Firstly, studies suggest that social, subcultural, and clinical factors interact with psychological attitudes of adolescents in determining the pattern of usage of the available local health care services. For instance, the Edinburgh research reveals an inverse relationship between areas of the city where there was direct psychiatric referral, and areas where there were low rates of direct referral, but high rates of self-poisoning, which were associated with indices of social disorganization (McCulloch et al. 1966; and Henderson 1965). Secondly, compared with the child, who is taken to a clinic by parents, and the adult, who assumes responsibility for his own health, the adolescent is less likely to submit to the former, or to be motivated to undertake the latter. Thirdly, some workers have pointed out that some adolescents fail to recognize and may even deny the existence of evident disturbance (Rutter and Graham 1973) and even when they acknowledge disturbance, they have a variable reluctance to consult available helping agencies. As this is likely to be allied to anxieties about confidentiality, we believe it could be partly overcome if wider publicity were given to the fact that young people over the age of sixteen are entitled to medical confidentiality and that medical practitioners are not at liberty to disclose such information to parents or any other authority (social services) without the adolescent's permission.

In the child service, both Rutter and Graham (1966) and Ryle (1965) claim that the available services are dealing with the most deserving cases. We can only speculate that this is likely to be true, too, of disturbed adolescents. But this refers only to the tip of the iceberg and the crucial question is what about the remainder.

While there is ample evidence that when clinical services expand and improve, the use of services rapidly increases. This appears to be true, too, with psychiatric disorders in adolescence (Evans and Acton 1972). These authors also report that only one-third of their referrals come from non-medical sources. It would be therefore reasonable to assume that when the integrated community services for adolescents improve, the majority of disturbed adolescents will still by one means or another be channeled into one of the traditional medical services such as general practitioners or their equivalent in colleges or universities and referred on from these to the adolescent psychiatrist when necessary. In these circumstances, it is essential that primary physicians in the community colleges or universities have more training in the problems and disorders of adolescence and further, more psychiatrists need to be specifically trained in adolescent psychiatry.

In planning health care facilities for adolescents all the above factors and more need to be taken into account. Comprehensive community programs for adolescents should, therefore, include a network of services ranging from statutory to voluntary and formal to informal—such as orthodox hospital inpatient, day patient, outpatient departments, and hospital self-referral walk-in clinics on the one hand, to informal agencies run by voluntary bodies on the other. It is essential for these to be loosely integrated with parallel youth services in the community such as social services departments, probation departments, youth associations, educational psychology departments, school counseling services, etc. An account and critical review of such services in the United Kingdom follows.

Manpower

In a recent review Schonfield points out that in the United States NIMH statistics reveal that outpatient psychiatric clinics serve more persons in the 10-19 year age group than in any other decade of life. Similarly in the United Kingdom prevalence studies show that a high proportion of adolescents are in need of specialized psychiatric help, but at present specific adolescent services are less well developed. However, it needs to be remembered that as it is not possible to equate prevalence with demand (Rutter and Graham 1966; Rutter et al. 1970) the requirements for staffing cannot be based on prevalence rates alone. Indeed, from their epidemiological survey, Rutter and Graham conclude that of those children showing psychiatric disturbance, a third were thought to need diagnosis and advice only; a third possibly required treatment and a third *probably* required treatment. Further, these authors report (Rutter and Graham 1973) that at mid-adolescence many of those with clear problems did not see themselves as needing help and would not necessarily accept it, even if offered. Manpower estimates are, therefore, even more complicated in adolescent psychiatry. Allowance has to be made for the lower rate of acceptance of treatment, for the high dropout rates in treatment (Rosen et al.

1964; Rosen et al. 1965; Kidd 1968) and for availability and use of child psychiatric, adult psychiatric, and other helping agencies. While dropout rates are similar in the United Kingdom and United States (Rosen et al. 1969; Rosen et al. 1965; Kidd and Dixon, 1968) there is a sharp contrast in offers of treatment to new referrals of 33 percent in the United States to 66 percent in the United Kingdom.

Garside et al. (1973) describe a dramatic increase of social workers and psychologists working in child guidance clinics, but a very much slower rate of increase of child psychiatrists. In an attempt to correct serious psychiatric staffing deficiencies, the Ministry of Health doubled their senior training posts between 1968 and 1971. Nevertheless, it was clear that the modest target for consultant psychiatrists by a Ministry Committee in 1955 (Underwood Committee) of one psychiatrist per 45,000 school children has only recently been achieved (1971) in relation to psychiatrists. Subsequently the R.M.P.A. (Royal Medico-Psychological Association, 1960 and 1965) recommended as a realistic minimum, one full-time consultant child psychiatrist per 200,000 general population (35,000 school population). Garside et al. (1973) recommend two levels of manpower targets, i.e., an ideal to provide a comprehensive service and a realistic minimum. The ideal would consist of one consultant psychiatrist, supported by one psychologist and two social workers, so that in relation to the 1971 situation the minimal full-time equivalent staff necessary for clinical activities should have been 243 consultants, 243 psychologists, and 486 social workers. With the present rate of training, it is unlikely that such minimal levels will be achieved before 1975. In a subsequent document produced by the manpower committee of the RCP (Royal College of Psychiatrists 1973) the recommendations differ only slightly from the ideal and realistic minimum levels proposed by Garside et al. (1973) for a population of 200,000 and consist of:

1. Ideal Level—two consultants and supporting junior staff.
2. Realistic Minimum—one and a half consultants and supporting junior staff.
3. A further expansion of the senior training sub-consultant grade.

In the most recent draft memorandum on Adolescent Psychiatry produced in 1974 (R.C.P.–Child Psychiatry Specialist Section) it is recommended that the number of adolescent psychiatrists be increased to at least equal those of child psychiatry. This suggestion does not seem to take into consideration the fact that estimates of staffing needs for child psychiatry were based on both preschool and school population, the latter of which already includes a substantial percentage of younger adolescents. Furthermore, a variable percentage of the older adolescents or young adults will inevitably always be seen by general psychiatrists, particularly in areas geographically remote from specialized units. As such, we estimate that adolescent psychiatrists would maximally cope with 50 percent of the disorders in the second decade of life and hence only about 25 to 30 percent of patient population in the first two decades of life. We therefore consider, in spite of the higher rates of disturbance in the adolescent section of the population, that a more realistic manpower estimate would be 50 percent of those recommended in child psychiatry.

While detailed statistics are not available, it is evident that adolescent psychiatry in the United Kingdom is one of the Cinderellas of the psychiatric subspecialties with ratios of adolescent psychiatrists to child psychiatrists running at 1 to 5 or more, rather than 1 to 2 as suggested above. There is little doubt, therefore, that establishment of training and consultant posts merit the highest priority in adolescent psychiatry as compared to general psychiatry and clearly even above that of child psychiatry.

We still need to indicate manpower recommendations in relation to nurses working in hospital adolescent units. As in child psychiatry, in adolescence there is unanimity of opinion that there should be a high nursing staff to patient ratios (about 1:1) together with permanence of staff in the adolescent unit (R.C.P. 1974; A.P.S.A. 1972). However, not only is there a major deficiency of trained staff even in established units, but there are also serious recruitment and training difficulties (Ackral et al. 1968; Garside et al. 1973; A.P.S.A. 1972). More recently a new National Nursing Board (Joint Board of Clinical Nursing Studies) has been established to plan curricula, monitor standards and accredit new or established postgraduate training programs (Brown et al. 1974) in the psychological management of children.

Provision of Facilities

Provision of health facilities for both children and adolescents in the United Kingdom was originally provided under the National Health Services Act (1946) and the Education Act (1944). Thus the facilities were based both on the National Health Service (hospitals) and the child and family guidance service of the local education authorities (community). This dualism has recently, in theory, been administratively resolved with the passing of the National Health Service Reorganisation Act, 1973, which came into force on April 1, 1974. The philosophy of the change and thus the intention of the Act is that the "health needs of the local community will be planned and provided for the first time within a single organisation. Local needs and priorities will be sorted and planned for in the context of national, regional and area plans" (Burbridge and Sichel 1972). The hope is for the establishment of a network of comprehensive health services which include both the community and the health service.

The child psychiatry services for children have been more fully developed than those dealing with adolescents. However, over the past ten years there has been an increase in the facilities for the latter. Thus services available under the Education Act catered for children of school age range up to fifteen for most children and eighteen to nineteen years for a small percentage. However, while community assessment and treatment of the early and mid-adolescent age range disorders were theoretically available in a number of centers, in practice the techniques of treating adolescents were not fully developed. A similar situation was present in the health service. In practice the main facilities for adolescents were based on the health services and were dependent on local developments and the experience and the running of outpatient clinics both in hospital departments and in the community. Further, the R.C.P. document wisely suggests that there should be outpatient clinics at every major general hospital serving a district (major segment of the community). The opposite argument is that community- and education- (either school or university) based programs provide better opportunities for reaching young people. There is, as yet, inadequate knowledge and experience to support a dogmatic policy concerning the organization of such services. Preliminary favorable impressions from a major action research program in Newcastle Upon Tyne, whose main theme is redeployment of mental health personnel (including psychiatrists) into the schools leads us to advocate at least experimentation with a two-pronged service base. We therefore believe that there should be available mental health services existing within schools where adolescents could have access to all types of psychological and psychiatric help. This would hopefully reduce the grave dropout problems described in the literature. We also have the impression that some of the more uncooperative parents would allow their children to receive help provided they were not personally involved. In other words, where services are not meeting the needs of adolescents, it is essential to be flexible about the redeployment of our specialist services. This is not dissimilar to developments in University Health Services where some of the physicians who have had psychiatric training (Ryle 1971) patently function as adolescent psychiatrists. Such a policy accepts that both home and school (Power et al. 1972; Gath et al. 1972; and Pritchard 1973) exert potent formative influences on personality development and personal adjustment.

The function of the psychiatrist in such community-based services would mainly be that of a consultant to other professionals accepting mental health roles (educational counselors, year tutors, psychologists, social services staff, etc.). However, the consultant in the hospital-based service would accept responsibility for assessment and treatment of the more severely disturbed adolescents and have a lesser community consultative role.

Prior to the establishment of specific adolescent services, adolescents at schools were not referred directly to psychiatrists working in child guidance clinics or hospitals. Instead they came via two school sources, i.e., school physicians or school psychologist; and yet many adolescents were at the stage when they would have preferred opportunities for self-referral. More recently the Edinburgh Psychiatric Adolescent Service (Evans and Acton 1972) reported that about a third of their referral came from non-medical sources *including self-referral.* In adolescence, therefore, for multiple reasons, some of which we have already discussed in detail, we especially endorse the steady erosion of the medical shiboleth that only medical practitioners may refer cases to consultant psychiatrists. However, for obvious reasons, there remains a strong case for sending a confidential report to the patient's primary physician, i.e., his/her general practitioner, to whom devolves the day-to-day medical responsibility.

The Educational Network of Services

It has been pointed out (Warren 1965; and Schonfeld 1971) that adequate psychosocial facilities for adolescents need to be based on a comprehensive and integrated network of hospital and community services. It is necessary to comment on the constituents of the educational networks which are available for the adolescent still at school. While the child guidance clinics with their team of educational psychologist, psychiatrist, and social worker have rapidly expanded in the United Kingdom, the other services are poorly developed. For instance, the educational counseling service within schools is relatively undeveloped, and the concept of a school social worker almost embryonic. Some of the larger secondary schools are seeking alternative ways of dealing with the major psychiatric problems confronting them. Some are exploring the use of special classes (adjustment classes) for maladjusted pupils, while others are experimenting with special classes for unmanageable (undisciplined) pupils. In addition there are the special schools for maladjusted pupils.

In 1968 statistics available from the Department of Education and Science revealed that 14.8 per 10,000 school population were receiving or awaiting special education. Garside et al. (1973) conclude that it is reasonable to suggest that as a realistic minimum, there should be twenty day or residential places per 10,000 school children for maladjusted pupils. It has currently become popular to estimate service needs in terms of a population unit of 200,000 which approximately includes some 35,000 school children. As about 30 percent of these will be younger adolescents it is not unreasonable to suggest that what is needed for them is one small special school. Furthermore, a general population of 500,000 would need about 50-60 places and could quite easily cater for a larger special school. As the Ministry of Health (D.H.S.S.) has already recommended twenty hospital beds per million general population for adolescents, it would appear that a total of 150 day and residential places could be considered as a reasonable, realistic minimum target for the next decade for a general population of one million. On the other hand, it needs to be appreciated that the expectations and demands from both parents and ordinary schools will rise as facilities increase, which may lead to increased demand. Further, there is evidence that many of the children currently placed in other types of children's establishments, or even what were formerly approved schools (correctional institutions), may be more appropriately located in maladjusted schools. Provision of such facilities has always to take into account geographical distribution of population.

**Day and Residential Facilities in
the United Kingdom**

So far we have discussed the facilities for younger adolescents. In this section we propose giving an account of the range of facilities for all adolescents. Dependent on the age of adolescents, their special day and residential needs are served by a variety of settings in the United Kingdom.

1. Health Service settings—day and inpatient units.
2. Education Service settings—day and residential maladjusted schools.
3. Social Service settings—family group homes, community homes and hostels for working boys or girls.
4. Forensic (Correctional Service) settings—Those for younger adolescents have now been transferred to Social Services, and have been renamed community homes, while those for the young adults (borstal institutions) remain unchanged.
5. Combinations of the above, i.e., forensic settings within the health service.

In this section we will mainly concentrate on hospital settings. There is general agreement (Warren 1965; Henderson et al. 1971; Lancet 1968; and R.C.P. documents 1974) that separate inpatient services are essential for adolescents, both because of their potentially socially disruptive behavior and their special educational/vocational needs (Barter and Langsley 1968), and also as the principles of treatment of adolescents on a day or inpatient basis are sufficiently different from child or adult practice to merit separate facilities and handling. There is a further consensus view that some older adolescents are more appropriately and effectively treated on adult wards (Warren 1965; R.C.P. 1974). But arguments for the more general admission of adolescents to adult wards (Hansen 1969) because of the vitality they might inject into group therapy exercises are questionable. There is always the danger with such latter arguments that they constitute rationalizations for local expedients.

The development of day and inpatient units can be compared with that of the outpatient services. Such units often tend to reflect the training and experience and the philosophy of care of the local physician, and the local medico-political pressures to meet the particular needs, more than reflecting the characteristics and special needs of the local population. The units which have developed can be broadly categorized as follows:

1. Units for the more neurotic type of disorders. These are usually short- or medium-stay departments, offering intensive psychotherapy in a more permissive regime, and tend to treat the neurotic disorders of adolescents with a better prognosis. However, when cases with more severe disorders are admitted, short-term hospital admissions should be part of a long-term therapeutic plan.

2. Units capable of coping with psychiatric disorders with a significant acting out or antisocial component. Forensic adolescent psychiatric units also cater for some of the patients. Such units tend to use more structured therapy programs (Capes 1973).
3. Hostel units in which the adolescent may continue a normal or near to normal life style during the course of treatment. These tend to be informal, with little structure, and often rely considerably on group therapy.
4. Long-term units for more serious mental disorders.
5. The Ministry of Health (Department of Health and Social Security) has recommended the establishment of a small number of high security units in which severely disturbed adolescents, particularly those showing abnormally aggressive or seriously irresponsible conduct, may receive treatment. Unfortunately there are still few in number.
6. Special units for subnormal or borderline subnormal adolescents who additionally suffer from psychiatric disorder.

The Ministry of Health in 1964 suggested that, as an initial target, there should be 20-25 adolescent psychiatric beds per million population, which should be supported by day places and hostels. This works out at about 1,000 to 1,200 beds in England and Wales. Using the Register of Adolescent Psychiatric Units (A.P.S.A. 1973) we estimate that there were, theoretically, about 550 beds for adolescents, i.e., about 11 beds per million population. However, a percentage of these are located in "all-age" children's units, and are technically not very suitable for seriously disturbed adolescents. Thus by 1973 we were only halfway to the target specified in 1964 and, furthermore, there is substantial variation from region to region throughout the country.

Such conclusions can, of course, be misleading. For instance, more recently Bruggen et al. (1973) have advanced cogent reasons, such as lack of adequate peer models, disruption of long-term relations important for maturation, etc., for questioning the rationale of inpatient admission for younger adolescents. Nevertheless, the case for special units in each population area of the country is strong, but the number of beds required will depend on the extent to which community-based day and residential services as described above have been developed. A high proportion of adolescents can, in fact, be kept out of the hospital if there is adequate network of outpatient and other community services. While hospital facilities are more obviously indicated for the more clear-cut psychiatric disorders which require specialized nursing/medical supervision and treatment, a high proportion of disturbed adolescents (especially those requiring more in the way of environmental support) can and should be accommodated by the community services or by the outpatient services which can provide intensive psychotherapy. It is evident, therefore that no one unit can or would be willing to provide for the whole range of adolescent patients, but, on the other hand, a leader in *Lancet* (1968) warns that "too much diversity of inpatient units might impair the cohesion of services in the local community." What has to be answered individually by each area is what is the correct pattern of services for the local community.

COMMENTARY

While over the last three decades there have been major advances in the development of mental health services for adults and moderate advances in those for children, it is only over the last decade that there has been an increasing recognition of the need for specific services for adolescents.

The case for such specific services has been strengthened by modern research consisting of epidemiological surveys and follow-up studies (albeit few in number), together with studies of the use made of facilities. Furthermore, the lowering of the age of onset of puberty has tended to magnify the contrast between childhood and adolescence on the one hand, and adolescence and adulthood on the other. Modern technology and rapidly changing life styles of modern society together with this early onset of puberty have served to highlight the psychological problems of this phase of life and, in consequence, have facilitated the appreciation of the need for such adolescent services. It is, however, likely that no small part of the awareness of the mental health needs of adolescents is due to direct or indirect increasing appeals for help by the young people themselves.

It is often asserted by those with particular training and expertise in adolescence that at no time in life does careful investment of skills produce greater rewards. Such views have led to recommendations of major expansion of mental health facilities to serve the adolescent population. In such a therapeutic climate there is the danger of a blind emulation of the child psychiatric and child guidance practices without benefiting from an appreciation of the shortcomings of such models (Rehin 1972; Levitt 1971; Eisenberg 1969; Carside et al. 1973). Simultaneously with service developments attempts need to be made to grasp the complex problems of clarification and diagnosis as an adjunct to studying the effectiveness of the diversity of services so that maximum support can be given to those developments which can be shown to be most psychologically and socially useful.

Further, as has been suggested in child psychiatry (Garside et al 1973) it is necessary to ascertain which disorders merit intervention by the sophisticated but expensive multidisciplinary teams and which, for instance, by the more economic but possibly equally effective use of community services which utilize psychiatrists in a consultative capacity only. Furthermore, there needs to be an appreciation and awareness that the diversity of developments described in this chapter must be in future based not on chance alone but rather on sound principles. These principles, in turn, need to be based on careful evaluation. Such evaluation should also apply to the different forms of therapy, i.e., dynamic, behavior, and psychotherapy. It is fundamental to such evaluation of treatment and services in adolescent that there should be some attempt to define age adequate behavior which can be used as an index of maturation (Capes 1973).

Finally, it is necessary to emphasize that referral rates are useful to planners in that they provide an index of the use made of services by the local community. However, in no way do they constitute indices of incidence or prevalence. While it is helpful to know the prevalence-usage ratio for a particular community, rates dependent on such ratios can be grossly misleading when applied to other communities as both prevalence and usage vary widely, not only between, but also within communities.

BIBLIOGRAPHY

Ackral, M.; Kolvin, I.; and Scott, D. McI. "A Post Registered Course in Child Psychiatry for Nurses." *Nursing Times* (April 1968): 53-55.

Annesley, P.T. "Psychiatric Illness in Adolescence." *J. Ment. Sci.* 107 (1961): 268-78.

A.P.S.A. *Report on Post-Registration Training of Nurses in Psychiatric Units for Adolescents,* 1972.

Barter, J.T. and Langsley, D.G. "The Advantages of a Separate Unit for Adolescents." *Hosp. and Commn. Psychiat.* 19, 8 (1968).

Brandon, S. "An Epidemiological Study of Maladjustment in Childhood." Unpublished M.D. thesis, University of Durham, 1960.

Brown, S.; Tweddle, E.; Kolvin, I.; and Scott, D. *The Child Psychiatric Nurse – Training in Residential Child Care.* Edited by P. Barker (In Press, 1974).

Bruggen, P.; Byng-Hall, J.; and Pitt-Aikens, T. "The Reason for Admission as a Focus of Work for an Adolescent Unit." *Brit. J. Psychiat.* 122 (1973): 319-329.

Caldbeck-Meenan J. "Screening University Students with C.M.T." *J. Psychosom. Res.* 9 (1966): 331-337.

Capes, M.; Gould, E.; and Townsend, M. *Stress in Youth.* Occasional Hundreds 1. (O.U.P. for the Nuffield Provincial Hospitals Trust), 1971.

Capes, M. "Evaluating Services for Adolescents." In *Roots of Evaluation,* Edited by J.K. Wing and H. Hafner, London: O.U.P., 1973.

Cornell Medical Index. K. Brodman, A.J. Erdman, I. Lorge, G. Wolff, and T.H. Broadbent. *J. Amer. Med. Assoc.* 140 (1949): 530.

Davies, B.; Mowbray, R.M.; and Jensen, D. "A Questionnaire Survey of Psychiatric Symptoms in Australian Medical Students." *Aust. N.Z. J. Psychiat.* 2 (1968): 46-53.

D.E.S. *Psychologists in Education Services (Summerfield Report),* London: HMSO, 1968.

D.H.S.S. *National Health Service Reorganization: Consultative Document.* D.H.S.S. Circular, 1971.

Education Act. London: HMSO, 1944.

Eisenberg, L. "The Post-Quarter Century." *Am. J. Orthopsychiat.* 39 (1969): 389-401.

Evans, J. and Acton, W.P. "Psychiatric Service for the Disturbed Adolescent." *Brit. J. Psychiat.* 120, 557. (1972): 429-432.

Garside, R.F.; Hulbert, C.M.; Kilvin, I.; van der Spuy, H.I.J.; Wolstenholme, F.; and Wrate, R.M. "Evaluation of Psychiatric Services for Children in England and Wales." In *Roots of Evaluation.* Edited by J.K. Wing and H. Hafner. London: O.U.P., 1973.

Gath, D.; Cooper, B.; and Gattoni, F.E.G. "Child Guidance and Delinquency in a London Borough." *Psychol. Med.* 2 (1972): 185-191.

Goldberg, D.P. "The Identification and Assessment of Non-Psychotic Illness by Means of a Questionnaire." D.M. Thesis, University of Oxford, 1969.

Goldberg, D.P. *The Detection of Psychiatric Illness by Questionnaire.* Maudsley Monographs, London: O.U.P., 1972.

Hansen, S. "Impact of Adolescent Patients on a Psychiatric Hospital" *Hosp. and Commn. Psychiat.* 20, 11 (1969).

Henderson, A.S.; Krupinski, J.; and Stoller, A. "Epidemiological Aspects of Adolescent Psychiatry" In *Modern Perspectives in Adolescent Psychiatry.* Edit. J.G. Howells. Edinburgh: Oliver and Boyd, 1971.

Henderson, A.S. "The Use of Psychiatric Services by Adolescents." In *Psychiatric Epidemiology.* Edit. E.H. Hare and J.K. Wing. O.U.P. for the Nuffield Provincial Hospitals Trust, 1965.

Henderson, A.S.; McCulloch, J.W.; and Philip, A.E. "Survey of Mental Illness in Adolescence." *Brit. Med. J.* 1 (1967): 83-84.

Hudson, W.W. "An Autelic Teaching Experiment with Ancillary Casework Services." *Amer. Educ. Res. Jnl.* 8, 4 (1971): 467-483.

Joint Board of Clinical Nursing Studies. *Outline Curriculum in Child and Adolescent Psychiatric Nursing for Registered Nurses.* Course No. 600. London: HMSO, 1973.

Kidd, C.B. and Dixon, G.A. "The Incidence of Psychiatric Illness in Aberdeen Teenagers." *Health Bulletin* 26, 2 (April 1968).

Kidd, C.B. and Caldbeck-Meenan, J. "A Comparative Study of Psychiatric Morbidity Among Students at Two Different Universities." *Brit. J. Psychiat.* 112 (1966): 57-64.

Kolvin, I. "Research into Childhood Psychoses—A Cross-Cultural Comparison." *Internat. J. of Mental Health.* N.Y.: I.A.S.P., 1974.

Kolvin, I. "Psychoses in Childhood—A Comparative Study." In *Infantile Autism: Concepts, Characteristics and Treatment.* Ed. M. Rutter. London: Churchill, Livingstone, 1971.

Lancet "Psychiatric Care of the Adolescent." Leading article, 1 (1968): 676-678.

Laufer, M. "A Psychoanalytical Approach to Work with Adolescents; A Description of the Young People's Consultative Centre, London." *J. Child Psychol. Psychiat.* 5 (1964): 217-29.

Levitt, E.E. "Research on Psychotherapy with Children." In *Handbook of Psychotherapy and Behaviour Change.* Eds. A. Bergin, and Garfield, S. New York: John Wiley, 1971, pp. 474-94.

Masterson, J.F. Jr. *The Psychiatric Dilemma of Adolescence.* London: J. & A. Churchill, 1967.

McCulloch, J.W.; Henderson, A.S.; and Philip, A.E. "Psychiatric Illness in Edinburgh Tennagers." *Scot. Med. J.* 11 (1966): 277-281.

Ministry of Education. Circular 179. London: HMSO, 1948.

Ministry of Education. *Report of the Committee on Maladjusted Children. (Underwood Report),* London: HMSO, 1955.

Ministry of Health. *Memoranda RHB 47 (13).* London: HMSO, 1947.

Ministry of Health. *In-patient Accommodation for Mentally Ill and Seriously Maladjusted Children and Adolescents.* HM (64), London: HMSO, 1964.

Mitchell, S. and Shepherd, M. "A Comparative Study of Children's Behaviour at Home and at School." *Br. J. Educ. Psychol.* 36 (1966): 248-54.

Mumford, E., et al. "Hospital-Based School Mental Health Project." *Amer. J. Psychiat.* 127, 7 (1971): 920-924.

National Health Service. D.H.D. Burbridge and G.R.M. Sischel. "The Philosophy of Change (England) 4. The Framework of the New Structure." *Health Trends.* HMSO, February 1974.

Offer, D. *The Psychological World of the Teenager.* New York and London: Basic Books, 1969.

Offer, D., and Offer, J. "Four Issues in the Developmental Psychology of Adolescents." In *Modern Perspectives in Adolescent Psychiatry.* Edit. J.G. Howells. Edinburgh: Oliver and Boyd, 1971.

Offer, D., and Offer, J.L. "Growing Up. A Follow-up Study of Normal Adolescents." *Sem. Psychiat.* 1, 1 (1969): 46-56.

Philip, A.E., and McCulloch, J.W. "Use of Social Indices in Psychiatric Epidemiology." *Brit. J. Prev. Soc. Med.* 20 (1966): 122.

Power, M.J.; Benn, R.T.; and Morris, J.N. "Neighbourhood, School and Juveniles before the Courts." *Brit. J. Criminol.* 12 (1972): 111.

Pritchard, C. "The Teacher and Aspects of Adolescent Psychiatry." In *The Proceedings of the Eighth Conference, Coventry, of the Association for the Psychiatric Study of Adolescents.* (A.P.S.A.) Econoprint Ltd., Edinburgh, 1973.

Register of Adolescent Psychiatric Units. *The Association for the Psychiatric Study of Adolescents.* (A.P.S.A.) Econoprint Ltd., Edinburgh, 1973.

Rehin, G.F. "Child Guidance at the End of the Road." *Soc. Wk. Today,* 2, 24 (1972): 21-24.

Rinsley, D.B. "Contribution to the Nosology and Dynamics of Adolescent Schizophrenia." *Psychiatr. Qu.* 46 (1972): 159-186.

Rosen, B.M.; Bahn, A.K.; Shellow, R.; and Bower, E.M. "Adolescent Patients Served in Out-Patient Psychiatric Clinics." *Am. J. Publ. Hlth.* 55,10 (1965).

Rosen, B.M.; Kramer, M.; Redlick, R.W.; and Willner, S.G. *Utilization of Psychiatric Facilities by Children: Current Status, Trends, Implications.* Nat. Inst. of Mental Health, Office of Program Planning and Evaluation, Biometry Branch, 1969 (Mimeo).

Royal College of Psychiatrists—News and Notes. "Norms for Staffing of

Psychiatric Services." *Child Psychiatry.* Supp. *B.J. Psychiat.*, (December 1973).

Royal College of Psychiatrists—News and Notes. Suppl *B.J. Psychiat.* (April 1974).

Royal College of Psychiatrists. *Memorandum on Adolescent Psychiatry*, 1974.

Royal Medico-Psychological Association. *Memorandum: The Provision of Psychiatric Services for Children and Adolescents*, 1965.

Royal Medico-Psychological Association. *Memorandum: The Recruitment and Training of the Child Psychiatrist*, 1960.

Rutter, M. and Graham, P. "Psychiatric Disorder in 10 and 11 Year Old Children." *Proc. R. Soc. Med.* 59 (1966): 382-87.

Rutter, M. "A Children's Behaviour Questionnaire for Completion by Teachers. Preliminary Findings." *J. Child Psychol. Psychiat.* 8 (1967): 1-11.

Rutter, M.; Tizard, J.; and Whitmore, K. *Education, Health and Behaviour.* London: Longmans, 1970.

Rutter, M. and Graham, P. *Psychiatric Disorder in 'Normal' Adolescents.* In Proceedings of the Eighth Annual Conference, Coventry, of the Association for the Psychiatric Study of Adolescents. (A.P.S.A.) Econoprint Ltd., Edinburgh, 1973.

Ryle, A. "University Psychiatric Services in the United Kingdom." In *Modern Perspectives in Adolescent Psychiatry.* Edit. J.G. Howells. Edinburgh: Oliver & Boyd, 1971.

Schonfeld, W.A. "Comprehensive Community Programs for the Investigation and Treatment of Adolescents." In *Modern Perspectives in Adolescent Psychiatry.* Edit. J.G. Howells, Edinburgh: Oliver & Boyd, 1971.

Sindos, L.K. "Program for the Encouragement, Motivation and Education of High School Drop-Outs." *Amer. J. Orthopsychiat.* 40 (1970): 512-519.

Warren, W. "A Study of Adolescent Psychiatric In-patients and the Outcome Six or More Years Later. I and II." *J. Child Psychol. Psychiat.* 6, 1-17; 6, 141-60, 1965.

Wing, J.K.; Birley, J.L.T.; Cooper, J.E.; Graham, P.; and Isaacs, A.D. "The Reliability of a Procedure for Measuring and Classifying Present Psychiatric State." *Brit. J. Psychiat.* 113 (1967): 499-515.

Chapter 9

The Care of the Handicapped Child in the United Kingdom

Kenneth S. Holt

INTRODUCTION

It is sometimes said that the value of any civilization may be judged by the concern it shows for its handicapped and dependent members. On the basis of this criterion the United Kingdom has been striving to be a reputable and worthwhile civilization for many years. Medically, in past years the strong and long-standing tradition of family general practice made medical care available to most children, and this was supported by special children's clinics organized by local health authorities and by a separate medical service for school children. The introduction of the National Health Service in 1948 strengthened this pattern by arranging that every individual, including children, was registered with a doctor whom they could consult whenever necessary.

Specialist medical care was also available upon referral, but the creation of specialist medical services specifically for handicapped children is a more recent development, stimulated by the changing pattern of child health and a growing demand for high quality of survival for all infants (Holt 1972). Voluntary and charitable organizations pioneered special education for handicapped children in the late eighteenth century. A century later education authorities were required to make special provisions for handicapped children. The first of a series of Acts was passed in 1893 (Elementary Education [Blind and Deaf Children] Act). Ever since then, a comprehensive range of special educational provision has been available to all handicapped children except the severely retarded ones (below IQ of approximately 60). These were regarded as ineducable, and health authorities supervised their care at home and in day and residential centers. In 1970 (Education [Mental Handicapped] Act), however, education authorities accepted responsibility for the education of all children including the severely retarded.

The contribution of the social services to the care of handicapped children over the years was examined recently (Seebohm Report 1968), and as a result it was recommended that they should play a greater part, especially with regard to the provision of nursery and welfare services for handicapped children.

Voluntary organizations have played and are continuing to play an important part in complementing the official services for handicapped children and in pioneering new types of help.

Thus, concern for handicapped children has evolved over many years, and the services for them are still being extended and improved. They are characterized by a wide base of national provisions complemented by the work of many voluntarily supported organizations. If some of the efforts appear to have too strong a charitable flavor, this is more than adequately balanced by a sincere desire to insure that services are available to all those who need them, and by a growing realization of the need for an integrated scientific approach to the handicapped. This last point is illustrated by the breadth of a current definition of the term handicap: "An interference with normal growth, or development, or capacity to learn, caused by a continuing disability of body, intellect or personality, of such a degree as to need extra care or treatment from the medical, nursing, social or educational services."

AN IDEAL OF COMPREHENSIVE CONTINUING CARE

Planning services for handicapped children is different from most medical planning, which is based upon dealing with a series of acute episodes. Successful planning must be *comprehensive*, and take account of all the needs and services involved, and must provide *continuity*, because however good the provisions may be at one particular stage, they will be rendered useless if the work is not linked up with the next stage. Figure 9-1 illustrates the ideal of a comprehensive and continuous service for handicapped children. It is against this background that the United Kingdom provisions will be discussed.

PREVENTION OF HANDICAP

Currently in the United Kingdom the majority of women arrive at pregnancy with a good knowledge of what it is all about; and healthy enough to see it through without danger to themselves or their fetus. This is the result of wide dissemination of knowledge about sex, child bearing, and the responsibilities of parenthood throughout the senior state schools, and of the good general healthy state of the population. Extensive trials are currently in progress to attempt to prevent congenital malformations from maternal rubella by giving rubella immunization to susceptible teenage girls (Dudgeon 1972).

The national perinatal survey of 1963 (Butler and Bonham) revealed

R E Q U I R E M E N T S	Prevention		Counselling
	Detection		Support
	Diagnosis		Vocational Placement
	Assessment	—	and Re-assessment
	Treatment	—	Teaching

Conception — Pregnancy — Birth — Preschool — School — Adult Life

P R O F E S S I O N	Geneticists		Other Medical Specialists
	Obstetricians		Therapists
	Paediatricians		Nurses
			Teachers
		Social Workers	

Figure 9-1.

that antenatal care was not always as satisfactory as it should be. This is being corrected and regular antenatal care with examination for rhesus incompatibility and, where appropriate, specialist advice and hospital treatment is available to everyone. Over 80 percent of deliveries are now carried out in hospital maternity units.

If there is any question of a risk to the fetus by genetically determined disorders, advice is available from regional genetic counseling referral centers. In appropriate cases, therapeutic abortion is recommended and carried out in order to prevent the birth of a seriously disabled body. These services are available to everyone through the health service.

The possibility and advisability of timing, spacing, and limiting pregnancies is widely known and practiced. This contributes to the health of children and lowers the prevalence of handicaps. A voluntary organization—The Family Planning Association—pioneered centers throughout the country at which contraceptive advice and materials could be obtained, and now this work is being absorbed into the National Health Service. In some parts of the country contraceptive materials are supplied freely as part of the service, and even vasectomy is being made easily available.

During pregnancy mothers are provided with dietary supplements, are discouraged from working for the last weeks of the pregnancy, and receive a weekly maternity payment for eighteen weeks amounting to approximately one-third of the average weekly income for women and a maternity grant equal to approximately the average week's income for women.

Improved medical care, especially the practice of immunization and use of antibiotics, has reduced the incidence of handicapping conditions secondary to such infections as poliomyelitis, tuberculosis, and rheumatic fever. Accidents, especially road accidents, however, have increased and contribute to the pool of handicapped children. This is likely to be a continuing and even increasing problem unless preventive measures are successful. At the present time a steady stream of health education propaganda is issued to try to reduce the number of accidents in the home and on the roads.

The fact that the various provisions mentioned above are available automatically to everyone through the National Health Service goes a long way towards the prevention of handicapping conditions in childhood in the United Kingdom.

DETECTION AND DIAGNOSIS: THE "AT RISK" CONCEPT

The "at risk" concept is both simple and sensible (Holt 1968). Case histories of disabled children reveal a higher than average incidence of illnesses, abnormalities, and complications during the antenatal, natal, and postnatal periods. Therefore, by identifying a group of infants with such histories, i.e., a group at increased risk, and giving them additional examinations, it should be possible to increase the success of both early diagnosis of disabled children and the prevention of complications. This concept was put forward almost simultaneously by Lindon (1961) and by Sheridan (1962), and led to the keeping of registers of "at risk" children by health authorities throughout the United Kingdom.

There have been several important outcomes of this endeavor. It was soon realized that keeping these registers did not provide the simple answer to early diagnosis. It was found that all handicapped children did not come from the "at risk" group. Although the incidence of disabled children in the "not at risk" group is lower than in the "at risk" group, the greater size of the first group means that it nevertheless contributes a considerable number to the total population of such children, and so it cannot be neglected. Other difficulties arose because the criteria for inclusion in the register were not well defined; insufficient attention was given to social risk factors; and the whole exercise was too isolated from active clinical work. Studies of the effectiveness of "at risk" registers showed that they were most useful when total resources (i.e., trained professional staff) were limited, and became less necessary when total population screening was possible with adequate resources (Alberman and Goldstein 1970). A move toward developmental screening of the whole infant population was made easier by a beneficial side effect of keeping the "at risk" registers. This work increased professional interest in the problems of young disabled children and the clinical skills of the doctors improved considerably. In 1967 Rogers reported that the percentage of children with specified handicaps diagnosed in the first year of life rose from 32 percent in 1959 (before the register) to 60 percent in 1964 (after four years of keeping a register). Moreover the improvement in early diagnosis was more evident in the "not at risk" group, illustrating the general effects of an improvement in clinical skills. This showed that there exists a group of experienced clinicians who could be deployed on whole infant population examinations.

Now it is advocated that all infants should be examined at selected ages. A working party on this subject recently recommended examination at the ages of 6 weeks, 6 months, 10 months, 18 months, 2 years, 3 years, and 4 1/2 years (Egan, Illingworth, and Mackeith 1969). This represents a lot of examinations and the ideal has not yet been agreed. There continue to be much active inquiry and discussion about the following topics; devising simple, reliable, and quick examinations; studies of the most effective methods and times of examination; studies of cost effectiveness; who should do this work (general family practitioners or primary pediatric physicians), and how they should be trained.

This year the National Health Service is being reorganized on more definite regional lines, which should promote this work. The creation of regional child health services will bring general practitioners, local authority, and hospital doctors closer together and will also facilitate monitoring of the services provided.

The most encouraging feature at present is a turning away from schemes designed just to detect abnormalities toward an increasing appreciation of the value of providing developmental advice for all children. Developmental diagnosis is now seen not as an end in itself, but as the basis of developmental guidance and training.

ASSESSMENT SERVICES

The need for assessment services for handicapped children arose out of three factors—the multiplicity of the problems of many handicapped children; the multiplicity of the helping professionals; and the fact that early diagnosis is sensible only if it leads to action carefully planned from the beginning and based upon adequate assessment.

Unfortunately the term assessment has been used indiscriminately and now means different things to different people. For clarification the following definition is repeated here: "Assessment consists of careful examination to detect all the defects which are present, interpretation of the significance of the findings with regard to the child's development, elaboration of a program of continuing care, and communication to all concerned."

In July 1968 the DHSS issued a statement recommending the establishment of district and regional assessment centers for handicapped children. In the light of subsequent experience it is preferable to interpret these recommendations with regard to district assessment *services* and regional assessment centers.

In both areas, the pattern of assessment is similar. It begins with the *diagnostic* phase in which all the medical, educational, and social aspects of the problems and of the child and his situation are identified and also all the assets which might be used in planning care and treatment. A composite picture is then built up from which it is possible to *interpret* the effect of this upon the child's development and to define treatment and teaching needs. This leads to the formulation of a plan of management which must then be *implemented.* *Communication* to all concerned, and particularly to the child and his parents, is essential. This process is illustrated in Figure 9-2. The district services are based upon population units of 100,000-200,000. The concerned professionals (e.g., pediatrician, other medical specialists, psychologist, social workers, teachers, therapists, etc.) work together and their efforts are coordinated by an appropriately trained pediatrician. (In the United Kingdom the term pediatrician refers to highly trained consultants. There will be one or two pediatricians in the population considered here.) This team is responsible for (a) the identification and assessment of all the handicapped children in the population, (b) insuring that facilities exist to enable their recommendations to be implemented, and (c) for providing continuing surveillance. Complex cases, probably amounting to between 5 and 10 percent of the children seen, are referred to the regional center for assessment, but are then referred back to their own district for continuing management and treatment.

The regional centers provide the district type service for their immediate area, but most of their work is concerned with referrals from other districts. These centers are usually purpose designed and staffed by full-time personnel. They have important responsibilities for training staff and the maintenance of a high standard of work throughout the region.

Currently district teams are forming in many parts of the country. Most of the principal cities now have regional assessment centers either established or in the process of development. Many of these are linked with children's hospital units and medical schools. The Wolfson Centre was set up by the Institute of Child Health of London University so that it could contain both a university department to carry out research in this subject and to train staff for other centers and district teams, and also a regional assessment center for a major sector of London.

Immeasurable advantages are enjoyed by having an assessment center

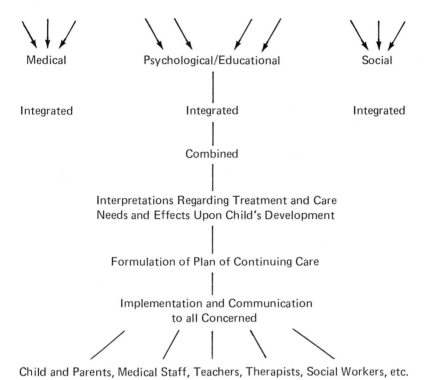

Figure 9-2. The Assessment Process, Diagrammatically

in which all the different professionals concerned can work together. It makes help given to the handicapped children more effective, and also provides professional work satisfaction. The work is arranged with a core team of three—a pediatrician, educational psychologist, and social worker. Each one is responsible for insuring that all the problems are dealt with in his own professional area, and for interpreting this information to the other two. He is also responsible for co-opting into the team whatever other professionals may be needed. This organization and illustrative examples are described elsewhere (Black, Holt, Huntley 1973). Examination in the individual's rooms is discouraged. The child is examined in parts of the building designed to be appropriate for the particular functions being examined. Thus one part is suitable for a study of communication disorders and another for a study of motor problems. A range of assessment procedures has been devised (Holt 1965; Holt and Reynell 1967; Reynell and Huntley 1971), and planned observation is used to reinforce the assessment (Holt and Reynell 1970). Much can be achieved by a small team such as this working throughout the day. At the end of the day the findings and opinions are reviewed and discussed with the child and his parents. Further visits are arranged as necessary until a comprehensive picture is obtained.

At the Wolfson Centre there is accommodation for two or three families to stay. This has been found to be one of the most useful services provided. The family seem to come face to face with their problems for the first time, and they feel they are in a sympathetic situation and able to discuss many of their problems. This work requires considerable skill and stamina on the part of the staff who have to build up the family reserves for the future.

All these services—at the district and regional levels, and including the residential facilities for families—are available as part of the National Health Service provisions. The handicapped children and their families do not have to make any financial contribution, nor is there any financial inquiry or barrier in connection with these services.

Although this is basically a medically initiated development, it is widely recognized that it will succeed only if close affiliation with educational and social services is achieved. At the district level there must be consumer feedback and satisfaction. At regional level there must be integrated policy development and training. It is probable that in time to come the development of assessment services will be seen as a tangible indication of medicine's acceptance of its preventive role and its responsibility to contribute its share along with education and social services to the promotion of child health and development.

EXPERIENCE OF TEAM WORK

The futility of isolated specialist medical work with respect to handicapped children is widely appreciated. Each specialist deals with those aspects which are of particular concern to himself and then usually either ignores any other requirements or else recognizes them and arranges a series of unrelated appointments with other specialist colleagues which the child and his parents find utterly confusing.

Teamwork does not develop easily. When professionals recognize the need to work together, they may swamp the patient with their multiple attentions or else be so busy communicating among themselves that the patient is left out in the cold. Attempts to run combined medical clinics do not always work satisfactorily because of the different tempo of work of the different specialists, i.e., surgeon and physician. Experience shows that in order to achieve good teamwork, one specialist has to accept the task of coordinating the work of all the others and of acting as an adviser and interpreter to the child and his parents. The British National Health Service provides a particularly good basis and model for setting up such integrated teams.

The coordinator of the medical team also acts as link man with other professional workers such as educators and social workers, and in many cases acts as the leader of this multidisciplinary team. Such teams cannot be created at short notice. They evolve gradually and this enables members to become familiar with their own roles and those of others, and to develop mutual respect for each others contributions. Such teams are now evolving successfully in several centers in the United Kingdom.

The case conference is a useful medium for the promotion of understanding and communication between professionals, and is much used by assessment teams. We have found that once teams are working well together, it is unnecessary to have a full conference about each patient. On the spot "mini conferences" are exceptionally useful because they enable constructive integrated advice to be given to the child and his parents without any delay. Formal conferences are very time consuming, often difficult to arrange at times and places to suit everyone concerned, and can seem intimidating to less experienced staff. We have found, therefore, that in order to get the fullest value from case conferences, their precise objective must be defined, and they must be arranged with much sensitive care.

TREATMENT, TEACHING, AND SOCIAL SUPPORT

Help is available in all three of these areas for every handicapped child. Following an assessment decisions are made about further investigations which are then carried out. On the medical side whatever medication, therapy or surgery is required is arranged. No charges are made to the child or his parents, nor are there any restrictions with respect to income or residential status.

The educational services are now statutorily responsible for the provision of appropriate education to all children from the age of five years whatever their disability and its severity, and they may make services available from the age of two years. With respect to handicapped children, the education services meet their responsibilities by integrating handicapped children into the ordinary school whenever this is possible (Anderson 1973), and by providing remedial teachers, special classes, and special schools.

The social services are responsible for the welfare of the handicapped. This includes the provision of home modifications and equipment, nurseries for young handicapped, and financial support in all those cases in which the presence of the handicapped child increases demands upon parents and requires extra care by day or night. The present value of this grant is best indicated by stating that it is equivalent to 15 percent of the average weekly income.

There are many voluntary organizations concerned with handicapped children. They fulfill a valuable complementary role to the official services. Some support research; others pioneer projects which if successful are often later taken over by the official services. Several organize special school or other facilities to meet particular needs. If a child requires a particular service which is available only in a voluntary society's school, then the local governmental authority will pay the fees.

PROFESSIONAL TRAINING

The adequacy and effectiveness of any service depend largely upon the quantity, quality, and experience, and training of its professional staff. Work with the handicapped, especially the severely and mentally handicapped, does not attract many professionals nor always the best ones. This is a problem which faces all countries. The situation in the United Kingdom is probably no more difficult than anywhere else, and so far as children are concerned it is usually easier to obtain staff to work with them than with adults. The development of assessment centers in the principal medical centers is doing much to enhance the status of the work. Within the National Health Service doctors are able to take up work with the handicapped and receive the same remuneration as their colleagues in other branches. Worries about loss of earnings from private practice seldom apply. A majority of the consultant pediatricians in the United Kingdom are employed full time in the health service. Many more pediatricians in the school medical and public health services work part time, but this is because they wish to do so and not in order to pursue private practice.

Medical training in this subject is very deficient but is being improved. Undergraduate training still contains relatively little on normal child development and there are as yet too few multidisciplinary assessment team models to which the students can be exposed. Curricula are being revised, however, to include more of this work and to emphasize the community aspects of medicine. The new medical schools, e.g., at Southampton and Nottingham, are pioneering schemes in undergraduate training.

The deficiencies in postgraduate training are being exposed and remedied. In the past relatively little postgraduate training was required to equip a doctor in the school health service to carry out a statutory duty concerned with the educational placement of handicapped children (Holt and Huntley 1973). From 1967 the Institute of Child Health of London University has run an annual full-time year's postgraduate course on Developmental Paediatrics and Child Assessment, and in the last year or two similar courses have been started or are being planned at other medical schools. In addition, training posts for pediatricians are being established in the new assessment centers.

Training courses for teachers concerned with special education have existed for many years. In recent years efforts have been concentrated upon improving the quality of these courses, increasing their number, and most important of all, developing full training courses for the teachers of the severely subnormal who previously had received only diploma courses.

Social and therapy services are the ones which are most deficient in trained and experienced staff. Sheer shortage of numbers and training facilities is the problem for the social services. All their field staff now work on a generic basis and deal with all problems. It is therefore very difficult to find workers with experience in depth in any particular aspect, such as handicapped children, who are not preoccupied with administration.

Therapists are not well paid and do not enjoy a career structure which offers encouraging prospects. Consequently many therapists leave their professions for marriage or other occupations after a few years. This situation is being reviewed and improved. For example, a recent report recommended the establishment of university level training opportunities for speech therapists and other improvements to their profession (D.E.S. 1969).

OUTSTANDING PROBLEMS

Although it is very pleasing to report recent improvements in attitudes to the handicapped, increased objectivity in their assessment and better provision of services, it would not be right to give the impression that all is perfect and that there are no outstanding problems. There are. The most important are the following:

1. The need to further increase the quantity and the quality of the services and provisions.
2. The need to make community care of handicapped children more effective and realistic. There is much talk of community care but little appreciation of its full meaning. For example, attendance at special schools often means that the child travels away from his local neighborhood and feels a stranger among local children when he is at home; and for some severely handicapped children community care still means that the parents cope as best they can at home.
3. The need to be able to arrange appropriate relief for families when it is needed. All too often identification of this requirement means that the child's name goes on a waiting list. There are some circumstances where prompt relief is needed and it would be useful to be able to supply this every time and not just in some cases.
4. The need to reach the unreachable. Some of the handicapped children most in need of help, many of whom are in the lower social classes, are often the most inaccessible to help. We still have to learn how to overcome this problem.
5. The need for more training opportunities for all groups of professional staff.

Clearly there is still much to be done. The traditional pattern of care together with the national health, educational, and social services form a sound basis for advances and it is encouraging that the recent development of assessment services is opening up the scientific study of the problems and more effective provision of help.

REFERENCES

Alberman, E.D. and Goldstein, H. "The 'At Risk' Register: a Statistical Evaluation." *Brit. J. Prev. Soc. Med.* 24 (1970): 129.

Anderson, E.M. *The Disabled School Child.* London: Methuen, 1973.

Black, J.M.M.; Holt, K.S.; and Huntley, R.M.C. "Comprehensive Assessment of the Needs of the Handicapped Child and His Family." In *Special Education in the New Community Services,* Ed. J.W. Palmer. Glamorgan: Ron Jones Publications, 1973.

Butler, N.R. and Bonham, D.G. *Perinatal Mortality.* Edinburgh: Livingstone, 1963.

Department of Education and Science. *Speech Therapy Services.* London: HMSO, 1969.

Dudgeon, J.A. "Congenital Rubella: A Preventable Disease." *Postgraduate Medical Journal Supplement,* No. 3 (1972): 48.

Egan, D.; Illingworth, R.S.; and MacKeith, R.C. "Developmental Screening 0-5 Years." *Clinics in Dev. Med.* 30 London: Heinemann, 1969.

Holt, K.S. *Assessment of Cerebral Palsy,* Vol. I. London: Lloyd-Luke, 1965.

Holt, K.S. "The 'At Risk' Concept." *Maternal and Child Care.* (July 1968): 145.

Holt, K.S. *The Quality of Survival.* Occasional Papers of the Institute for Research into Mental Retardation 2. London: Butterworths, 1972.

Holt, K.S. and Huntley, R.M.C. "Mental Subnormality: Medical Training in the UK." *Brit. J. Med. Ed.* 7 (1973): 197.

Holt, K.S. and Reynell, J.K. *Assessment of Cerebral Palsy,* Vol. II. London: Lloyd-Luke, 1967.

Holt, K.S. and Reynell, J.K. *Observation of Children.* National Association for Mental Health Publications, 1970.

Lindon, R. "Risk Register." *C.P. Bull.* 3 (1961): 481.

Reynell, J.K. and Huntley, R.M.C. "New Scales for the Assessment of Language Development in Young Children." *J. Learning Disabilities* 4 (1971): 549.

Rogers, M.G.H. "The Risk Register—A Critical Assessment." *Med. Officer* 118 (1967): 253.

Seebohm, F. *Report of The Committee on Local Authority and Allied Personal Social Services.* London: HMSO, 1968.

Sheridan, M.D. "Infants at Risk of Handicapping Conditions." *Mth. Bull. Ministry of Health Lab. Serv.* 21 (1962): 238.

Part II:

Sweden

Chapter 10

The National Health Service in Sweden

Malcolm Tottie and Helen M. Wallace

HISTORY OF THE DEVELOPMENT OF NATIONAL HEALTH SERVICE AND NATIONAL HEALTH INSURANCE IN SWEDEN

In Sweden, as in many other countries, the first health services were developed with the ecclesiastical organization. They were mainly concerned with sick, poor people, and persons with mental problems. During the Middle Ages, there was a number of foundations giving medical service and assistance to poor people, mainly based on voluntary contributions. In Stockholm, the foundations were all amalgamated in 1527 to a single institution on one of the islands of the city. This hospital could be described as a hospital and old-age home and in 1551 it was moved to a rather large institution with different wards for old-age persons, children, psychotics, patients with venereal disease, and invalids.

During the centuries, social care and medical care were combined, because both services concerned people who had to be taken care of. This mixture of sick and socially dependent people has continued to the present time.

During the eighteenth century, responsibility for the social services was delegated to the local authorities. During the same period, the development of the hospital system started. The first real hospital, Serafimerlassarettet in Stockholm, was inaugurated in 1752. One of the main reasons for starting this hospital and a number of others was to care for patients with venereal disease.

Sweden has had a pattern of a strong state and strong central government since the early 1880s. Its engagement in wars stimulated the need of returning soldiers for hospital care, and was an impetus to the development of hospitals for care in general and for the treatment of venereal disease. In 1818

Sweden levied a uniform head tax on citizens to finance one class of hospitals called "cure-houses" that were establshed to care for returning soldiers and others infected with venereal disease. In time, venereal disease came under control, but the head tax remained as a primary source of funding for Swedish hospitals until the 1860s. The state helped to support hospital-based physicians, and also supported the development of a health officer medical corps at local levels (in cities and counties), and especially in outlying areas.

In 1862, the Swedish government moved to the development of the län or county. The country was divided into twenty-five counties and three municipalities; they were given responsibility for the general hospitals, and also they were given taxing power, including property, personal income, and part of the liquor tax. From 1861 to 1904, the number of hospitals increased from 46 to 75, and the number of hospital beds from 2,960 to 7,856. The hospital and the hospital-based specialist became the core of the free health service in Sweden, accounting for the heavy emphasis on inpatient care and for the high bed-to-population ratio.

By 1900, voluntary benefit associations and insurance societies organized by trade unions were established. One of the needs was for the provision of physicians' services outside the hospital; gradually, more associations and societies began to add physicians' services. By 1910, there were 2,400 registered funds, covering 13.4 percent of the adult population. From 1910 until 1947 (when the compulsory health insurance law was enacted) and 1955 (when it went into effect), there were government commissions set up to consider and make recommendations for health care for the people. The separation of inpatient and outpatient hospital care had occurred; the pattern of the outpatient "polyclinic," staffed by hospital-based physicians, had developed; there were physicians in private practice without hospital affiliations; and universal health insurance was frequently discussed.

In 1947, the Swedish Parliament enacted the first compulsory health insurance act covering physicians' outpatient services and selected drugs; this went into effect in 1955. The next step was to regionalize the hospital system into seven regions, but with counties and municipalities retaining control and ownership, and with the state participating with assistance for separate staff and facilities which the hospital would need.

In 1960, Parliament recommended that the County Councils cooperate in setting up seven hospital regions to provide their populations with the most specialized clinical services at the regional hospitals. In 1961, the county was given responsibility for the public health officers, and in 1967, for mental hospitals. In 1970, the Seven Crown Reform was enacted (when a patient sees a doctor under the National Health Service, he was required to pay the National Health Service a fee of 7 Kroner, about $1.75); this was an effort to make hospital physicians' services more accessible to patients, to incorporate and strengthen outpatient ambulatory care in the National Health Service system, and to resolve the problem of payment of physicians' services in inpatient and outpatient care. The fee of 7 Kroner has now been raised to 12 Kroner (about $2.70).

ORGANIZATION OF GOVERNMENT IN SWEDEN

The Cabinet and Ministries

Although Sweden has a king, who is head of state, political power rests with the Cabinet and the party (or parties) it represents. There are at present nineteen ministers in the Social Democratic Cabinet. The prime minister has twelve heads of ministry: Justice, Foreign Affairs, Defense, Health and Social Affairs, Communications, Finance, Education and Cultural Affairs, Agriculture, Commerce, Labor and Housing, Physical Planning and Local Government, and Industry. The present Cabinet also includes six ministers without portfolio; one of these is in charge of Family Policy; another deals with educational matters; the other four consist of one in foreign affairs, one in civil service affairs, and two legal consultants. The ministries are small units, concerned with: (1) preparing the government's bills for Parliament on budget appropriation and laws; (2) issuing laws and regulations and general rules for the administrative agencies; (3) international relations; (4) higher appointments in the administration; and (5) certain appeals from individuals [2].

The Ministry of Health and Social Affairs has seven units. One deals with social insurance, one with social welfare programs, two with public health services, and the other three with legal matters, planning and budgetary questions, and international relations [2].

Commissions of Inquiry

The preparation of legal or other measures of the government is as a rule not done exclusively in the ministries. The government calls upon a group of experts to serve on a Commission of Inquiry, to study, investigate, and prepare a report on specific subjects. Such a method has been used recently in such areas as abortion, sex education, maternity care, dental care, etc. [2].

Table 10-1. Budget of National Government—Sweden—1968-69

(Expenditures in millions of dollars)	
Social Welfare	$2,061
Defense	1,047
Education	1,193
Total expenditures	7,517

Source: S.A. Lindgren, *Health Services in Sweden—Planning and Implementation* (Stockholm: National Board of Health and Welfare, 1970).

Planning
Considerable emphasis is placed on both central and regional planning [3, 4, 5].

Research
The Ministry of Education and Cultural Affairs is responsible for the universities (six) and most of the research councils, and hence for most of the basic research. Most of the ministries are in charge of a sector of applied research. Most basic research in Sweden is conducted at universities and professional schools. The total cost of universities and professional schools during the year 1972-73 was 1,400 million Kroner. Also in that year, 47.0 million Kroner was allocated for the Medical Research Council, and 11.2 million Kroner to the Social Science Research Council [5].

A variety of research institutes exist to cover special fields. Examples of this are the National Institute of Public Health, the National Bacteriological Laboratory, the Institute of Occupational Health. In 1968 the government established an institute for the planning of hospitals, including equipment standards, information processing methods, data systems, etc. [5]

HOSPITAL CARE

When the first hospital had been inaugurated in the capital at the end of the eighteenth century, hospitals were developed in nearly all the provincial capitals. From then up to the present time, there has been significant development within hospital service, and the history of the medical service in Sweden is very much related to the building of hospitals. To start with, the County Councils were responsible for the venereal disease hospitals only. In 1864, the Royal Regulations gave the County Councils direct responsibility for the medical care given at the general hospitals. The mental hospitals and the medical officers were the responsibility of the central government during the nineteenth century and the beginning of this century.

When the County Councils were instituted in the year 1863, the total number of general and venereal disease hospitals was 46, of which 40 were distributed within the different counties. The total number of beds was 3,007. The number of beds increased each year. The cost per day was not very high. In 1910, the daily cost per bed was Kr. 2.60 (approximately $0.60). In 1897, the first County Council hospital was divided into one section for surgery and one for internal medicine. Today, nearly all the hospitals are divided into different sections. In 1971 there was a total of 877 hospitals with a total number of beds of 134,458.

The central government is responsible only for two large teaching hospitals—the Karolinska hospital together with the Serafimerlasarettet in Stockholm—and the Akademiska hospital at Uppsala. These hospitals are run in collaboration with the corresponding County Councils.

During the period mentioned, it was realized that the mental hospitals run by the central government and some by the largest communities were lagging behind as a consequence of the slow development of treatment and rehabilitation of the mentally ill. These hospitals were also very often constructed as huge institutions, mainly intended for custodial care and not for treatment aiming at readaptation of the mentally sick. Newer treatment methods, to a great extent, altered the situation for the mentally sick. It became quite clear that the County Councils should provide medical care for the mentally sick also. All the mental hospitals were therefore, through a parliamentary decision, transferred to the County Councils in 1967. They are now partly integrated with the general hospitals and partly still forming bigger institutions attached to other big general hospitals.

Tuberculosis hospitals were in the beginning of this century supported by the municipalities and the central government. The enormous change in this disease has diminished the need for special hospitals for patients with tuberculosis. The number of deaths per year has decreased from 10,000 in 1909 to about 350 in the year 1971. The tuberculosis hospitals have therefore been changed to hospitals for treatment of other kinds of lung diseases or to institutions for other purposes.

For treatment of infectious diseases, the local authorities had organized a great number of small hospitals of a very limited character. When the responsibility had been taken over by the County Councils, these small hospitals were closed and the wards for infectious diseases were transferred to other hospitals. They now have other infectious diseases. At the same time there is some reserve capacity in case of very serious emergencies.

Sweden is divided into seven medical care regions, each with an average of slightly over a million inhabitants. This system is designed to prevent expensive duplication of services which might lack a sufficient population base. A *regional hospital* is a central hospital with a higher degree of specialization. It is usually affiliated with a medical school and plays an important role in medical research. Regional hospitals have 1,200-2,300 beds. Thoracic surgery, neurosurgery, pediatric surgery, urology, plastic surgery, dermatology, rheumatology, radiation therapy, and certain types of cardiology are among regional specialties. A *central general hospital* has 12-20 or more specialized wards. There is usually one central general hospital per county. In some counties, there are several. The smallest type, the *general hospital*, ordinarily has four medical chiefs of staff: one each for medicine, surgery, radiology, and anesthesiology. Each county has at least one central general hospital of 800-1,000 beds serving the whole county and containing a number of specialist departments—often around 15.

Special purpose hospitals were once common and are being replaced. For example, children's hospitals are replaced by children's wards; maternity homes by maternity wards, homes for the handicapped by orthopedic wards at larger hospitals. Special mental hospitals are no longer built; psychiatric care has been merged into the regular medical care system in the form of psychiatric clinics.

The number of *private hospitals* is very small.

The picture of the hospital services today is that there is a number of fairly well-developed hospitals all over Sweden. The hospitals can be classified into two categories, viz., those handling emergencies and other serious cases—general hospitals—and those providing long-term care—nursing homes. The type of beds existing in Sweden in 1972 may be classified according to Table 10-2.

In 1971, there were approximately 1.4 million admissions to the hospitals, of which approximately 65,000 were to general hospitals. The average length of stay in general hospitals is 11.1 days. (In 1920, this figure amounted to 29.8 days.)

ORGANIZATION OF HEALTH SERVICES

Administrative Organization

The central administration of health services in Sweden is divided between the Ministry of Health and Social Affairs, and the National Board of Health and Welfare. The authority of decision is thus shared between the two.

The National Board of Health and Welfare has six departments (see Figure 10-1). Responsibility for child health is in Department HB, with a full-time pediatrician in charge; responsibility for maternal health and family planning is in Department SN with a part-time obstetrician as consultant; responsibility for the handicapped and mentally retarded is in Department LÅ. Thus, there is no one unit at central government level responsible for the health care of mothers and children. Nevertheless, the specific units mentioned above are responsible for their own sections of the overall field [2].

Local Administration—The County [2, 7]

For the purpose of administration, Sweden is divided into twenty-five counties. Each county, plus the cities of Stockholm, Malmo, and Gothenburg, is responsible for most aspects of health care, including outpatient and

Table 10-2. Hospital Beds According to Type of Care, 1972

Type of Care	No. of Beds
Short-term, somatic diseases	50,000
Long-term, somatic diseases	34,000
Convalescent care	2,000
Adult psychiatry	25,000
Child and adolescent psychiatry	900
Psychiatric nursing-homes	7,100
Care of epileptics	150
Care of mentally retarded	20,000

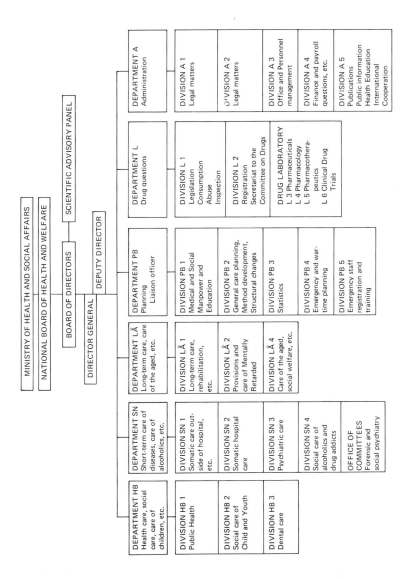

Figure 10-1.

Table 10-3.   Composition of Staff—Dec. 31, 1968—Sweden

Type	*Number*
Physicians	7,223
Dentists	2,448
Nurses and certain medical technicians	22,865
in laboratory work	1,868
Physical therapists	1,266
Enrolled nurses	7,958
Nursing assistants in psychiatric care	11,852
Dental assistants and technicians	3,430
Other nursing personnel	42,069
Subtotal	98,907
Administrative hospital staff	8,480
Domestic staff in hospitals	19,949
Total	127,540

Source: S.A. Lindgren, *Health Services in Sweden—Planning and Implementation* (Stockholm: National Board of Health and Welfare, 1970).

inpatient care for all illness, injury, deformity, and childbirth. Each county has a County Council which is responsible for administering the health and medical services. Each County Council is governed by a popularly elected body and has a medical services board, elected by the County Council, as the executive body of the medical care work. The County Councils have their own powers of taxation and in this way cover most of the expenditures for health and medical care. They also receive certain grants or subsidies from the central government for their work; this subsidy system is used by the central government to stimulate the development and strengthening of needed basic health services; for example, for several decades, this subsidy system was used in the field of maternal and child health, until the pattern of basic MCH services was firmly established, so that the County Councils would be certain to be able to continue them. Presently, subsidies from the central government are used for mental health, nursing, and district medical officers. The County Council is responsible not only for health care including hospital services, but also for certain types of education and vocational training. Approximately 75-80 percent of County Council expenditure is on medical care and related services. From the time of the creation of County Councils, one of their most important functions has been to manage hospitals and other types of medical care. The County Councils are thus in charge of the smallest dispensaries as well as the large central hospitals.

Under the medical care activities of the County Councils are the district nurse organization; the maternal and child welfare programs; the mental

Table 10-4. Outpatient Visits to Hospitals and Specialized Clinics, Sweden—1968

Type of Care	Number of Visits (thousands)
Surgery	5,508
Medicine	2,480
Psychiatry	507
Other	673
Total	9,168

Outpatient Visits to Certain Health Units Outside Hospitals
Sweden—1968

Unit	Number of Visits (thousands)
P.H. Nurses	3,740
District M.O. Stations	3,383
Child Health Centers	1,964
Maternity Centers	973
TB Dispensaries	448
Total	10,508

Source: S.A. Lindgren, *Health Services in Sweden—Planning and Implementation* (Stockholm: National Board of Health and Welfare, 1970).

institutions; the public medical services administered by the medical officers; the public dental care programs in central and district dental clinics. In addition, the County Councils have certain social welfare functions, including children's homes, infant nurseries, maternity homes, correctional institutions, and special homes. There are twenty-one county-operated schools of nursing (in addition, there are twelve others in Sweden).

Local Administration—The Municipality [2, 7]

Sweden had 464 municipalities. In 1974, this number was reduced to 270. The powers and duties of the municipalities include a large number of services: housing, roads, sewerage and water supply, basic education, public assistance, child welfare, treatment of alcoholics, environmental and food hygiene. The municipalities have the right to levy income taxes and receive the revenue of a modest tax on real estate.

National Governmental Supervision [8]

In many respects the County Councils possess independent authority. Nevertheless the central government has several ways of influencing the

Table 10-5. Expenditures of the Primary Municipalities in 1970—Sweden

Expenditures	S. Kr. Mill	%
Education	8,923	24
Welfare	5,716	16
Health and Medical Services	2,587	7
Industrial Activities	5,394	15
Urban Construction (roads, streets, etc.)	4,130	11
Housing and Property Management	3,808	10
Other	6,249	17
Total	36,807	100

Source: The Swedish Institute. "Local Government in Sweden." In *Fact Sheets on Sweden.* (Stockholm, November 1972).

Table 10-6. Source of Funds for Health Care in the County, Sweden

Source	% of Total
Local taxation	70%
From national government	13
From health insurance	7
Patients' fees	1
Other	8
Total	99%

Source: S.A. Lindgren, *Health Services in Sweden—Planning and Implementation* (Stockholm: National Board of Health and Welfare, 1970).

health and medical services provided by them. This is done through its authority to decide whether to establish new public service positions for doctors and through its duty to inspect all medical care activities. The Medical Appeals Board, attached to the National Board of Health and Welfare, investigates complaints of malpractice or neglect on the part of medical personnel. Approval of blueprints for construction or alteration of medical facilities is also handled on the national level by a special board of medical and social welfare buildings.

THE ORGANIZATION OF MEDICAL CARE IN SWEDEN [8]

All activities in the field of public health in Sweden, including medical care, are either operated or controlled by public authorities.

Brief History of Development

Swedish medical care has undergone major reforms in recent decades. In 1951, the County Councils were given responsibility for the care of the chronically ill, who previously received aid through what was then called the poor relief system. Care of chronic illness was thereby put on an equal footing with other medical care.

In 1955, national public health insurance was introduced, guaranteeing a certain income in case of illness. The daily payment is based on a person's normal annual income. The previous system of voluntary medical insurance excluded many persons who, for reason of disability or injury, urgently needed protection from loss of income during an illness.

In 1963, the County Councils took over the national system of district medical officers, who until then had been employed by the central government. In 1967, the County Councils assumed similar responsibility for mental health care. The counties thereby gained uniform authority over most of Swedish medical care.

In 1969, the Social Insurance System assumed a greater share of the cost of medicines. Outpatients pay a maximum of 15 Kroner for medicines prescribed on any one occasion by a physician.

In 1970, a uniform charge for outpatient care was introduced. The purpose of this so-called Seven Crown Reform was to lower the fee for outpatient medical care at hospital clinics and district medical officers, thereby making ambulatory outpatient care more available and reducing hospitalization. Simultaneously, publicly employed physicians were placed on a regular salary— i.e., a patient no longer pays a doctor a direct fee. The salary for county-employed physicians covers both inpatient and outpatient care. All physicians with equal positions and equal length of service are on the whole paid the same salary for the same number of working hours [8].

Medical Practice [7]

There are approximately 10,000 doctors in Sweden at present. There is a recognized shortage of doctors, and admissions to medical schools have increased so that by 1980 the number will be increased to 20,000. Three-fourths of the physicians are public employees, and one-fourth are in private practice.

General medicine is practiced by private practitioners and district medical officers employed by the County Councils. Most of the general practitioners work in single practice, but there is a trend toward group practice, which in the case of private practitioners also includes specialists. There are about 3,000 general practitioners in Sweden; among them are 400 private practitioners and 800 district medical officers.

Specialized medicine in Sweden is practiced by two types of physicians, namely, private practitioners and hospital physicians. The hospital physicians are employed by the County Councils and work full time at the hospital. The number of specialists in Sweden is approximately 7,000; of this number, 450 are pediatricians and 480 are obstetricians.

Other Medical and Health Services [8]

A large percentage of accidents and illnesses are handled on an outpatient basis. Local health districts offer the services of one or more physicians at each local office. The district medical officer is frequently the first contact a sick person has with the medical care system. If necessary, this doctor can contact a specialist and refer the patient to him for additional examination and treatment.

District medical officers also make house calls, but their time for this is limited. In Stockholm, a special emergency telephone exchange has been established, with doctors providing this.

The district nurse, like the district medical officer, meets patients in her office and makes home calls. On the District Medical Officer's Instructions, she provides health care and counseling. She also supervises the care provided to patients in their homes, obtains certain technical aids needed by the sick and the handicapped, gives first aid in case of accidents, does examinations, and helps solve public health problems. Her services are free of charge.

A person who is ill over a long period and receives home care can under certain circumstances be granted an allowance from the county to pay for an attendant. The county or municipality can also provide home nurses or attendants. If technical aids are requested, these are provided free of charge after proper testing in the hospital or in the home.

The Swedish health services have been informally regionalized for a long time because of county and major municipality responsibility for ownership, funding, and operation of hospitals. Since 1961, the public health officers, who were employed for the state, became part of the county and major municipality health services. The health officers are in charge of environmental and communicable disease control, MCH, public health nurses, and nurse-midwives. Since 1955, the income of private practitioners has come essentially from the compulsory health insurance related to out-of-hospital (including hospital outpatient departments) medical services.

Ambulatory care in Sweden is given mainly at the outpatient services of the general hospitals for approximately 50 percent of the total number of visits. The ambulatory service is provided by 1,400 medical officers who are appointed and paid by the central government. These services have from 1963 been taken over by the County Councils and the medical officers are now to an increasing extent grouped together in "vordcentraler" (health centers) which are responsible for about 25 percent of the total number of ambulatory visits; 25 percent of the ambulatory visits are made to private practitioners. The total number of ambulatory visits was twenty million in 1971.

The principle for the medical care system is to provide the individual with an optimum of care at the right time. Health centers are being developed in such a way that they can provide good general and specialist care without necessarily having to refer a patient to specialists in a hospital. At the same time, smaller hospitals are being closed or transferred to institutions for long-term care. It is planned that small hospitals will exist in the future only in very remote areas. The forming of health centers will be different according to the different needs and geographical areas, and there may be some with 3-5 physicians, mainly generalists with some preference for some specialities. In the bigger health centers, there may be up to fifteen physicians, of which approximately two-thirds should be specialists and the rest generalists. These health centers are planned to function as service centers as is the case in one pilot area—Tierp in the Uppsala region—with the idea of one center covering more or less the whole needs of an individual.

The next trend of high importance is the development of more possibility for long-term care under the supervision of a physician responsible for a given area covering both hospital beds and home care.

Preventive Health Services

Regarding preventive health services, the MCH services are run by the County Councils and cover nearly every expectant mother and new-born child. More than 99 percent of the babies are born in hospitals, and it is planned that the supervision of the child will provide complete health supervision from birth, during the younger years and into the school years through the school health services. At the same time, the services for family planning are under development within the same sphere. The cost of preventive health care is not paid by health insurance. Maternal and child care, tuberculosis services, and immunizations are provided free of charge by the County Councils. To assist medical officers with preventive medical services and health education activities, there are about 2,000 district health nurses, providing free-of-charge service.

Dental Health Service

The public dental service is also the responsibility of the County Councils. They are through dental health centers providing treatment free of charge for children and youth up to the age of sixteen. Thereafter, the dental care service is given on a very low fee scale. The dental care is paid by the insurance to 50 percent. Expensive prostheses are heavily supported financially.

MEDICAL EDUCATION IN SWEDEN [9]

There are six medical schools in universities in Sweden. First-year students are currently admitted at the rate of 1,026 per year.

It is planned to double the number of doctors from approximately 10,000 in 1968 to 20,000 in 1980. In 1972, there were 13,000.

Medical education has been shortened from 6½ to 5½ years, mainly by doing away with the nine-month internship. The 5½ year basic curriculum is followed by a compulsory general service period of twenty-one months, which is divided as follows: six months each in medicine, surgery, and OPD; and three months in psychiatry. The basic medical education has the following content:

Term I-II — Anatomy, histology, medical statistics, medical genetics

Term III — General chemistry, medical chemistry

Term IV — Medical physics, physiology, psychology

Term V-VI — Pharmacology, medical microbiology, pathology, clinical chemistry, clinical psychology, clinical subjects (including medicine, surgery, methods of clinical investigation, radiology, nursing and physiotherapy, social medicine and psychiatry, and development psychology). Clinical stage, part one.

Term VII-VIII — Medicine, surgery, clinical chemistry, clinical physiology, clinical bacteriology, radiotherapy, X-ray diagnosis, Clinical stage, part two.

Term IX — Dermatovenereology, Communicable diseases, Emergency medicine, Psychiatry

Term X — Ophthalmology, ENT, Forensic Medicine
— Hygiene, Neurology, Social Medicine

Term XI — Obstetrics, gynecology, infancy
— Pediatrics, child and youth, psychiatry

Medical specialty postgraduate training last 4-5½ years. There is a separate program for postgraduate education for general practitioners for three years.

SOCIAL INSURANCE IN SWEDEN

History

Important milestones in history are the creation of National Health Insurance in 1955, and the decision to introduce a General Supplementary

Table 10-7. Doctors in Sweden—1960-1980

	1960	1965	1968	1972	1975	1980
Total number of doctors	7,095	8,696	9,930	12,877	16,000	20,500
Full-time doctors	6,386	7,700	8,738	11,281	14,000	17,500
Population per doctor	1,070	880	800	632	525	430

Source: The Swedish Institute, "Medical Education in Sweden," In *Fact Sheets on Sweden* (Stockholm, Feb. 1973).

Table 10-8. Population per Health Personnel

	Per Physician	Per Dentist
USA	(1967) 650	(1967) 2,020
Sweden	(1970) 760	(1970) 1,110
England & Wales	(1967) 860	

Source: National Board of Health and Welfare, *Public Health in Sweden 1970* (Stockholm, 1972).

Table 10-9. Number of Physicians with Specialist Qualifications, Sweden—1970

Type	Number
Anesthesiology	116
Pediatrics	443
Pediatric Surgery	27
Orthopedics	180
Plastic Surgery	12
Obstetrics and Gynecology	481
Neurology	106
Child and Adolescent Psychiatry	69
Ophthalmology	213
Otolaryngology	316
Rehabilitation	4
Total Number of Specialists	6,904

Source: National Board of Health and Welfare, *Public Health in Sweden* (Stockholm, 1972).

Pension in 1959. From January 1, 1963, the National Health Insurance Act, the Basic Pension Act, and the National Supplementary Pension Act have been combined in a single National Insurance Act. Other important reforms in the field of social insurance are the improved health insurance from 1967; the introduction in 1968 of rebates on pharmaceutical preparations; pension increments in 1969; the uniform tariff for doctors' consultations from 1970; and in 1970 the extension of advance pension rights.

Organization

The National Insurance system is under the administration of twenty-six regional insurance offices. These are independent bodies centrally managed and inspected by the National Social Insurance Board, which also handles grievances.

Table 10-10. Number of Dentists—Sweden—1964-70

Type	1964	1965	1966	1967	1968	1969	1970
Pedodontics	24	27	30	35	38	47	56
Orthodontics	58	71	78	84	101	107	128
Other	34	42	54	61	71	81	117
Total	116	140	162	180	210	235	291

Source: National Board of Health and Welfare, *Public Health in Sweden* (Stockholm, 1972).

General Coverage

The National Insurance Act covers health insurance and pension insurance (basic and supplementary pension). All Swedish citizens are insured under the National Insurance Act. All insured persons are registered with an insurance office from the month in which they reach the age of sixteen.

Health Insurance

Allowances for Medical Expenses. Allowances for medical expenses cover various payments made in connection with treatment by a doctor, a dentist (in certain cases), and at a hospital. They also include reimbursements for the costs of other care and treatment, travel costs, and discounts on pharmaceutical preparations.

A uniform tariff applies to the public outpatient services. The charges are 12 Kr. for visiting a doctor and 20 Kr. for a home visit.

On January 1, 1974, a national dental insurance scheme began, in which half the cost of dental treatment is refunded. Dental costs in excess of 1,000 Kr. qualify for 75 percent reimbursement.

Payment for hospital care in connection with sickness or maternity is usually paid up to the amount which corresponds to the costs of care in a public ward at the local hospital.

Compensation is made for travel for medical or dental care, in excess of 6 Kr.

Reimbursement for the charges for other types of treatment (convalescent care, physical therapy) amounts in principle to three-quarters of the actual expenditure.

Rebates on purchases of drugs are made directly by the pharmacy. The maximum payable by the patient on each occasion is 15 Kr. Certain drugs for the treatment of chronic and serious disease are free.

Sickness Benefit and Maternity Benefit. Sickness benefit is compensation paid for income loss due to illness. It reimburses about 80 percent of the income loss in the most common income brackets. It is calculated according to estimated annual income. The lowest sickness benefit paid is 6 Kr. per day, which is the *basic sickness benefit.* Among those who receive this are female and male insureds who earn no income from gainful employment (home spouses). Payments made in excess of this sum are *supplementary sickness benefit.* The maximum amount paid is 52 Kr. per day. The period for which sickness benefit can be paid is unlimited in principle. Usually sickness benefit is paid from and including the day after the person becomes ill. In certain cases, *a children's bonus* is paid, amounting to 1, 2, or 3 Kr., depending on the number of children.

Home spouses and students who are not insured for any supplementary sickness benefit can take out a *voluntary sickness benefit insurance.* For a low premium, they can then receive a total sickness benefit of 15 Kr. per day.

A woman delivering a child receives a *maternity benefit* of a lump sum, 1,080 Kr. A gainfully employed woman is entitled to *supplementary sickness benefit in connection with childbirth* for 180 days, provided she has been insured for a supplementary sickness benefit of at least 7 Kr. per day during 270 or more days prior to delivery. On January 1, 1974, the present maternity insurance was replaced by a *parental insurance* assuring parents of support during six months after birth of a child. Parents are free to decide which of them will stay home and look after the baby during these six months; they can also divide the time between them.

Pension Insurance

The national pensions scheme covers the basic pension and national supplementary pension (ATP). Both are calculated according to a "base sum," which follows the general level of prices and is adjusted each month.

Basic Pension. An *old age pension* normally begins at sixty-seven years. For a single person it amounts to 90 percent of the base sum and is now 6,750 Kr. per year. If husband and wife are both pensioners, the pension amounts to 70 percent of the base sum for each, or a combined pension of 10,220 Kr. In addition, they receive municipal housing allowances and pension increments.

A person of sixteen or more whose working capacity has been reduced by at least half due to sickness, mental retardation, physical disability or other handicap can obtain an *advance pension* if the disability is permanent.

A *widow's pension* is paid (a) to a widow who is thirty-six years of age, provided she was married for at least five years; a full pension is paid if the widow is fifty; (b) to a widow having the custody of a child under sixteen.

A *children's pension* is paid to children under sixteen on the death of one or both parents.

Specific Benefits under the Basic Pension Scheme. A *children's allowance* is paid to pensioners with children under sixteen living at home.

A pensioner unable to look after himself and needing daily help can receive a *disability allowance.*

A *nursing allowance* is made to children under sixteen who are disabled and cared for at home.

A *housing allowance* can be made as a bonus to the old-age or other pensions.

National Supplementary Pension (ATP). These are supplementary amounts available to a person who has had a working income in excess of the base sum for at least three years, and been credited with "pension-carrying income." They are available as supplements to old-age pension and widow's pension. A children's pension from ATP is paid to children under nineteen on the death of one or both parents.

FINANCIAL INFORMATION

In 1972, the Gross National Product was 199,000 million Kroner. The national government budget for the fiscal year 1973-74 was 67,104 million Kroner. Of this, 29 percent goes to social welfare programs, 16 percent to education, and 12 percent to defense.

In 1972, the total labor force in Sweden was approximately 3.9 million people. The average hourly income for a male industrial worker was 13.5 Kr., which means a gross annual income of 27-30,000 Kr. per year.

The national income tax is progressive, while the local income tax is a fixed percentage of income.

The Cost of Social Welfare Services
Data for 1971 are shown in Table 10-14. Total social welfare

Table 10-11. How National Insurance is Financed—Sweden

Type of Insurance		Source
1. Health Insurance	1A.	Insured persons' own contributions
	B.	Employers' contributions
	C.	State Grants
2. Basic Pension	2A.	Insured persons' own contributions
	B.	State grants
3. National Supplementary Pension (ATP)	3A.	Employers' contributions
	B.	Own contributions from certain insured persons (who do not have any employer)

Source: The Swedish Institute, "Social Insurance in Sweden," In *Fact Sheets on Sweden* (Stockholm, Feb. 1973).

Table 10-12. Swedish Social Insurance Benefits

1. *Health Insurance*

   A. *Allowances for Medical Expenses*

   Care by a doctor
   Dental care
   Care at a hospital
   Travel
   Other care and treatment
   Pharmaceutical preparations

   B. *Sickness and Maternity Benefits*

   Basic sickness benefit
   Supplementary sickness benefit
   Children's bonus
   Voluntary sickness benefit
   Maternity benefit
   Supplementary sickness benefit
   on childbirth

2. *Industrial Injuries Insurance*

   Allowances for medical expenses
   Sickness benefit
   Life annuity
   Grant in case of death

3. *Pension Insurance*

   A. *Basic Pension*

   Old age pension
   Advance pension
   Widows' and children's pension

   B. *Supplementary Pension (ATP)*

   Old age pension
   Advance pension
   Widows' and children's pension

4. *Special Benefits under the Basic Pension Scheme*

   Children's allowance
   Disability allowance
   Disability compensation
   Wife's allowance
   Housing allowance

5. *Unemployment Insurance*

   Daily benefit
   Children's benefit

Source: The Swedish Institute, "Social Insurance in Sweden," In *Fact Sheets on Sweden* (Stockholm, Feb. 1973).

Table 10-13. Economic Comparison—1970—Gross National Product per Capita

USA	$4,531
Sweden	3,873
United Kingdom	1,998

Source: The Swedish Institute, *Sweden in a Nutshell* (Stockholm, 1972).

Table 10-14.   Expenditure on Social Welfare in Sweden—1971 (in thousands of Kroner)

Type	Total	Source			
		National	Municipal & County	Employers	Insured People
Sickness	14,487,608	2,758,346	7,740,402	2,569,217	1,419,343
Sickness insurance	4,766,559	777,999	–	2,569,217	1,419,343
General health service, hospitals, midwifery	8,603,479	1,707,849	6,895,630	–	–
Temperance welfare	252,299	198,753	53,546	–	–
Care of mentally deficient	522,304	58,079	464,225	–	–
National dental service	342,967	15,666	327,301	–	–
Accidents at Work & Industrial Safety	248,911	26,799	–	222,112	–
Occupational injury ins.	231,158	9,046	–	222,112	–
Industrial safety	17,753	17,753	–	–	–
Unemployment	2,311,447	1,986,573	200,307	–	124,567
Unemployment benefits & insurance	596,259	449,385	22,307	–	124,567
Employment exchange & occupational guidance	211,203	211,203	–	–	–
Retraining of unemployed	547,985	547,985	–	–	–
Public works & locality allowances to enterprises	956,000	778,000	178,000	–	–
Old Age, Disablement, etc.	17,945,502	5,910,312	2,381,289	6,651,307	3,002,594
Old age and premature pensions	9,108,500	5,466,450	991,200	–	2,650,850
Gen. supplementary pensions	7,003,051	–	–	6,651,307	351,744
Care of cripples	362,852	278,133	84,719	–	–

Old age homes	912,668	—	912,668	—	—
Assistance in home or other facilities for aged	558,431	165,729	392,702	—	—
Families and Children	6,342,044	3,916,831	1,967,556	201,982	255,675
General child allowances	2,144,274	2,144,274	—	—	—
Rent allowances to families with children	857,097	681,000	176,097	—	—
Children's pensions	315,550	36,850	—	247,450	31,250
Allowances paid in advance	267,787	200,840	66,947	—	—
Mothers and infants welfare	437,494	44,837	—	136,982	255,675
Children's day homes, nursery schools, etc.	868,929	134,684	734,245	—	—
Home help service	195,504	52,335	143,169	—	—
Holidays for children & housewives	5,422	5,422	—	—	—
Public child welfare	382,447	84,681	297,766	—	—
School meals	549,332	—	549,332	—	—
Assistant for education	513,758	513,758	—	—	—
General Assistance	494,025	46,165	447,860	—	—
Social assistance	478,732	30,872	447,860	—	—
Other assistance	15,293	15,293	—	—	—
Injuries Received in Military and War Accidents	20,231	20,231	—	—	—
Total	41,849,768	14,665,257	12,737,714	9,644,618	4,802,179
Central Administrative Costs	205,217	196,517	—	8,700	—
Total	42,054,985	14,861,774	12,737,714	9,653,318	4,802,179

Source: National Central Bureau of Statistics, *The Cost of Financing of the Social Services in Sweden in 1971* (Stockholm, 1973).

expenditure for 1971 was 42,056 thousand Kroner, of which over one-third came from national funds, one-third from municipal and county funds, almost one-quarter from employers, and over one-tenth from insured people. National funds were used most to support pensions, child allowances, the general health service, old age pensions, the care of the handicapped, the care of children in day homes and nursery schools, and school meals. Employers' funds were used most to support the general supplementary pensions and sickness insurance. Funds from insured people were used to support pensions and sickness insurance (Table 10-14).

The cost of medical care has increased enormously. During the last six years, there has been an average annual increase of approximately 15 percent, and the medical care expenditure takes approximately 4.5 percent of the GNP, whereas at the same time education is responsible for 5.1 percent and military defense for 3.7 percent.

The cost of a hospital bed per day has increased greatly and now amounts to Kr 350 ($78) or more per day. Between 70-80 percent of the cost for the care in a hospital is due to personnel costs, which is a consequence of intensified service and shorter working hours.

In view of rising costs, there has been a considerable interest in finding solutions to limit the steadily increasing costs. Some investigations have been made within the National Board of Health and Welfare in collaboration with the County Councils and the local municipalities. According to principles accepted by all, it has been agreed that to achieve its best effectiveness, medicine has to be closely integrated into the whole field of social welfare. This integration is highly stressed in the planning of future development.

Health Economics from the Patient's Point of View [7]

The health insurance is supervised by the National Social Insurance Board, which is also under the Ministry of Health and Social Affairs. Insurance is compulsory. Benefits include free care for hospitalized patients, doctors' services, and the pharmaceutical prescriptions at reduced cost for patients in ambulatory care. Dental care has just been included.

On January 1, 1970 Sweden developed a new payment scheme for ambulatory care operated by the County Councils. The patient has to pay 12 Kroner per consultation. This fee includes consultation as well as laboratory examination in connection with the consultation. The County Councils receive on request from the social insurance a remuneration of 31 Kroner per consultation. (Patients attending a private practitioner receive reimbursement from the social insurance system according to a specific reimbursement scheme. The patient receives 75 percent of the amount that is stated in the reimbursement schedule for the type of consultation in question.)

The patient's traveling expenses which exceed 5 Kroner are paid. Expenses for staying overnight and for a companion are paid in certain cases.

Prescribed pharmaceutical preparations are paid for by the patients at reduced prices, and do not exceed 15 Kroner. Certain medicines (i.e., insulin) prescribed by a doctor are obtainable free of charge.

The patient is not charged for inpatient care; unlimited inpatient care is free, except for individuals over sixty-seven years, where there is a maximum of 365 days. Free hospitalization includes medical treatment, surgery, laboratory examinations, and drugs. The hospital sends an invoice for 10 Kroner per day to the regional social insurance office.

The health insurance system in Sweden includes a number of provisions for facilitating a visit to a doctor or a dentist or a hospital or a convalescent home. The fee for the ambulatory service is now Kr 12 ($2.70) if the doctor is appointed by the County Council, and Kr 20 ($4.50) for a home visit by the same doctor. The social insurance system pays the County Council Kr 48 ($10.50) for each visit. The insurance gives a daily allowance and provides a reduction of the price of pharmaceutical preparations. Preparations on prescription can never cost more than Kr 15 ($3.30). The private practitioner is free to charge whatever he wants. The patient is for the time being reimbursed three-fourths according to a fixed fee scale. This gives in practice a reimbursement of about 60 percent.

SUMMARY

The development of the health services in Sweden is a result of the willingness of the counties to develop their services among the guiding principles given by the National Board of Health and Welfare and the Swedish National Institute for Planning and Rationalization of Health Services.

Rising costs have forced all authorities concerned to try to develop more exact tools for planning for the future. It is quite clear that each county now has to provide short-term and long-term plans not only for their building activities but also for administration and educational activities. It is hoped that this will result in better planning and that it may be possible to better utilize existing resources which will stimulate a balanced development. All the new knowledge required puts more emphasis on setting priorities when further resources become limited.

Certain trends are occurring. There is more emphasis on developing ambulatory care. Health centers are being developed, some of which are being linked to hospitals. The pattern of group practice of physicians is being developed and encouraged. Mental health care is being integrated into general health care. Dental health care is being included. Regional planning is being implemented to provide specialized care. Home care is being developed.

REFERENCES

1. Anderson, O.W. *Health Care: Can There Be Equity?* New York: John Wiley & Sons, 1972.

2. The Swedish Institute. "Swedish Government in Action." In *Fact Sheets on Sweden*. Stockholm, Dec. 1972.

3. The Swedish Institute. "Central Planning Sweden." In *Fact Sheets on Sweden*. Stockholm, Aug. 1972.

4. The Swedish Institute. "Regional Development Policy in Sweden." In *Fact Sheets on Sweden*. Stockholm, Oct. 1972.

5. The Swedish Institute. "The Organization and Planning of Swedish Research." In *Fact Sheets on Sweden*. Stockholm, April 1972.

6. The Swedish Institute. "Local Government in Sweden." In *Fact Sheets on Sweden*. Stockholm, 1972.

7. Lindgren, S.A. *Health Services in Sweden—Planning and Implementation*. Stockholm: National Board of Health and Welfare, 1970.

8. The Swedish Institute. "The Organization of Medical Care in Sweden." In *Fact Sheets on Sweden*. Stockholm, Aug. 1972.

9. The Swedish Institute. "Medical Education in Sweden." In *Fact Sheets on Sweden*. Stockholm, Feb. 1973.

10. The Swedish Institute. "Social Insurance in Sweden." In *Facts on Sweden*. Stockholm, Feb. 1973.

11. National Central Bureau of Statistics. *The Cost and Financing of the Social Services in Sweden in 1971*. Stockholm, 1973.

12. The Swedish Institute. "General Facts on Sweden." In *Facts on Sweden*. Stockholm, June 1973.

Chapter 11

Maternal and Child Health in Sweden

Helen M. Wallace

INTRODUCTION

Sweden is a country of eight million people. It had had a long history (almost 100 years) of social insurance, largely organized through voluntary benefit associations and insurance societies. In 1955, the National Health Insurance Law went into effect, requiring compulsory insurance for the payment of health care. This covers diagnostic, treatment, rehabilitation care on an inpatient and ambulatory basis, drugs, appliances, etc.

Responsibility for delivering health and medical care has been decentralized to the twenty-five counties and three large cities. Approximately 75-80 percent of County Council expenditure is on medical and health care. One of the most important functions of the County Council is to manage hospitals and other types of medical care, and to provide such services as mother and child welfare programs, district nursing, mental institutions, public dental care programs, and public medical services administered by the medical officers. They also operate children's homes, infant nurseries, maternity homes, and correctional institutions. Maternal and child health services are provided at the county level free of charge.

MATERNAL HEALTH, FAMILY PLANNING, AND ABORTION

Demographic Data

Live Birthrate. The birthrate in Sweden has been low for several decades. Since 1964, it has been decreasing further. In 1971, it was 14.1 per 1,000 population. Practically 100 percent of all live births now occur in hospitals in Sweden (Table 11-1).

Table 11-1. Marriage Rate, Birthrate, and Infant Mortality Rate Per 1,000 of the Mean Population in Sweden

Year	Marriage Rate	Birthrate	Infant Mortality Rate
1950	7.33	16.45	0.35
1955		14.78	0.26
1960	6.70	13.66	0.23
1965	7.75	15.88	0.21
1966	7.83	15.80	0.20
1967	7.19	15.42	0.20
1968	6.63	14.29	0.19
1969	6.07	13.51	0.16
1970	5.38	13.70	0.15
1971	4.92	14.14	0.16
1972		13.8	

Source: *Population Changes*, Central Bureau of Statistics, (Stockholm, 1973).

Marriage Rate. The marriage rate has been decreasing since 1940. In 1971, it was 4.9 per 1,000 population (Table 11-1).

Average Age at First Marriage. In 1971 this was 26.4 years for men and 24.2 years for women. For men, this has remained stationary since 1965; for women, it has increased slightly since 1965.

Illegitimacy. While this has traditionally been high, since the 1960s it has increased significantly. In 1971, it was 21.6 percent. While the birthrate to married parents has decreased, that to unmarried parents has increased. It has increased in the age groups of women 15-19, 20-24, 25-29, 30-34, and 35-39 years (Tables 11-2 and 11-3).

Table 11-2. Illegitimacy in Sweden Percentage of Live Births Out of Wedlock

Year	Percentage in Wedlock	Percentage Out of Wedlock
1930	83.7	17.3
1940	88.2	11.8
1950	90.2	9.8
1960	90.6	9.4
1965	86.2	13.8
1970	81.6	19.4
1971	78.4	21.6

Source: RFSU Statistik. *Befolkningen, Sexualvanor, Aborten, Gonoré, Sexualbrott, Internationellt* (Stockholm, May 1973).

Table 11-3. Number of Live Births Per 1,000 Unmarried Women in Different Age Groups—Sweden

Age Group	1940	1950	1960	1970	1971
15-19 years	12.9	19.4	18.7	24.7	27.1
20-24 years	23.6	31.1	29.7	46.7	56.3
25-29 years	17.3	22.2	27.5	39.8	45.9
30-34 years	12.6	16.1	17.9	29.7	30.7
35-39 years	7.9	9.1	10.7	14.3	15.2
40-44 years	3.0	3.4	3.9	4.4	3.8
45-49 years	0.3	0.2	0.3	0.1	0.3

Source: RFSU Statistik, *Befolkningen, Sexualvanor, Aborten, Gonoré, Sexualbrott, Internationellt* (Stockholm, May 1973).

Maternal Health Services

The National Board of Health and Welfare has a unit on Maternal Health and Family Planning, with a part-time obstetric consultant.

Maternal health care is delivered through maternal health centers, of which there are 282 in Sweden; 99 of Type I and 183 of Type II [1]. In 1970, 115,402 women received care there, with an average of 11.9 visits per woman.

Maternal Health Centers Type I are connected with a hospital department of obstetrics and gynecology, and headed by an obstetrician. Maternal Health Centers Type II are headed by a district medical officer or some other physician. They are sometimes combined with a child welfare center.

Standards for maternity care have been developed [1]. This includes medical and dental care, and such laboratory tests as screening for Rh and ABO incompatibility, syphilis, and bacteriological culture for suspected gonorrhea. Optional tests include cytological screening for cervical cancer, examination for detection of asymptomatic bacteriuria, and chest X-ray during the second trimester.

Most prenatal care is provided by nurse-midwives. Whenever a complication is suspected, the woman is referred immediately to an obstetrician; if confirmed, she will continue under the care of an obstetrician. Thus, there is screening for high risk women, and their care is then the responsibility of the obstetrician. In rural areas, this is a problem due to the shortage of specialists.

Most normal deliveries are done by nurse-midwives. Women with complications are delivered by obstetricians. The system of medical and hospital care makes this easy to implement, except in remote rural areas.

Contraceptive advice is a regular part of postnatal care.

Courses for expectant parents are given by the nurse-midwives.

Maternal health care is free under the National Health Service, as are medications.

Presently, there are more than fifty hospitals with departments of obstetrics and gynecology, with full-time medical staff. They have about 70 percent of the total 3,600 maternity beds.

Maternal Mortality

Sweden has one of the lowest maternal mortality rates in the world—1 per 10,000 births. Major remaining causes are infection, toxemia, and hemorrhage. Abortion has disappeared as a cause of maternal death. There are 9-10 annual maternal deaths in Sweden. There is no organized plan for routine review and study of each maternal death (Table 11-4).

Family Planning in Sweden

The status of family planning in Sweden varies among the twenty-five counties and three large cities.

In general, considerable *information* about family planning is available—via sex education in schools, information on hospital intrapartum and postpartum services, and at the time of the postpartum visit to the Maternal Health Center.

In regard to family planning *service*, two geographic examples will illustrate the situation. In the city of Stockholm, advice is free; the patient pays the full price for the pill and the IUD. In Umea (in the north of Sweden, a community of 60,000 with a medical school), the patient pays 12 Kr. for the visit to the doctor, plus the full cost of supplies; in Umea, there is reported to be a nine-month waiting list for family planning service.

In a study done in 1967 in Sweden, 85 percent of people 18-30 years of age reporting intercourse were using a contraceptive, mostly the condom [2]. In this study, 73.2 percent at latest intercourse were using some method of contraception, mostly the condom [2].

The median age of first intercourse was 17.6 years. Premarital intercourse is very common. A large number of sexual partners is common; the median for men is 4-5, and for women 1-2 [2]. (Tables 11-6 through 11-10.)

Abortion

History. The law on abortion in Sweden was restrictive until 1921. In 1921, while the law did not sanction abortion under any circumstances, nevertheless abortions for undisputable medical reasons had been unofficially sanctioned for some time. During the 1920s, the number of "criminal" abortions began to rise rapidly, and during the first half of the 1930s about seventy women a year died from the sequelae of abortion. In 1934, a commission was appointed and made recommendations; the present law on abortion took effect on January 1, 1939. Under this law, therapeutic abortion is permissible under certain medical, humanitarian, and eugenic conditions: (1) when because of

Table 11-4.   Maternal Mortality—Sweden—1955-1970

	1955	1960	1965	1966	1967	1968	1969	1970
Infection	5	3	–	1	–	2	3	2
Toxemia	17	10	6	3	4	2	3	2
Hemorrhage	6	7	–	4	4	2	1	1
Uncomplicated Abortion	9	4	2	2	1	–	2	–
Abortion with Fever	–	–	1	–	1	–	–	–
Other Complications	16	14	8	4	7	4	2	6
Total Maternal Deaths	53	38	17	14	17	10	11	11
Total Maternal Deaths per 100,000 Deliveries	49	37	14	11	14	9	10	10
Total Maternal Deaths per 100,000 Live and Still Births	49	37	14	11	14	9	10	10

Source: National Board of Health and Welfare, Stockholm, 1973.

Table 11-5. Data on Contraception Services in Sweden

Total number of females	1,000,000
Under 45 years – 936,000	
45-49 years – 64,000	
18-44 years – 475,000	
No sex experience	17%
Had intercourse in month preceding interview	54%
Had live births	110,000
Number of live births prevented	300,000
Induced abortion – 20,000	
Use contraceptive – 280,000	
Infertile	10%
Women at risk	200,000
Women without contraceptive, have births	400-500,000

Source: G. Geijerstam. Conference. 1973.

Table 11-6. Use of Contraceptives at First Sexual Intercourse for Individuals Aged 18-30 Years—Sweden—1967

	Male	Female	Both
Number of persons 18-30 years reporting intercourse	252	247	499
No contraception	15.1%	17.3%	16.2%
Condom	58.4	41.3	54.5
Pessary	2.5	0.0	1.4
Coitus Interruptus	23.6	29.2	26.5
Other	0.4	2.3	1.4

Source: RFSU Statistik, *Befolkningen, Sexualvanor, Aborten, Gonoré, Sexualbrott, Internationellt* (Stockholm, May 1973).

disease, deformity, or weakness in the woman, the birth of the child would endanger her life or health; (2) when the woman was impregnated under certain conditions set forth in the penal code, particularly if she was made to submit to intercourse against her will, as in rape; or if she was impregnated before she was fifteen; (3) when there is reason to believe that the expected child will inherit a mental disease, mental deficiency and/or a severe disease or deformity of other nature, either from its mother or its father.

In 1946, the law was amended to broaden the medical indications into socioeconomic as well as purely medical indications. Thus was added the

Table 11-7. Use of Contraceptive at Latest Sexual Intercourse According to Age and Sex—Sweden—1967

	Male		Female		Both
	18-30	*30-60*	*18-30*	*30-60*	
No. of persons	220	429	202	382	1,233
Condom	44.1%	46.4%	32.3%	28.0%	38.0%
Pessary	7.4	6.9	6.4	10.6	8.0
Pill	25.8	9.6	26.6	6.1	14.2
IUD	1.1	0.6	1.7	1.0	1.0
Chemical Method	0.5	0.0	2.3	1.1	0.8
	78.9	63.5	69.3	46.8	62.0
Other					
Douche	0.3	1.1	2.1	2.8	1.7
Safe period	4.3	5.0	3.9	3.0	4.1
Coitus interruptus	11.8	16.7	15.6	21.6	17.2
Total	16.4	22.8	21.6	27.4	23.0
Total not receiving contraceptive	12.3	17.8	19.4	25.1	19.3
Total without contraceptive	12.1	22.9	24.4	41.0	26.8

Source: RFSU Statistik, *Befolkningen, Sexualvanor, Aborten, Gonoré, Sexualbrott, Internationellt* (Stockholm, May 1973).

following: abortion is also permissible when, in view of the woman's living conditions and other circumstances, it can be assumed that the birth and care of the expected child will seriously undermine her mental or physical health.

In June 1963, an act was passed providing for another form of indication for abortion: when there is reason to assume that the child will suffer from severe disease or deformity because of injury during fetal life.

In 1965, an abortion committee was appointed to review the situation and consider the question of free abortion. A report submitted in 1971 recommended that all restrictions be removed. Parliament has not yet acted on this.

Abortion in Practice at Present

A woman considering abortion may go to one of the special advisory centers on abortion. These centers are sometimes independent institutions, but as a psychiatric evaluation of the applicant may play a role in the procedure, some of them are associated with hospital psychiatric departments. The applicant is given a thorough gynecologic examination to check on the state and length of pregnancy, and on the advisability of an abortion. Authorization for

Table 11-8. Sexual Debut at Each Age in 1967—Sweden

Years	Male 18-30	Male 30-60	Female 18-30	Female 30-60	Total
13	1.8	0.2	0.6	0.2	0.5
14	4.2	3.2	1.4	0.4	2.1
15	13.3	6.7	5.6	1.6	5.8
16	18.7	13.5	17.5	7.5	12.7
17	19.8	18.1	18.6	14.3	17.1
18	17.7	21.0	26.2	19.8	20.9
19	10.8	9.4	12.3	13.5	11.4
20	6.4	11.6	9.0	14.8	11.6
21	3.6	3.6	5.1	6.8	4.9
22	2.5	2.7	1.8	5.4	3.5
23	0.4	2.2	0.2	3.5	2.1
24		0.4	0.5	3.0	1.2
25	0.5	4.1	0.7	5.2	3.5
26	0.3	1.3	0.5	1.3	1.0
27		0.6		0.6	0.4
28		0.6		0.4	0.4
29		0.4		0.3	0.3
30		0.4		1.4	0.6
Median Age	16.6	17.4	17.2	18.5	17.6

Source: RFSU Statistik, *Befolkningen, Sexualvanor, Aborten, Gonoré, Sexualbrott, Internationellt (Stockholm, May 1973).*

abortion can be obtained from either the National Board of Health and Welfare, or from two doctors in combination. The special Social-Psychiatric Committee (which is composed of an obstetrician, a psychiatrist, a geneticist, and a woman) reviews reports on the applicant which are submitted usually by a psychiatrist, an obstetrician, and a social worker.

When permission for an abortion is granted, it must be done in a public hospital by an obstetrician or surgeon. As a rulé, it must be done before the end of the twentieth week of gestation.

For teenagers, it is relatively easy to secure an abortion. For example, in 1965-69, 85 percent of those under fifteen years of age who applied for an abortion secured one.

The cost of abortion is covered by National Health Insurance. Some counties have an abortion bureau, in which there is no charge. In other counties, the patient may have to pay 12 Kr.

Reasons for the need for a change in the abortion law, may be summarized as follows: (1) the law is interpreted more liberally than it is

Table 11-9. Status of Group at First Time of Sexual Experience—Sweden—1967

| | Male | | Female | | |
	18-30	*30-60*	*18-30*	*30-60*	*Total*
Number	271	688	257	678	1,894
Unmarried	98.5	100.0	98.0	95.4	98.1
Married	1.5	0.0	2.0	4.6	1.9

Source: RFSU Statistik, *Befolkningen, Sexualvanor, Aborten, Gonoré, Sexualbrott, Internationellt* (Stockholm, May 1973).

Table 11-10. Number of Sexual Partners at Each Age—1967—Sweden

| | Male | | Female | | |
	18-30	*30-60*	*18-30*	*30-60*	*Both*
No. of persons	271	688	257	678	1,894
One partner	19.7	15.0	40.1	40.3	28.4
2	10.9	10.1	21.8	24.0	16.9
3	8.0	8.8	14.8	13.5	11.2
4	5.4	6.1	4.0	6.6	5.9
5	12.3	12.3	6.8	7.9	9.9
6-7	5.0	6.3	3.0	3.3	4.6
8-9	1.9	2.6	2.6	0.6	1.8
10-12	11.3	14.3	3.5	2.2	7.9
13-15	7.0	5.9	0.5	0.6	3.4
16-19	0.4	1.4	0.5	–	0.6
20-29	9.6	8.9	1.6	1.0	5.1
30-49	2.9	3.6	0.6	–	1.7
50	5.8	4.6	0.2	–	2.5
Median	4.5	4.8	1.5	1.4	2.4

Source: RFSU Statistik, *Befolkningen, Sexualvanor, Aborten, Gonoré, Sexualbrott, Internationellt* (Stockholm, May 1973).

written; (2) in some regions, doctors have a more rigid, judgmental attitude; (3) the procedure may be too time consuming.

In 1970, of the 16,100 abortions done, 7,645 were done in unmarried women, 6,796 in married women, and 1,659 in divorced women. Of the 16,100, 163 were done in girls under fourteen years; 3,425 were done in girls 15-19 years [2].

CHILD HEALTH

Organization of Services

The National Board of Health and Welfare has six departments, one of which has responsibility for child health with a full-time pediatrician in charge.

At the local level, there are twenty-five counties and three large cities which are responsible for the financial support and administration of the health and hospital services, with subsidies from the central government for certain aspects of health work. There are 464 local municipalities responsible for certain services, including child welfare. Each county has a head doctor for child health, who is a pediatrician recruited largely from the Department of Pediatrics of a hospital. In the beginning, they spent half of their time in the hospital and half in the child health services; now it is 20 percent and 80 percent respectively.

Infant Mortality

Infant mortality in Sweden is of special interest, because Sweden has the lowest infant mortality rate in the world, and it has had for some years. Furthermore the infant mortality rate in Sweden has continued to decline. In 1971, the infant mortality rate was 11.1 per 1,000 live births (Tables 11-13 and 11-14).

The greatest decline in perinatal mortality in Sweden has occurred around the immediate birth process (stillbirths and first day of life); this decline has been approximately 43 percent in the period 1960-72. In contrast, the decline in other time periods in the first year of life has been as follows:

Table 11-11.   Abortions—Sweden—1970

	Granted by National Board of Health and Welfare	Authorized by Two Physicians	Total
Total number	6,604	9,496	16,100
Under 20 years of age	1,433		
Reasons			
Eugenic	3		3
Disease	95		1,004
Weakness	2,427		5,861
Anticipated weakness	3,968		8,874
Risk of fetal injury	70		69
Humanitarian	41		227

Source: National Board of Health and Welfare, *Public Health in Sweden* (Stockholm, 1972).

Table 11-12.   Therapeutic Abortions in Sweden—1950-1970

Year	# of Births	# of Applic. for Abortion Received by Nat'l. Bd. of H&W	Applic. Granted No.	Applic. Granted %	# of Abortions Done Auth. by Bd. of H&W	Auth. by 2 Doctors	Emer-gency	Total	Indication for Abortion Dis.	Weak-ness	Antic. Wkness.	Human-itarian	Eug-enics	Risk to Fetus
1950	117,754	6,361	5,149	81	4,786	1,096	7	5,889	1,790	2,965	565	18	544	
1954	106,907	6,079	4,792	79	4,488	599	2	5,089	1,855	2,533	542	47	110	
1958	107,175	4,366	2,830	65	2,376	445	2	2,823	1,528	1,432	188	60	67	
1962	108,632	4,257	2,957	69	2,772	431	2	3,205	1,265	1,675	162	89	12	
1966	124,591	6,499	5,782	89	5,375	1,876	3	7,254	1,467	4,433	1,205	78	9	59
1968	113,033	7,554	7,072	93	6,499	4,441		10,940	1,025	5,186	4,521	128	4	76
1970	111,079	7,548	7,220	97	6,604	9,496		16,100	1,004	5,861	8,874	227	3	69

Source: The Swedish Institute, *Therapeutic Abortion and the Law in Sweden* (Stockholm, Jan. 1973).

Table 11-13.   Infant Mortality Rate in Selected Countries (Per 1,000 Live Births)

Country	Year	Rate
Sweden	1971	11.1
Netherlands	1971	11.1
Finland	1971	11.8
Japan	1971	12.4
Iceland	1970	13.2
Norway	1969	13.8
Denmark	1970	14.2
France	1971	14.4
Switzerland	1970	15.1
Lichtenstein	1969	16.7
New Zealand	1970	16.7
Australia	1971	17.4
England & Wales	1971	17.6
E. Germany	1970	18.8
Canada	1970	18.8
U.S.A.	1971	19.2
Ireland	1970	19.6
Singapore	1971	19.7
Scotland	1971	19.9
Belgium	1970	20.5
Czechoslovakia	1970	22.1
Luxembourg	1971	22.5
Israel	1970	22.9
U.S.S.R.	1971	22.9
N. Ireland	1971	23.0
W. Germany	1971	23.2
Bulgaria	1971	24.9

Time Period	% Decline
The first week	36.6
The first week, exclusive of the first day	28.8
The first month	36.2
The first month, exclusive of the first day	29.7
Postneonatal (1-11 months)	17.8

Geijerstam has shown that one of the major factors in the difference in the perinatal mortality rate between Sweden and the United States is the incidence of low birth weight [3]. For example, in 1964-65, the incidence of

Table 11-14. Marriage Rate, Live Birthrate, Illegitimacy, and Infant Mortality Rate—Sweden

Year	Marriage Rate*	Live Birthrate*	Percentage of Live Births Born Out of Wedlock	Infant Mortality Rate**				
				Total	First Day	First Week	First Month	Postneonatal
1901-05		26.1		91.0				
1921-25		19.1		59.9				
1931-35		14.1		50.1				
1941-45		18.8		31.0				
1950	7.73	16.5	9.8	21.0				
1955		14.8	9.9	17.4				
1960	6.70	13.7	11.3	16.6	6.4	12.3	13.8	2.8
1961		13.9		15.8	5.1	11.3	13.1	2.7
1962		14.2		15.3	5.3	11.1	12.4	3.0
1963		14.9		15.0	5.0	11.0	12.3	3.2
1964		16.0		14.2	4.5	10.5	11.7	2.5
1965	7.75	15.9	13.8	13.3	4.5	9.6	10.6	2.7
1966	7.83	15.8	14.6	12.6	4.0	8.9	10.3	2.3
1967	7.19	15.4	15.1	12.9	4.4	9.4	10.5	2.4
1968	6.63	14.3	15.1	13.1	4.6	9.4	10.9	2.2
1969	6.07	13.5		11.7	3.7	8.2	9.3	2.4
1970	5.38	13.7	19.4	11.0	3.6	8.1	9.2	1.8
1971	4.92	14.1	21.6	11.1	3.6	7.8	8.8	2.3

*Per 1,000 population
**Per 1,000 live births

low birth weight was 8.2 percent in the United States, and 4.4 percent in Sweden; in the birth weight group 1,000 grams or less (where mortality is the highest), the incidence was 0.6 percent and 0.2 percent respectively; in the birth weight group 1001-1500 grams (where mortality is next highest), the incidence was 0.7 percent and 0.4 percent respectively; in the birth weight group 1501-2000 grams, it was 1.5 percent and 1.0 percent respectively; and in the birth weight group 2001-2500 grams, it was 5.4 percent and 2.9 percent respectively. (Table 11-15)

The birth weight distribution of live births in Sweden has been practically unchanged from 1965 to 1970.

Early neonatal mortality (within the first week of life) in Sweden has declined from 1965 to 1970 in birth weight groups of 1000 grams or less, 1001-1500 grams, 1501-2000 grams, and 2001-2500 grams.

According to Geijerstam, hospitals in Sweden with a department of obstetrics and gynecology with obstetric specialists had a higher proportion of low birth weight births, and also had a higher perinatal mortality rate, than hospitals without an obstetric specialist staff [3].

Possible reasons for the lower infant mortality rate in Sweden and for the continued decline in infant mortality can be summarized as follows:

General Reasons

1. A homogeneous population
2. A high standard of living, with a high level of education, housing, nutrition
3. The existence of the national health service
4. The existence of social insurance, including sickness benefit, maternity benefit, children's allowance
5. More even distribution of the quality of medical and health care
6. Some regionalization of services—i.e., perinatal services for high risk mothers and infants.

Medical and Health Reasons

1. *Maternal Health*
    a. A high percentage of deliveries in hospitals
    b. Availability of abortion service
    c. Some availability of family planning service
    d. A network of maternal health centers, with screening for high risk pregnancy and referral to obstetricians for care
    e. Transfer of women with complications to better maternity services
    f. Classes for expectant parents
    g. Most "normal" obstetrics is done by nurse—midwives
    h. Cautious anesthesiology in delivery.

2. *Child Health*
    a. Lower incidence of low birth weight, compared with the United States

Table 11-15.   Early Neonatal Mortality—Sweden—1965-65, and 1970

Birth Weight Group	Percent of Live Births		Early Neonatal Mortality Sweden—1965	Sweden 1970			
	U.S.A. 1964	Sweden 1965		Number Born	% of Total	Number Died Within 7 Days	Mortality %
1000 Gm or less	0.6%	0.2%	88.1%	111	0.2	95	85.6
1001-1500 Gm	0.7%	0.4%	47.6%	216	0.4	89	41.2
1501-2000 Gm	1.5%	1.0%	15.4%	481	0.9	62	12.8
2001-2500 Gm	5.4%	2.9%	4.8%	1,668	2.9	57	3.4
Total	8.2%	4.5%					
2501 Gm or more	91.8%	95.5%	0.3%				

Sources: (1) G. Geijerstam, "Low Birth Weight and Perinatal Mortality," *Public Health Reports* 84 (November 1969): 939-948. (2) National Board of Health and Welfare, *Public Health in Sweden* (Stockholm, 1972).

a. Intensive care units for newborn, with some transport service
b. Presence of pediatrician at all deliveries of high risk women in most obstetric services
d. Training in resuscitation of the newborn
e. High registration and supervision of infants at child welfare centers.

Some of the areas at present without adequate recent data are the effects of out-of-wedlock pregnancy, age distribution of the mothers, and possible differences in reporting on perinatal and infant mortality. Nor are there data on incidence of handicapping conditions in infants and children, which are associated with prenatal or perinatal factors.

Care of Newborn Infants
In addition to screening the maternal health population and to bringing high risk women under the care of an obstetrician, there is now a policy to have a pediatrician present at the delivery of high risk women. This is now possible except in the remote rural areas. There has been training of physicians and nurses in resuscitation of the newborn.

Regional perinatal centers, with intensive care units for the newborn, are now available. Some transport service is also available.

Neonatal screening is done routinely in the hospital for phenylketonuria, galactosemia, tyrosinemia, and fructose.

Child Welfare Centers
There are approximately 1,200 child welfare centers in Sweden; 392 are of Type I (connected with a Department of Pediatrics of a hospital and directed by a pediatrician); 881 are of Type II, located in other facilities, and directed by a medical officer [4]. About half the children are supervised by Type I and the other half by Type II (Table 11-16). The other main staff of the child welfare centers consists of nurses; some effort is being made to add psychologists and social workers to strengthen the mental health aspects.

The service is completely free of charge. It consists of preventive measures, including medical examinations, screening for vision and hearing, immunization, and counseling. All mothers receive a home visit by a nurse within two weeks of delivery; the baby is brought to the child welfare center at the age of 2-6 weeks. Almost 100 percent of children in the first two years of life are supervised by the child welfare centers, and 69 percent of the 2-7 year olds are. During the first year of life, a child is seen 4-5 times. Immunization is done for smallpox, diphtheria, tetanus, pertussis, and poliomyelitis. BCG vaccine is given before the baby is discharged from the hospital newborn service. Counseling of the mother includes feeding, hygiene, childrearing, safety, and accident prevention. Efforts are made to encourage breast feeding; in 1970, 35 percent of babies were breast fed for two months or more; 15 percent for four months or more; and 7 percent for six months or more [5].

Table 11-16. Scope of the Child Welfare Service—Sweden

	Live Births	One Year	2-7 Years
Number of children in Sweden	114,484	109,430	715,362
Supervised Children			
Number	112,775	107,898	495,551
Percentage of total	99	99	69
Enrolled during first month	94		
Visits to the doctor per supervised child per year	4.5	1.6	0.8
Home visits (by Nurse) per supervised child per year	2.7	0.5	0.4

Special regulations have been drawn up by the National Board of Health and Welfare, and adopted for use by the child welfare centers [4].

Health Screening for Four Year Olds [7]

This screening began in 1969. The objectives are to prevent or treat early diseases and injuries which may be handicapping; and to promote continuing health supervision for the older preschool child.

The screening consists of a home visit by a nurse. It includes a health check of the child's general clinical status, urinalysis, hearing and speech screening, screening for visual acuity and strabismus, dental checkup, check of psychological health, follow up and casefinding of handicaps. It includes interview with parents about problems, behavior, speech, and general development.

Of the twenty-eight County Councils (including the three large cities), twenty carried this out; 24,000 children were examined. Of this number, 6900 (24 percent) were referred to a specialist for the following specific conditions:

Dental	— 25.6%	Surgical	— 5.0%
Vision	— 21.7%	Speech	— 4.1%
ENT	— 10.1%	Hearing	— 2.9%
Psychological	— 8.6%	Special health problem	— 2.3%
Pediatric	— 8.1%	Referred to psychiatrist	— 1.9%
Orthopedic	— 7.2%	Other	— 2.4%

At Uppsala, a recent effort has been made to evaluate the four-year-old examination. The following was found:

		Results of Specialist Exam		
Area	Rate For Screening	Minor Problem	Major Problem	Handicap
Psychological	5.2%	2.0%	1.0%	0.1%
Physical	10.5%	3.7%	0.8%	0.1%
Vision	11.4%	1.7%	2.5%	0.0%
Hearing	3.6%	1.0%	0.3%	0.0%
Speech	3.5%	1.1%	0.4%	0.0%
Totals	34.3%	9.4%	5.1%	0.2%

Battered Children

There is a special committee of the National Board of Health and Welfare working on the problem of battered children. Guidelines were drawn up in 1969. A special survey is being done of three large cities. Cases are reviewed and referrals are made to social workers, the court, etc.

Day Care in Sweden [6]

Day care of children in Sweden is of several types.

1. *Day Nursery.* This receives children aged six months to seven years, when the parents are at work outside their homes. They are open five days a week (Monday-Friday) 6:30 A.M.-2:00 P.M.
2. *Free-Time Center.* This receives children aged 7-15 years for part of the day, when the children are not at school and the parents work outside their homes. They are open on Monday-Friday 7 A.M.-6 P.M., and on Saturday 7 A.M.-2 P.M.
3. *Nursery School.* This receives children aged 4-7 years, for three hours a day Monday-Friday, from either 9-12 noon or 1-5 P.M.
4. *Family Day Nursery.* These are private homes which receive children for a longer or shorter time of the day while the parents work outside their homes. Each Family Day Nursery may accept up to four children in the preschool age.

Extent of Services. According to Table 11-17, there is space at present for 212,000 children. It is estimated that 20 percent of the need is being covered at present.

Need for Services. There is a special need for day care for certain groups of children or because of special problems: (1) Parents are working; (2) One-parent families; (3) Children of school age who have no one at home to take care of them when school is over each day; (4) Children with special

Table 11-17. Number of Places and Enrolled Children in
Preschool Program

| | Day Nurseries | | | | |
Year	# Places	# Children	# Children in Nursery Schools	Free Time Centers	Family Day Nurseries
1955	10,000		27,800		
1960	10,300		38,400		
1965	11,900		52,100		
1966	13,400		56,400		
1967	16,100				
1968	19,200	21,400	58,100		
1969	25,200	28,700	62,800		
1970	29,200	22,500	71,900		
1971		39,904	82,282		
1972		52,000	105,000	10,000	45,000

Source: B. Rosengren, *Preschool in Sweden* (Stockholm: The Swedish Institute, 1973).

needs—physical or mental handicap, behavior problems, etc.; (5) Because of the low birthrate and the smaller number of children per family, some children have no siblings and need experience with other children.

Age Allocation of Children. Up to the present, children are assigned by age groups, as follows: 6 months-1 year, 1-2 years, 2-3 years, etc. It is proposed that children be assigned differently: up to 2½ years; 2½-7 years—for children and their siblings.

Health Program. This is the responsibility of the local social welfare unit in the county. In some communities, this is provided through the child health services.

Size of Group. This is variable. It may be as large as 75-100 children.

Location. Services are located near where parents and children live. In a few instances they have been located where mothers work—hospital, industry. The problem with this is that if the mother becomes unemployed, the child loses his place in day care.

Financial Aspects of Day Care. Day care is supported as follows:

Source	% of Cost
National	35
Local Community	45
Parents	20

There is a graded fee for parents; the more they earn, the more they pay. Many parents find it expensive. The fee in 1973 was 1-34 Kroner per child per day (at that time, $1 was worth 4 Kroner).

Building costs vary, but the average is 11-15,000 Kroner per child for a child center in a separate building.

Operating costs are estimated to be 8,500 Kr. per child per year in a day nursery, 6,500 Kr. in a free time center, 1,500 Kr. in a nursery school, and 6,000 Kr. in a family day nursery.

Government grants are available to establish a child center. In addition, loans are available for furniture and other equipment.

Care of Handicapped Children in Day Care. It is estimated that at least 10 percent of children have special needs. It is planned to include them in regular day care. Units admitting handicapped children will be smaller in size. This includes all types of handicaps. It is mutually advantageous to children and less expensive to accept handicapped children into regular day care. To what extent special services for handicapped children are funded in regular services is unknown.

Mortality in Preschool Children

Sweden has the lowest reported mortality in the age group of children 1-4 years (Table 11-18).

SCHOOL HEALTH

Organization of Services

At the national level, the National Board of Education is responsible for the school health program. There is a pediatrician in charge. In addition, there is a part time consultant on school meals. There is a sectional unit for social welfare matters in schools. There is currently some discussion about moving this into the National Board of Health and Welfare, and combining it with the child health service.

At the local level, there are twenty-five counties and three major large cities. For the school health program, there is a county medical officer who serves as a medical advisor to the County Board of Education.

At the local (municipality) level, the local education authority appoints school doctors and nurses. In some of the larger cities, there are doctors who are full-time directors of the school health program. The County Council

Table 11-18. Mortality of Children—1-4 Years of Age in Selected Countries (Rate Per 1,000 Children)

Country	Rate	Period
Sweden	2.4	1965-67
Denmark	3.1	1966-67
England & Wales	3.2	1965-67
Ireland	3.4	1965-67
U.S.A.	3.6	1965-67
White — 3.2		
Nonwhite — 6.0		
Norway	3.6	1965-67
Scotland	3.6	1965-67
France	3.6	1965-67
Belgium	3.7	1965-66
Netherlands	3.8	1966-67
Australia	3.8	1965-67
Israel	3.8	1965-67
Canada	3.9	1965-67
Germany (W)	4.2	1965-67
New Zealand	4.3	1965-67
Italy	5.0	1965-67
Japan	5.1	1965-66
Poland	5.1	1965-66
U.S.S.R.	9.6	1966-67

Source: Metropolitan Life Insurance Company, *Statistical Bulletin*, March 1971.

provides a district nurse for the health service in the comprehensive school (first nine grades). In all there are about 900 doctors working in schools; most are part time. There are no qualifications established for the school medical staff; some doctors are pediatricians.

There is a ratio of one nurse to 1,000-1,200 pupils. There is a psychologist in each comprehensive school. There are social workers in secondary schools; some in schools of grades 7-9.

A special school psychiatrist is employed in Stockholm, and in some other municipalities. Each county has a mental welfare center for children and youth, with branches in several municipalities.

Population Served

This consists of approximately 1½ million pupils. It includes all pupils in the comprehensive and secondary schools; pupils at special schools for the handicapped; pupils at special schools for the mentally retarded; pupils in schools of nursing; pupils in folk high schools.

Content of the School Health Program

The purpose of the school health program is to maintain and improve the health of pupils regarding physical, mental, and social factors relating to their health. The school health service is looked upon as an important component of the pupil welfare service, and is aimed at helping teachers to understand the physical and mental health of pupils so as to allow for these factors in their teaching. The school health staff is responsible for making recommendations to prevent health hazards, i.e., accidents, hygenic conditions, the pressure of work, etc.

Health inspections or class inspections are carried out on all pupils. A note is made of all pupils who should be followed up more closely. In large schools, the nurse will hold office hours daily, the doctor usually once a week. Pupils may come in independently to see the nurse, or may be referred in by a teacher, psychologist, welfare officer, or parent. The school nurse takes care of minor accidents. Medical care is provided in special schools (boarding) for children with impaired sight or hearing. Some steps are being taken for the school to provide gynecology service in some schools, including a contraception service.

Health examinations are carried out routinely in grades 1, 4, 7 and 9. This includes measurement of height and weight, urinalysis, and vision and hearing screening. Urinalaysis consists of albumin, glucose, and bacteriuria. All of this is done by the nurse, except the hearing test which is done by special staff from the local authority. The health examination includes the doctor's examination. There is some experimentation under way for a special health examination at the child's entrance to school, or shortly after entrance. The purpose is to do a better evaluation of each child in greater depth.

Immunizations

These are a continuation of those done in infancy and the preschool periods. They consist of the following:

Type	Grade
Polio vaccine	1
Diphtheria, tetanus	2
Smallpox	4
BCG vaccine	8 or 9, if indicated

Dental Care. Dental care is provided to children in primary school free of charge.

School Lunches. These are provided to children in primary school free of charge; also to some children in secondary school.

Records. Preschool health records, kept by the child welfare centers, are transferred to the school at age seven.

Cooperation with the Child's Home. Parents are requested to fill out a questionnaire as part of the examination in grade one, and are invited to attend the examination. They are informed of the results of the examination and of the recommendations. There is opportunity for parents to contact the school nurse and/or doctor to discuss their child.

Cooperation with Teachers. There is contact between teachers and nurse, to decide on individual pupils requiring close observation.

For individual children with special problems a weekly conference of classroom teacher, nurse, social worker, and psychologist is held to discuss and make a plan for the child.

Teachers play an important role in the school health service in their health teaching, which includes health and living, sex education, and information on alcohol, tobacco and drugs.

Sex education begins in grade one. It continues according to the handbook. At grade eight, the biological part is added. It is taught in religion, biology, and civics. Sex education is taught by the teacher.

Major Problems in Pupils. These were described as vision; behavior problems of youth 14-16 years; orthopedic problems; drugs, alcohol, and tobacco; sex; school dropout; juvenile delinquency.

Sex Education in Sweden

Sweden is one of the few countries where sex education is compulsory in the schools. It was introduced into the school curriculum in the 1940s and became a required course in 1956. The first government report (Handbook) was published in 1945, and was revised in 1956. It was redone in 1968. The government set up a Swedish State Committee for Sex Education, which has just completed its report.

Table 11-19. Percentage of Age Groups in Education—Sweden

Age Group	Number of Years in School	1940	1950	1960	1965	1970	Type of Education
7-15 years	9	79	85	92	98	99	Compulsory
16-18 years	1	10	25	34	44	75	Secondary
19-24 years		5	10	17	21	60	

Source: The Swedish Institute, *Sweden in a Nutshell* (Stockholm, 1972).

Since the publication of the earlier handbook, many changes have occurred in society and customs in Sweden. There is more free discussion. Sex debut occurs at an earlier age. The need is to help the teenager to find his way into society. The Church is reported to have lost its influence. The age of sexual maturation is lower. Access to contraceptives is easier. Abortion is free. Sexual behavior has changed more among teenage girls than boys.

The old handbook in sex education stated that sex was morally wrong and psychologically dangerous. The new handbook, which is just about to be published, will stress the need for couples to help each other, respect each other, and have a good relationship. The committee has accepted sex experience in the teenager.

The handbook on sex education covered the following topics:

1. Structure and function of the sexual organs
2. Development of fetus and pregnancy
3. Labor
4. Sex and youth
5. Children born out of wedlock
6. Abortion
7. Venereal disease
8. Contraceptives
9. Sterilization
10. Sexual abnormalities
11. Menopause
12. Welfare measures to help in setting up a family
13. Welfare measures in pregnancy, confinement, and nursing
14. Welfare measures for the care and training of adolescents.

Sex education has been taught in biology, social studies, religion, and other classes.

In addition to general sex education in the classroom, the school nurse does considerable sex education with individual teenagers on an individual basis.

HANDICAPPED CHILDREN

Introduction

The national health service makes available medical, hospital, and health services at almost no charge to the individual patient. This section describes the special provisions for the care of handicapped children, which have been made available in the presence of a national health service.

Organization of Services [15, 16]

The National Board of Health and Welfare is responsible for the central government health and welfare activities for the handicapped, and the National Board of Education for the educational aspects. Within the National Board of Health and Welfare is one of the six major departments, Department LÅ; included in this are a separate Division for Long Term Care and Rehabilitation, and a separate Division on Care of the Mentally Retarded.

Medical treatment is the responsibility of twenty-five counties and the three largest cities. The counties and cities are divided into seven regions for the organization of specialized services, such as centers for handicapped children.

In 1971-72, a new step was taken at central, county, and municipal levels to create councils for the handicapped in order to achieve better coordination of services.

Relevant Legislation

Relevant legislation for the handicapped consists of the Act on Medical Care, which makes the County Councils responsible for all medical and related services. The National Board of Health and Welfare acts as the central supervisory agency.

The National Insurance Act provides for old age and disability pensions, daily sickness benefits, and certain contributions to medical care, including ambulatory care and physical therapy.

The Social Welfare Act regulates the responsibility of the municipalities for residual needs not covered by social insurance and other major provisions, and contains a general clause intended to improve services for the handicapped.

The Education Act makes the municipalities responsible for almost all educational services below university level, including most special education. The National Board of Education acts as the supervisory agency.

The Act on Provisions For Certain Mentally Retarded Persons in 1968 provides for the right to preschool education; special education; vocational education and training; medical care; services in institutions, special hospitals and small hostels; occupational centers for those who cannot obtain employment on the open market or in sheltered work; rehabilitative services for those living at home. Almost all these services are free and financed mainly out of local taxes by County Councils.

Voluntary Agencies

There are a number of voluntary organizations concerned with handicapped children in Sweden. They include organizations for such categorical groups as the blind, the deaf, locomotor handicaps, rheumatism, victims of traffic accidents and poliomyelitis, multiple sclerosis, diabetes, heart and lung patients, allergy, psoriasis, mental retardation, and mental health. There is also a joint organization, the Central Committee of the Organizations of the Handicapped, serving seventeen of the national associations for the handicapped, with a total membership of close to 200,000. They promote services and legislation, better social security rights, social activities, special and adult education, technical aids and appliances, public planning for housing, recreation, etc.

Case Finding of Handicapped Children

Case finding of handicapped children is carried out through the following organized steps primarily.

Screening of Newborn Infants. For all newborn infants born in hospitals (close to 100 percent of all infants), there is routine screening for phenylketonuria, galactosemia, tyrosinemia, and fructose. A blood sample is taken and sent to a central laboratory in Stockholm.

Examination of Newborn Infants. The health assessment of all newborns in the hospital after birth is intended to identify evidence of congenital malformations, birth injury, or other handicapping condition.

Health Supervision of Infants and Preschool Children. Close to 100 percent of infants and children are under health supervision of the Child Welfare Centers during the first two years of life. In addition, the routine examination of four year olds is being implemented.

Health Screening For Four Year Olds [14] —This began in 1969. The objectives are to prevent or treat early diseases and injuries which may be handicapping; to promote continuing health supervision for the older preschool child. It consists of a home visit by a nurse. It includes a health check of the child's general clinical status, urinalysis, hearing and speech screening, screening for visual acuity and strabismus, dental checkup, check of psychological health, follow up and case finding of handicaps. It includes interview with parents about problems, behavior, speech and general development.

Health Supervision of Children of School Age. The routine health examination of children is carried out in grades 1, 4, 7, and 9. This includes measurement of height and weight, urinalysis, vision and hearing screening, and the school doctor's examination.

Operation of Registers

Register of Congenital Malformations. A register has been established of children reported to have a congenital malformation in the newborn period. Reporting is done by hospital maternity departments. Data reported to the National Board of Health and Welfare are reviewed monthly by two pediatricians from medical schools. The purpose of this is to provide surveillance in order to identify an unusual occurrence of any type of congenital malformation.

Register of Handicapped Children. This is in the process of being instituted. It will be used for follow up of handicapped children and their families.

Diagnostic, Treatment, and Rehabilitation
Services

The country is divided into seven regions. The plan is for each region to have a major central pediatric clinic with habilitation department for handicapped children. This facility provides diagnostic and treatment services on an inpatient and outpatient basis; special education; physical therapy; social work; training in activities of daily living.

In 1954, it was proposed that there be at least one hospital department for rehabilitation in each of the twenty-five counties and three largest cities. By 1972, this had been achieved in about one-third of the counties. In addition, there are about fifty hearing centers connected with departments of otolaryngology and/or audiology of hospitals.

Medical care of physically handicapped children is usually under the direction of a pediatrician. Medical care of mentally retarded children is usually under the direction of a child psychiatrist.

Education of Handicapped Children

Slow learners obtain special instruction in classes for slow learners, or in special instruction. In 1969-70, there were more in special classes, although large numbers in both types of educational placement.

Children with immaturity receive special instruction in special classes or in special instruction. In 1969-70, there were large numbers in both types of instruction.

Children with difficulties of adjustment (emotionally disturbed) received instruction in special observation classes, where pupils receive all their instruction for varying periods of time.

Children with reading and writing disorders mostly receive special teaching, not in special classes.

Children with sight disorders (mainly the partially sighted) receive special teaching, not in special classes. The prevalence is 0.1-0.3 percent for a mild to medium defect (in the better eye after correction) in the compulsory schools (first nine grades). There are two special schools for children with severe visual defects (blind); one which has children of compulsory and secondary educational level, the other for multiply handicapped children.

Children with impaired hearing of a moderate degree are placed in an ordinary class with support of special teaching. There are four special schools for the deaf.

Children with speech disorders receive special teaching.

There is a small number of children with orthopedic handicaps in special classes.

There are large numbers of mentally retarded children in special schools and classes. Since 1968, the County Councils have been required to arrange classes for all mentally retarded children.

Table 11-20. Children in Special Classes in the Compulsory Schools and Children Receiving Special Training—Sweden (1969-70)

Type of Child	Type of Education Placement	Children	No. of Classes
Slow Learners	Special Class	23,240	2,251
Slow Learners	Ordinary Class	17,751	
Immaturity	Special Class	5,105	533
Immaturity	Special Teaching	4,843	
Difficulties in Adjustment	Observational Classes	748	113
Reading & Writing Disorders	Special Classes	5,217	474
Reading & Writing Disorders	Special Training	56,494	
Sight Disorders	Special Classes	70	11
Sight Disorders	Special Teaching	400	
Blind	Special School	160	
Blind	Special School for multiply handicapped	100	
Blind	Regular Secondary	52	
Hearing Disorders	Special Classes	594	100
Hearing Disorders	Special Teaching	471	
Speech Disorders	Special Teaching	20,106	
Orthopedic (Motor)	Special Classes Elementary	508	91
	Secondary	74	
Mental Retardation	Special Schools	9,100	

Source: K. Lundstrom, *Special Teaching in Sweden* (Stockholm: National Board of Education, October 1970).

Note: There are approximately 900,000 children aged 7-16 years in the compulsory schools (grades 1-9).

In general, the current policy in Sweden is to integrate the handicapped child or adult into as normal a setting as possible. Examples of this are to have them live at home (parents' home, own home, group living in apartment); attend a day nursery with nonhandicapped children; attend a regular or separate class in a regular school, with nonhandicapped children. The reasons for this are similar to those in the United States—that integrated education can be organized in more schools which will reduce the distance from home; that handicapped children and youth, to prepare themselves for life, need to learn to be together with normal children, just as normal children need to learn about the existence of handicaps.

Transport

Most urban communities, but few of the rural communities, have organized transportation services for the handicapped, usually in taxi cabs, supplemented by cars and buses with special equipment. There are restrictions on travel not connected with work, medical care or rehabilitation. There is a committee proposal on national aid to municipalities for transportation services, which has not yet been acted upon.

Appliances

The national government provides funds for the total cost ($28 million in 1972) of technical aids for the handicapped. This includes hearing aids, wheelchairs, prostheses, optical aids (but not ordinary glasses), typewriters, tape recorders, dishwashing machines, braces, surgical boots, walking sticks, invalid vehicles with or without motor, etc. Repairs for such equipment are also covered. The aids must be prescribed by medical specialists at hospitals, but some may also be prescribed by district medical officers and district nurses. Considerable interest has also been shown in the development in the medico-technical field, i.e., in the development of improved technical equipment for the handicapped.

Living

The intent is that, wherever possible, the handicapped live outside of institutions in the community in as normal a setting as possible. Aside from living in their own or parents' home, substitutes have been set up, such as hostels or group homes in ordinary residential areas. National subsidies have been available to convert and equip individual homes and flats to meet the housing and living needs of the handicapped.

In various municipalities, measures have been introduced to increase the possibilities for the handicapped to live in their own homes. Social workers are employed, housework patrols are set up, and special services to help in running the homes have been organized.

Home care workers are employed to take charge of the household during short periods and look after children, where due to illness, childbirth, etc., the mother is unable to look after the home.

Removal of Barriers

Steps have been taken to remove architectural barriers for the handicapped. These include unnecessary steps, narrow passages, narrow elevators or lack of them, unsuitable toilets, etc. The Building Code of 1966 and amended in 1971 requires that all public buildings be designed to make them accessible and usable by handicapped people; this applies to new buildings under reconstruction. Work is being done on standards regarding the interior design of new dwelling units.

Vocational Rehabilitation [17]

The National Labor Market Board, working in collaboration with local authorities and other national agencies, has developed a number of methods for providing and creating jobs for the handicapped. It has a special vocational rehabilitation service for the handicapped. In 1971, it had 100,000 applicants, compared with 96,000 in 1970. In 1970, almost 5,000 handicapped persons were in systematic work training, and 19,000 started vocational training. At the end of 1970, there were 28,000, most of them working for union wages, in various forms of protected work, mainly in sheltered workshops, office work, and on open air projects.

Among the services offered are psychological aptitude tests, employment tests, industrial arts training, education, sheltered workshops, semi-sheltered employment at special in-plant work places subsidized by the government, archive work (sheltered employment for white collar workers in offices) for different public agencies, and in special work relief projects for the handicapped. The National Labor Market Board offers employer subsidies for alterations of working place facilities required to render a handicapped person capable of functioning on the premises, plus subsidies of various kinds of $1,000-$1,200 a year for each handicapped person placed in his employment. An additional subsidy is also available for a handicapped person already on his payroll.

Special Social Welfare Benefits
for the Handicapped [15, 16]

Handicapped persons who have reached the age of sixteen years receive a disability pension under the national basic pensions scheme, if they have lost their working capacity because of their handicap. Disability pensions of this kind are paid to over 200,000 persons. A full disability pension is equivalent to the old age pension paid to a single person. In addition to this, there is a municipal housing allowance (subject to a means test) and in some cases certain special handicap allowances. Many handicapped persons also receive compensation from the state industrial injuries insurance, from traffic injuries insurance, or from voluntary insurance based on agreements between the employers' and employees' organizations. The government pays for technical aids and appliances. Handicapped persons in need of special fixtures in the home can obtain a state grant toward the necessary adaptation.

Day Care for the Handicapped

Efforts are being made to integrate handicapped children into the regular preschool programs (day nurseries, family day care homes, nursery schools, and free-time centers). It is estimated that at least 10 percent of children in these programs will have special needs, requiring the adaptation of the program to the individual child.

Special Services for the
Mentally Retarded [10]

On July 1, 1968 new legislation for the mentally retarded was enacted. This prescribes the activities of the County Council; each County Council will have a special board for mentally retarded, including a director. Full-time medical directors served in 1973 on boards in nine counties; in other counties, the person is usually the head physician of the hospital child psychiatry department. The duties of the County Board are to ensure that the mentally retarded are provided with the services they need. The County Councils are required to make a five-year plan for the care of the mentally retarded. The legislation required that the County Board for the mentally retarded be sure that information and case finding be provided. It required that the board keep a register of persons receiving care, with notes of measures taken.

Data are being accumulated on prevalence of mental retardation, showing the highest prevalence (7.1 per 1,000 population) in the age group 7-16 years, with a lower prevalence before and after school age. Of the people drawing disablement pensions and sickness benefit in January 1966, 17.3 percent (27,875) were mentally retarded. It is of interest that 71 percent of the youth 16-19 years receiving pensions are mentally retarded.

Sweden has some 200 special schools for the mentally retarded including residential homes. Altogether, some 8,500 pupils are given instruction, about half of whom live in their own homes. Practically every County Council has a special boarding school for the mentally retarded. In addition, there are two special boarding schools for mentally retarded children with difficulties in social adjustment, plus two special boarding schools for pupils with behavioral disorders. There is a special school at a hospital for mentally retarded children with severe orthopedic handicaps. Boarding homes for children from special schools have begun to be built.

The law prescribes vocational education for all young people. At present there are about sixty occupational centers and twenty-five sheltered workshops for the retarded.

There is a recommendation in favor of small institutions for residential care, with greater proximity to the patients' own home, and allowing more visiting.

Sweden has 132 residential homes which care for about 7,900 adult retardates. Twenty-two of these also care for children. Sweden has a total of 47 residential homes for 2,200 children.

At present there are six special hospitals, one for each of the seven regions in Sweden. The objective is to provide specially trained personnel and consulting specialists. The intent is to link each regional hospital with a university and research center. Each regional hospital is to provide medical evaluation and supervision, orthopedic care and physical therapy, genetic studies, vocational testing, training in activities of daily living, and clinical research.

It is anticipated that there will be a shift in care from residential homes to care in the parents' homes, other homes, or hostels.

Day nurseries are to be provided for the mentally retarded, combined with a kindergarten, to relieve the families of day care. Leisure time activities are to be provided.

The cost of care is free. This includes medical care, hospital care, education, board and lodging, travel to and from school, day care, employment homes, dental care, speech, and physical therapy.

Children with Impaired Hearing

It is estimated that about 0.5 percent of all pupils need to attend a special school for the deaf, while 1 percent need special teaching in a hearing class or individually. In nine grades (with approximately 900,000 pupils aged 7-16 years in compulsory school), some 1,000 pupils are estimated to have a mild to moderate hearing defect; approximately 450 have a more severe loss. There is also one more annual group of about 50 pupils, since those with a severe hearing loss have a ten-year compulsory schooling (7-17 years).

Attendance at kindergarten level is voluntary. For the preschool period, attempts are made to work with parents to develop teaching of the child in the home by the parents. Almost all County Councils operate a kindergarten for children with hearing disorders. These kindergartens are run as day schools and accept children from the age of five years. There is an increasing trend to accept younger children with hearing defects in ordinary kindergartens, where there are specially trained teachers to work with speech and language training.

At the age of seven years, in considering the child with hearing loss for school placement, the child has an extensive medical, audiological, psychological, and pedagogical evaluation. In the nine-year compulsory school, it is possible to arrange both special hearing classes and teaching in "clinics" for partially hearing pupils. Hearing classes exist in about fifty municipalities in Sweden. Pupils can obtain both classroom amplifiers and their own hearing aids. Children are taught by specially trained teachers. The city of Stockholm has set up a special secondary school (grades 10-12) for pupils with hearing loss.

The teaching of deaf pupils is divided into four regions. In each region there is a school for the deaf, covering seven grades. There are also three national special schools—one for pupils who do not have serious linguistic or speech disorders, one for deaf pupils who are mentally retarded, and one for deaf pupils with emotional disorders and for pupils who can hear but not speak. With the introduction of the nine-year compulsory school, effort is made to give pupils a chance to live at home, especially during the early school years, through collaboration between the small number of special schools for the deaf, and the larger number of special classes for children with hearing loss around the country. The compulsory school for the deaf consists of ten grades. Special training is provided in lip-reading, and language development. The aim is to give pupils at the special school for the deaf language, speech, and lip-reading ability.

All education of students with severe hearing loss after the ten-grade compulsory school is voluntary. There are a three-year secondary school, a two-year continuation school, and a two to three year vocational school, which have been incorporated into the regular school system in one city, with a total capacity for fifty children a year.

The government bears the responsibility for all costs of teaching pupils with severe hearing loss and for their medical care; for the cost of hostels and foster homes. For children away from home, travel to and from home is paid for by the government at the beginning and end of each term.

Children Who Are Blind or Partially Sighted [9]

The number of registered children up to seven years of age with a handicapping visual defect is about 300, of whom about 250 are in their own homes. As soon as a visually handicapped preschool child is found and reported, his home is visited by a special consultant attached to one of the special schools; subsequent visits are made once or twice a year. Suggestions are made regarding toys, a grant for the care of the child, a housing grant, a tape-recorder, a day nursery, an appropriate school, etc. A one-week course is held annually for parents of preschool visually handicapped children. There is a special home which can accommodate eight children. In addition, children with multiple handicaps at the age of five years can be accepted into one of the special schools. Evaluation of the child is carried out by ophthalmologists and teachers.

For children of school age who are partially sighted, special classes exist in the three largest cities for a total of 62 pupils. An additional 800 children are being taught in primary school in their home communities.

For children with a severe visual loss, there are two special schools in Sweden; one is for 110 children with only a visual problem; the other is for 100 children who have another handicap as well (deaf, epilepsy, mobility, etc.). Admission to either requires a team evaluation. Each school provides medical and dental care, tuition, board and lodging, the cost of which is covered by the national government.

A small number of visually handicapped students attend universities and technical colleges. About fifty partially sighted students do so per year.

There are about fifty blind pupils receiving secondary school education with the help of itinerant teachers.

Equipment such as talking books, talking newspapers, newspapers in Braille, tape recorders, books in large print, a Braille library, and other technical aids are available from the Association of the Blind. This also includes optical devices.

The Association of the Blind provides an information service; recommendation for a recreational program to be supported and developed by the County Councils; youth clubs for young people with a visual handicap organized in collaboration with Lion Clubs.

The partially sighted are granted subsidies and loans to assist them at their place of employment. Sheltered employment is available. An employer hiring a partially sighted worker receives a subsidy.

The Association of the Blind operates a technical factory of the blind, manufacturing various supplies, and employing about thirty visually handicapped workers.

REFERENCES

Maternal Health, Family Planning, and Abortion

1. National Board of Health and Welfare. Model Regulations For Maternal and Child Health Service. Stockholm. 1970. 1 page.
2. RFSU Statistik. Befolkningen, Sexualvanor, Aborten, Gonoré, Sexualbrott, Internationellt. Stockholm. May 1973. 99 pages.

Child Health

3. Geijerstam, G. Low Birth Weight and Perinatal Mortality. Public Health Reports 84: 939-948, November 1969.
4. National Board of Health and Welfare. Model Regulations For Maternal and Child Health Service. Stockholm. 1970. 11 pages.
5. Ragercrantz, R. and Groth, C.G. Essentials of the Swedish National Program For Preventive Child Care. Published by the National Board of Health and Welfare. Stockholm. 1971. 6 pages.
6. Rosengren, B. Preschool In Sweden. The Swedish Institute. Stockholm. 1973. 36 pages.
7. Social styrelsen Informer. Health Screening For Four Year Olds. Stockholm. Undated. 8 pages mimeographed.

School Health

8. RFSU. Befolkningen, Sexualvanor, Aborten, Gonoré, Sexualbrott, Internationellt. Stockholm. May 1973. 99 pages.

Handicapped Children

9. Association of The Blind. Swedish Blind Welfare—72. Stockholm. 1972. 54 pages.
10. Grunewald, K. The Mentally Retarded In Sweden. Published by The Swedish Institute. Stockholm. 1973. 44 pages.

11. Herner, R. Services For The Handicapped. Published by the Swedish Institute. Stockholm. 1969. 40 pages.
12. Lundstrom, K. Special Teaching In Sweden. National Board of Education. Stockholm. October 1970. 30 pages mimeographed.
13. Moultan, K. Rehabilitation In Sweden. Published by the Swedish Institute. Stockholm. 1967. 40 pages.
14. Social styrelsen Informerer. Health Screening For Four-Year-Olds. Stockholm. Undated. 8 pages mimeographed.
15. The Swedish Institute. Social Policy and How It Works. Stockholm. 1972. 35 pages.
16. The Swedish Institute. Social Benefits In Sweden. Stockholm. 1972. 71 pages.
17. The Swedish Institute. Active Manpower Policy In Sweden. In Fact Sheets On Sweden. Stockholm. April 1972. 4 pages.

Chapter 12

Infant Mortality in Sweden

Stig Sjölin

Swedish infant mortality figures have atracted worldwide interest mainly for two reasons. One is that reliable statistics have been available for the whole country since 1749, which is longer than in any other country. The other is that the Swedish infant mortality rate has for long been the lowest in the world and therefore, a challenge to other countries. Before trying to explain how Sweden came to be the constant record holder in infant survival, infant mortality figures for the whole period from 1749 should first be presented.

CHANGES IN INFANT MORTALITY

During the second half of the eighteenth century infant mortality remained approximately at 200 per thousand live births, somewhat higher for boys than for girls (Figure 12-1) [7]. Already at the beginning of the nineteenth century, however, a decline is noted, and after 1810 a gradual and mostly steady fall has taken place, leading to about 100 per thousand in 1900 and the low figure of 10.8 per thousand in 1972 [7, 9]. Consistently boys have suffered a greater loss than girls. In 1972 the infant mortality rate for boys was 12.7 in comparison with 8.8 per thousand for girls.

It is interesting to see that infant mortality through the years seems relatively uninfluenced by environmental disasters like famine, war, and cholera epidemics, which all had a marked effect on mortality among older children (Figure 12-2) [7]. The three mortality peaks visualized in Figure 12-2 for older children were caused by famine in 1773-74, by war with Russia in 1808-09 followed by epidemics of different infectious diseases, and by cholera epidemics during the 1850s and 1860s in combination with famine in 1868 and 1869 [14]. It should also be observed that the fall in infant mortality was almost linear from

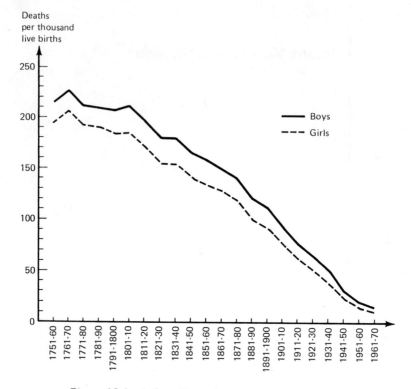

Figure 12-1.   Infant Mortality in Sweden, 1751-1970.

1840 to 1950, but also that it thereafter has been less rapid and now seems to decline more slowly (Figure 12-3).

Mortality figures for different periods of the first year of life are available from 1891 and show clearly that the early neonatal death rate (first week) remained about the same until 1940 (Figure 12-3) [7]. This also holds true for the stillbirth rate, which means that the perinatal mortality was not at all affected by those factors that had such a pronounced effect on infant mortality as a whole. The slight increase in the perinatal death rate during the 1920s and 1930s was probably due to an increasing rate of hospital deliveries during these years (from about 10 to 65 percent) and an improved reporting of live births and early neonatal deaths. It is only after 1940 that the perinatal mortality has continuously and slowly decreased from 45 per thousand in 1940 to 14 per thousand in 1972 [7, 9]. Still, however, about 70 percent of the infant deaths occur during the first week of life.

SOCIOECONOMIC FACTORS

A striking feature of the change in infant mortality in Sweden is that an impressive decrease occurred quite early, long before modern, scientific medicine

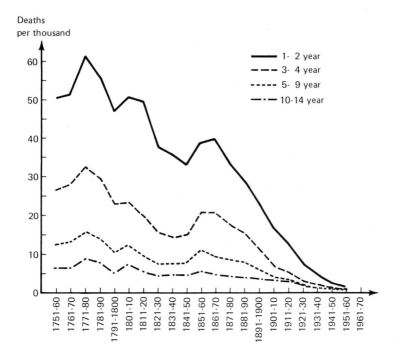

Deaths
per thousand

— 1- 2 year
--- 3- 4 year
····· 5- 9 year
—·— 10-14 year

Figure 12-2.   Mortality Among Children Aged 1-14 Years in Sweden,
1751-1970

could exert any influence on its status, long before information about bacteria,
viruses, vitamins, and antibiotics was known, and long before modern surgery
played a role. Obviously, the causes of the early continuous decline in infant
mortality must be sought outside medicine itself. Unfortunately, no detailed
statistics are available concerning causes of death before 1910. It is therefore not
possible to establish with certainty the conditions or measures that brought
about the decrease in infant mortality during the nineteenth century. If we
extrapolate from what we subsequently have learned, there seems to be every
reason to infer that the general economic expansion and the improved standard
of living and education during the nineteenth century constituted a basis for the
improvement.

The close correlation between socioeconomic conditions and infant
mortality has been demonstrated repeatedly, at different times and in different
places. For Sweden it is documented that people in rural areas during the
nineteenth century generally led a healthier life than people in the cities.
Especially housing and food were better and people also were better protected
against contagious diseases. The lower infant mortality in rural districts in
Sweden up to 1920 is probably explained mainly by factors of this kind (Figure
12-4) [7]. Today no such difference exists. The significance of breast feeding for

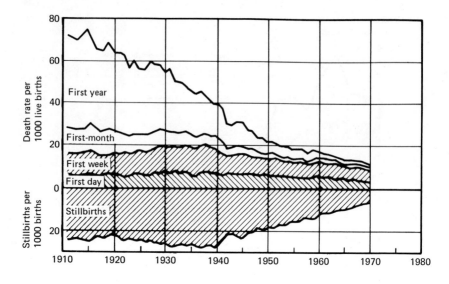

Figure 12-3. Infant and Perinatal Mortality in Sweden, 1910-1970

the infant's health was widely recognized at least since the middle of the eighteenth century [12, 15] and probably more closely observed in the rural areas.

The basic importance of socioeconomic factors for infant mortality can also be demonstrated by a comparison of infant mortality in different Swedish counties (Figure 12-5). Still in 1936-1940 infant mortality was much higher in the three most northern, rather remote and relatively poor counties of Norrbotten, Västerbotten, and Västernorrland than in the more central or southern counties such as the counties of Uppsala, Göteborg, and Bohus. This difference has now been eliminated, and in 1971 the northern county of Västernorrland noted the lowest infant mortality of all counties, 8.2 per thousand, while the southern county of Kronoberg had the highest figure, 13.7 per thousand [8].

The marked influence of the economy of the families on infant mortality was demonstrated by Rietz regarding the Stockholm population of legitimate infants born in 1918 to 1922 (Table 12-1) [11]. The difference in infant mortality between low- and high-income families was at that time quite great. Today the difference is probably completely erased, but there are no recent studies to confirm it.

After the beginning of the nineteenth century the general socioeconomic conditions in Sweden have improved continuously and during the last fifty years in particular more and more people have benefited in the economic development. It is hard to tell which parts of the social development have meant

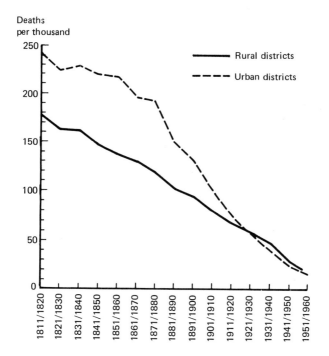

Figure 12-4. Infant Mortality in Rural and Urban Districts in Sweden, 1811-1960

most for the health of infants but improved maternal and infant nutrition in combination with increased knowledge of infant care must have been of early and fundamental importance. Today it is not only significant that Sweden is a highly industrialized country with the highest per capita income in Europe, but also that the total income is more equally distributed than in any other industrialized country and that the social and health insurance system is well developed and compulsory since 1955. There are very few poor people and no one needs to live in real poverty. It seems most likely that the favorable socioeconomic development was the major cause of the falling infant mortality during the nineteenth century and that its effect has been considerable also during the twentieth century.

The Role of Medicine

It was probably not until the end of the nineteenth century that medicine came to exert an influence on infant mortality. The discovery at this time of many of the pathogenic bacteria established a scientific basis for all those sanitary measures that were to prove of utmost significance for the health of the people. It is worth emphasizing here that it was not until the sanitary

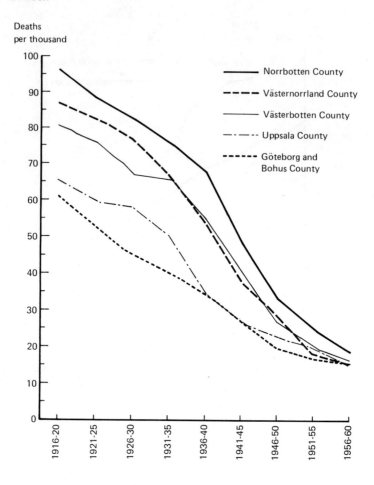

Deaths per thousand

Norrbotten County
Västernorrland County
Västerbotten County
Uppsala County
Göteborg and Bohus County

Figure 12-5. Infant Mortality in Five Swedish Counties, 1916-1960

measures were applied on a large scale that a significant effect on the population was obtained. The children in particular seem to have gained from these measures. The continuing fall in child mortality during the first decades of the twentieth century is undoubtedly explained, for the most part, by general sanitary measures combined with improved personal hygiene. Because of a general increase in income and better food storage and transportation facilities it also became easier to meet the nutritional needs of the population. Infant mortality fell from about 100 per thousand in 1900 to about 50 per thousand in 1930 (Figure 12-1).

During the last fifty years medical research and progress have come to mean more and more for the continuing decrease in infant mortality. A

Table 12-1.   Infant Mortality Among Legitimate Infants Born 1918-1922 in Stockholm in Relation to the Income of the Family

Family income, Swedish Crowns	Infant Mortality per thousand live born
less than 4000	48.9
4000-6000	38.3
6000-10.000	31.9
more than 10.000	14.3

Source: E. Rietz, "Sterblichkeit und Todesursachen in den Kinderjahren," *Acta Paediat* 9, Suppl 3 (1930).

comprehensive illustration of the changes that have taken place during the last decades is seen in Table 12-2 [1]. Infectious diseases and diseases of the respiratory and digestive systems have lost a great deal of their role as leading causes of infant deaths. For example twelve infants per thousand died from respiratory tract diseases in the period 1911-1915, while in 1966-1970 the corresponding figure was only 0.4. A long series of preventive and curative measures have contributed to this development, e.g., syphilis serology and pulmonary X-ray in all pregnant women, early diagnosis and treatment of Rh-isoimmunization, improved possibilities to prevent and treat obstetrical complications, improved analgesia during delivery, antibiotics against bacterial infections in mother and child, more effective treatment of asphyxia in the newborn, systematic vaccinations of most infants against tuberculosis, smallpox, diphtheria, pertussis, tetanus and polio, vitamin D-prophylaxis against rickets, early proper treatment of diarrhea, etc.

Table 12-2.   Leading Causes of Death Per 100,000 Children Below One Year of Age in Sweden in 1911-1915 and 1966-1970

	1911-15	1966-70
Diseases of the newborn		750
Congenital anomalies	2,890	300
Diseases of the respiratory system	1,200	40
Diseases of the digestive system	900	30
Infectious diseases	710	20
Tuberculosis	200	0
Accidents		70
Other and unknown causes	1,320	10
Total	7,220	1,220

Source: A.M. Bolander, Personal communication.

It is, however, not medical research alone that has created opportunities for this development. A series of organizational changes have contributed and made possible the use of research results for the benefit of the population.

One of the most characteristic features of Swedish obstetrics during the twentieth century has been the decreasing number of home deliveries and the corresponding increase in hospital deliveries. In 1920 about 90 percent of the deliveries took place at home, while in 1960 the figure was 0.6 and in 1972 0.02 percent [6]. The decrease was most rapid from 1935 to 1950. Parallel to this development, the number of beds in the hospital obstetrical departments has increased and the simple, poorly equipped delivery homes have disappeared. Today, the majority of the deliveries occur in hospitals with complete obstetrical and pediatric day and night services. In the Uppsala region for instance, 73.4 percent of the 96,733 deliveries in 1964-1968 took place in such hospitals, while the rest occurred in smaller hospitals without immediate access to obstetricians and pediatricians, but where midwives and surgeons were available day and night [5]. It should be added that risk pregnancies as often as possible are referred to the hospital obstetrical department for delivery. A seemingly unexpected result of this is a higher perinatal mortality in the most specialized hospitals. In the Uppsala region, for instance, the perinatal death rate was 18.2 per thousand births in 1964-1968 in the most specialized hospitals compared to 13.8 in the less specialized [5]. Worthy of note is also the fact that the specialized obstetrical departments of hospitals are distributed rather evenly over the country. This implies that it is only in the most northern part of the country that deliveries in the future to some extent will have to be performed in smaller hospitals which are not fully equipped to care for complicated deliveries. The expansion of obstetrics has been accompanied by a similar expansion of pediatrics, which can be illustrated by the increase in the number of hospital beds. In 1921 there were 0.30 beds per 1,000 children below the age of 15. In 1970 this figure had raised to 1.5 [14, 15]. Today there is at least one hospital department of pediatrics in each county.

It is obvious that all these changes in the delivery conditions have markedly improved the possibilities to treat more acutely, more effectively, and more accurately the different complications that may occur to the fetus and the newborn baby before, during, or after delivery. The organizational changes meant that obstetricians and pediatricians were more forcefully than ever before faced with perinatal illness and death, which in its turn from about 1940 led to active and systematic joint attempts to combat perinatal mortality. At the same time, and partly as a result, better technical equipment was developed and made available for clinical use in the hospitals. As a rule the local authorities during these years took pride in facilitating the construction of modern hospitals and furnishing them with appropriate equipment.

An analysis of the medical influences on perinatal and infant mortality must include an attempt to evaluate the general health supervision of pregnant women and of children introduced in 1938 in Sweden. It is hard to determine exactly the role of MCH in this complex system of influences, but it seems most likely that different types of general and specific preventive and educational activities within the framework of MCH have contributed substantially to the improved maternal and child health. The total prevention of scurvy, rickets, and congenital syphilis may serve as undisputable examples. The development of the MCH services was quite rapid. Already in 1950 more than 60 percent of the pregnant women and about 90 percent of all infants were regularly supervised [14]. Today the corresponding figures are for pregnant women about 95 percent and for infants 99 percent [4]. On an average each pregnant woman makes about four visits to the doctor and eight to the health nurse, and each infant makes five visits to the doctor and three to the nurse, who on an average also makes about three home visits to infants.

Certain other factors, which are more or less specific for Sweden should also be mentioned as explanation of the very low total infant mortality. It is well known that a birth order over three involves a higher neonatal death risk than a lower birth order. Since the number of children per family (mean 1.5) is lower in Sweden than in many other countries this tends to lower infant mortality. Of greater importance, however, is the low incidence of low birth weight infants (2,500 grams or less) in Sweden; in 1965 4.5 percent against 8.2 percent in the United States in 1964 [2]. As the perinatal mortality is considerably higher among low birth weight infants (Table 12-3) and preterm infants (Table 12-4) [3, 5], this means that infant mortality can be reduced by the prevention of preterm deliveries. In fact, Geijerstam [2] has calculated that

Table 12-3. Perinatal Mortality by Birth Weight in the Uppsala Region in 1964-1968 with 96,733 Total Births

Birth Weight, gm	Perinatal Deaths Per Thousands Births
1000 or less	925.1
1001-1500	587.3
1501-2000	253.7
2001-2500	74.5
2501-3000	19.1
3001-3500	6.5
3501-4000	4.4
4001-4500	4.1
4501 or more	7.1
Total	16.9

Source: National Board of Health and Welfare, *In-Patient Statistics from Hospitals in the Uppsala Region 1964-1968*, Newborn Infants, Patient Statistics No. 12 (Stockholm, 1973).

Table 12-4. Perinatal Mortality by Length of Gestation in the Uppsala Region in 1964-1968 with 96,733 Total Births

Weeks of Gestation	Perinatal Deaths Per Thousand Births
28 or less	709.9
29-32	335.6
33-36	102.7
37	44.7
38	27.1
39	11.6
40	6.9
41	5.0
42	6.6
43	8.8
44	8.8
45 or more	15.8
Total	16.9

Source: National Board of Health and Welfare, *In-Patient Statistics from Hospitals in the Uppsala Region 1964-1968*, Newborn Infants, Patient Statistics No. 12 (Stockholm, 1973).

the difference in infant mortality between Sweden and the United States would be almost eliminated if the U.S. incidence of low birth weight could be reduced to the Swedish level, which has been prevalent at least since the 1930s. In this connection, it may be stressed that the decreasing perinatal mortality in Sweden after 1940 with all probability has been caused mainly by the joint efforts made by obstetricians and pediatricians to improve the handling of pregnant women, deliveries, and newborn infants. In a recent study, however, it was shown that the largest part of the variation in perinatal death could not be explained by fifteen of the most common variables known to influence perinatal death [10]. The result indicates a multifactorial and complex cause-effect relationship. Low infant mortality figures can probably be obtained in a country only if social, economic, and medical measures are combined and applied in a large scale on the entire population concerned.

It is tempting to speculate on how low the future infant mortality rate might be. We all know that some deaths seem unavoidable and that it will also be impossible to prevent all fatal congenital malformations. For Sweden it seems reasonable to predict a very small and slow further decrease. It should also be realized that infant mortality figures no longer are useful indicators for the future Swedish child health planning. New and more refined indices, better describing the state of health and social adaptation of the children, are needed.

SUMMARY OF FACTORS PLAYING A ROLE
IN SWEDEN'S LOW INFANT
MORTALITY RATE

The most important factors, that have caused the steady decline in infant mortality in Sweden, cannot be defined unequivocally or with any degree of precision. With all probability there has been an interplay of different factors. These factors have been of different importance at different periods. For a long time it was almost only the mortality after the first week of life that was influenced. Not until recently also the neonatal part of infant mortality started to decrease.

1. During the nineteenth century a general improvement in living conditions, in economy, housing, and nutrition probably played the major role. Famine and epidemics became more and more rare.
2. At the end of the nineteenth and at the beginning of the twentieth century a more and more systematic application of general sanitary measures on the whole population contributed most.
3. During the twentieth century parents learned to take better care of their infants, and in particular infant feeding practice improved.
4. Medicine itself did probably not influence infant mortality to any great extent until the beginning of the 1920s, from which time more effective preventive and curative measures were developed and eventually also used for the benefit of the whole infant population.
5. The decrease in perinatal mortality after 1940 is probably mainly the result of the combined efforts of obstetricians and pediatricians, who from that time cooperated to develop and apply new methods of medical treatment both to the mother and the newborn.

REFERENCES

1. Bolander, A.M. Personal communication.
2. Geijerstam, G. af. "Low Birth Weight and Perinatal Mortality." *Publ Health Reports* 84 (1969): 939.
3. Lubchenco, L.O.; Searls, D.T.; and Brazie, J.V. "Neonatal Mortality Rate: Relationship to Birth Weight and Gestational Age." *J Ped* 81 (1972): 814.
4. National Board of Health and Welfare. *Public Health in Sweden 1970.* Stockholm 1973.
5. National Board of Health and Welfare. *In-patient Statistics from Hospitals in the Uppsala Region 1964-1968.* Newborn infants. Patient statistics No. 12. Stockholm, 1973.
6. National Board of Health and Welfare. *Förlossningsvårdens organisation.* Socialstyrelsen redovisar No. 35. Stockholm, 1973.

7. National Central Bureau of Statistics. *Historical Statistics of Sweden.* Part I Population. 1720-1967. 2nd Edition. Stockholm, 1969.
8. National Central Bureau of Statistics. *Population Changes 1971.* Part 3. Stockholm, 1972.
9. National Central Bureau of Statistics. *Statistical Abstract of Sweden, 1973.* Stockholm, 1973.
10. Pettersson, F.; Melander, S.; and Lagerberg, D. "Perinatal Mortality." *Acta Paediat Scand* 62 (1973): 221.
11. Rietz, E. "Sterblichkeit und Todesursachen in den Kinderjahren." *Acta Paediat* 9, Suppl. 3 (1930).
12. Rosén von Rosenstein, N. *The Diseases of Children and Their Remedies.* London: T. Cadell, 1776.
13. Sjölin, S. and Vahlquist, B. "Child Health in Sweden." *Acta Paediat Scand* 63 (1974).
14. Strom, J. "The Fall in Infant Mortality in Sweden and Its Causes." *Norde Med* 50 (1953): 1285.
15. Vahlquist, B. "The Diseases of Children and Their Remedies." In *Nils Rosén von Rosenstein and his Textbook on Paediatrics. Acta Paediat.* Suppl. 156. 1964, p. 30.

Chapter 13

Day Care of Children in Sweden

Bodil Rosengren

INTRODUCTION

The debate on the family in Sweden has been characterized during recent years by a pronounced consciousness of the relationship between the living conditions of families and social development as a whole. Discussion has centered on the extent to which the surroundings in which a child grows up influence his personality development, choice of education and future career, and living conditions. The debate has also focused on how families' living surroundings influence the opportunities of adults to shape their own lives after their own desires and abilities.

Family politics has, thus, taken two important directions. Firstly, it has been increasingly considered as a stage in the improvement of living conditions for low-wage earning families with children. Further it is concerned with contributing toward the attainment of a division of work and roles within the family and society, which will provide both men and women with greater opportunities for developing their personal potential.

The point of departure for politics of the family has increasingly become that both parents should be able to be gainfully employed. This is taking place through measures adopted in the areas of extension in the facilities for day care of small and younger children provided by the community. Attention is also being directed toward other forms of services for families with children where both parents are gainfully employed or where there is only one parent.

A whole range of social reforms has been introduced to improve the lot of families with children. Universal family allowance and an accommodation allowance enabling families with low incomes to enjoy a spacious and modern home, present examples of these. Sweeping school reforms, a vigorous expansion in child care and preparations for general nursery schooling, extensive housing developments aimed at families with children, improvements in the general environment, a long list could be drawn up.

The basis for the economic support to families with children remains the child allowance, which consists of 125 Swedish kronor per month and per child, distributed equally to all children aged under sixteen. The aim is to even out the economic situation between families with and without children.

During recent years economic support has been more and more directed toward families with children, who have low incomes, many children, and high housing costs. An example of this is the rent allowance. The background to this has been the debate surrounding equality which has taken place. Rent allowance takes the form of a basic sum per child plus a compensation for high housing costs. This assistance is subject to a means test and is gradually reduced with higher income.

All these innovations have implied considerable changes for the better. At the same time, a series of general structure changes have affected the child's environment, urbanization, increased mobility, disruption of households, greater stress from the outer environment through new obtrusive media, densely built-up areas which bring people closer together physically but also increase their anonymity, larger school units, etc.

Today's Swedish family is therefore vastly different in its function, size, and composition from the family in previous times. To a greater and greater extent gainful employment has become located outside the home and the child has therefore become screened off from the working life of the adult world. Improvement in education has entailed that more and more women find it natural to form permanent close ties with the labor market, even after they have had children. The employment intensity of married women in Sweden has risen steeply in the past few decades. Since the mid-sixties, married women have accounted for the greater part of the rise in the number of people in the labor force, and this despite a relatively heavy influx of immigrant labor. The employment intensity of married women even rose during the recession of 1970-1972. Married women are expected to constitute the largest increment to the labor force during the remainder of the 1970s as well.

The employment intensity of mothers with children declines as the number of children increases, and increases in proportion to the age of the youngest child. This applies throughout the entire period. On the other hand, there have been considerable changes in average employment intensity. In 1965, 46 percent of women with children under seventeen were employed, as against 61 percent in 1972. The lowest employment activity, approximately 33 percent, occurred in 1972 among mothers with one or more children, the youngest child being under three years old. The difference in employment intensity between mothers with one, two or more children practically disappeared by the time the youngest child reached the age of eleven. The proportion of gainfully employed women with children under seventeen rose by over 11 percent between 1968 and 1972. Employment rose in all groups except the youngest, where there was a decline in the number employed. Probably this was due to a rise in the number of students in this age group (Table 13-1).

The objective for family policy that everyone—men and women— should be able to combine gainful employment and care of the children, under conditions which both provide security for the children and do not necessitate unreasonable double jobs, has been manifested in the extensive reforms in the Parliament of 1973. Two important proposals were the following:

1. The maternity allowance was converted into a parents' insurance with a guaranteed minimum for a six-month period in connection with the birth of the child. The parents' insurance implies that for the time following the birth of the child, the parents themselves can decide which of them will remain home to take care of the child and be thereby entitled to parenthood benefit, which is not less than 25 Swedish kronor per day. The reform is a significant indication from the community that both the mother and the father share responsibility for the child's development. Adopted children are also included in the parents' insurance. For adopted children who are *over* eight months old, parenthood benefit is payable for twenty days, and the parents may divide it between them as they will. This applies to adopted children under ten years of age.

2. The right to sickness benefit for a gainfully employed mother *or* father who must stay home from work to look after an occasionally ill child in the family. Sickness benefit also includes the opportunity for a father to remain home to take care of the older children when another child is born in the family. This reform provides an important increase in security for gainfully employed parents. The reform also implies the indication that it should be considered entirely natural that either mother or father stays home from work when necessary if their children are ill.

An absence of this nature should, thus, be able to occur for both parents and should not, as it has previously, be charged to women when the

Table 13-1. Employment Intensity Among Women With Children Under 17—By Age

		Relative Labor Force Rates			
Age	*1968*	*1969*	*1970*	*1971*	*1972*
16-19	53.3	40.2	35.2	37.7	32.1
20-24	44.9	44.4	49.5	52.9	55.6
25-34	41.4	46.9	50.5	52.1	53.7
35-44	42.4	46.7	51.0	52.6	54.1
45-54	22.0	29.8	44.7	53.4	58.4
16-54	42.1	45.8	49.7	52.1	53.7

debate arises with regard to equal salaries and equivalent prospects for promotion. A vigorous debate is also taking place on the husband's right to share the responsibility for housework, and for the children's care and upbringing, to develop his full potential, and to enjoy close contact with his children.

A debate has recently arisen in Sweden regarding working hours in relation to the situation of parents with small children. One of the demands which have been raised is that future reductions in working hours should preferably take the form of reductions in the working day and not, for example, the working week. The question of a general reduction in working hours for the parents of small children with a reduction in salary has also been taken up. A decrease in the working hours of *both* parents should mean that the time each child remains in the day-nursery or a family day-nursery could be reduced to 5-6 hours per day. This question is still just at the discussion stage. There are naturally many aspects to a reform of this nature—not the least the economic, but the debate illustrates the interplay between measures for promoting equality on the labor market, in child care and in home.

AN INCREASING NEED OF DAY CARE
FOR CHILDREN

Much of the support given by the community to children of preschool age and children at the junior level thus consists of grants designed to raise the standard of living of the family and child. Various types of social insurance offer families and their children a basic security. Less attention, however, has been paid to the fact that the conditions under which children grow up are determined also by residential construction and housing policy, by the way in which the residential environment is shaped by leisure facilities within and outside the area. Working life itself, and its conditions, hours, wage rates etc., also have a decisive bearing on the child's life, via the parents' opportunity to function as suppliers, as individuals, and in relation to their children.

The preschool (i.e., day-nurseries, nursery schools), the school, the free-time centers (i.e., day-nurseries for school children primarily those in the 7-9 age group), and other public preventive child care, together with health services for children, are the means by which the community can offer a complement to the family, which influences the childrens' development more directly. Therefore the continued rapid extension in community child-care facilities is equally important as a further increase in cash support to families with children. One of the necessary conditions for making upbringing a process of interplay between the children, their parents, and the community is a day care of children that incorporates different forms of part-time, half-day, and full-day activity, and which can enter the child's life at an early stage. Various further measures are needed for the child, within the family and home, to ensure optimum conditions of upbringing; such measures include efforts to establish a properly functioning system of parent training.

The year 1973 therefore was an important one to all Swedish children from the age of six months until they start school, which in Sweden is at the age of seven. Then the Parliament passed a Government Bill, which means that after almost forty years discussion for and against child care facilities provided by the community we have a Preschool Act. By this Act the local authorities, the municipalities, are obliged by law to meet the right of children to attend preschool, either in day-nurseries or in nursery schools.

The Government Bill emphasizes the fact that it is an important aim of family politics to increase the security of children. It is important to a child to spend his time rich in varied experiences together with both parents but also to spend a stimulating time together with other children. The conditions under which children grow up and their emotional contact during the preschool ages are of great importance to the individual's continuous development and consequently to the whole development of society. The aim to increase the security of children also means to give all children the opportunity of having living conditions which stimulate and develop their personalities. Unfavorable conditions while being a child restrict the individual's chance of personality development and could cause troubles in later years. Young people's choice of education and of a profession is still strongly connected with prejudice against sex roles and with the parents' social consciousness and educational background instead of with the child's innate capacity and interests. Children with physical, mental or social handicaps, and immigrant children belong to those who at some point often have an initial position of life inferior to others and who for that reason may need a special support and stimulation to their development.

To sum it up, it is important to children and to parents that day care of children is organized in such a way that parents feel safe and may rest assured that the children are taken care of in an adequate way, which also means a complement to the upbringing and care the child will get in his own home.

The overriding aims of the preschool drawn up in the Government Bill indicate what fundamental personality resources it is important to concentrate upon, and promote pedagogically. From the psychological, pedagogical, and sociological aspects alike, the preschool emerges as an entirely necessary support to the child's long-term development into a mature and active adult, who can function both as an independent individual and in cooperation and interplay with others as a democratic human being.

The preschool should endeavor, in cooperation with the parents, to offer every child the optimum conditions to develop his emotional and intellectual, physical and social resources in a rich, many-faceted manner.

In this way, the preschool can lay the foundation for the child's development into an open, considerate person with a capacity for empathy and cooperation with others, and an ability to arrive at his or her own judgments and solutions.

The preschool should lay in the child the foundation for a willingness to seek and utilize knowledge to improve both his own and others' condition of life.

THE MAIN POINTS OF THE PRE-SCHOOL ACT

By the Parliament's decision, it is now laid down by law that:

1. A general preschool, with a minimum of three hours' attendance per day, covering to begin with all six-year-olds, shall be introduced from 1975. The local authorities are obliged by law to assign all children a place in a nursery school, once they reach age of six unless they already hold a place in a day nursery. This general preschool for six-year-olds should be free of charge. Through information and calling up actions, local authorities are to encourage all six-year-olds in the district to participate in nursery school activities.

In those exceptional cases where the parents reject the preschool, the primary issue is what is best for the child. If the child is placed in a nursery school against the definite will of its parents, conflict can arise that will ultimately have a negative effect on the child. In such cases, the local authority should establish contact with the parents with a view to inducing an understanding for the child's situation and needs before school starts.

Otherwise, it would be the duty of the local authority to see that the child's personality development was promoted in another way, e.g., by activities in a play-group. This could apply, for instance, to a child with few peer contacts, a child that is oversensitive to introduction to a larger group of children. In such case, it is naturally of particular importance that the local authority gradually assist in preparing the child, gently and carefully, for the onset of compulsory schooling, so that this is not experienced as a shock. In exceptional cases where a child fails to continue in the preschool later in the year, the local authority is to establish renewed contacts.

The Parliament has considered it important to establish the general preschool in law, to create guarantees that all six-year-olds are actually reached and given places. The child's right to attend a preschool cannot be considered as guaranteed, simply by places made available for those whose parents have reported an interest. In such a case, there is a risk that many of the worse-off children (immigrant children, children from socially and financially inadequate environments, children isolated in sparsely populated areas, etc.) who most need the preschool would be left out of things. It is in respect of these children that the preschool demands most resources but it is for them too that it is most essential.

In those instances, however, where case finding activities indicate very grave shortcomings in the child's situation, ultimate resort can naturally—as at present—be made to custody under the Child Welfare Act. To a greater extent than previously, the preschool should be able even in such cases to constitute a positive aspect of family—therapeutic work, before the question of custody arises.

The demand for a general preschool implies certain special efforts, over and above those already planned by the local authorities, for between 5,000 and 10,000 children. A high proportion of these children live in sparsely populated areas. Owing to their own and the family's isolation, the children there need to establish an early contact with other adults and peers via the preschool. For purely practical reasons, it is often best to provide a two-year preschool for children living in such areas. Owing, for instance, to long distances to and from the preschool, it is often possible to arrange a preschool then only for 2-3 days a week, for a total up to ten hours per week (nursery schools in urban areas cover at present fifteen hours per week).

It is stated that the preschool should cover 525 hours per year. Such local authorities by reason of long distances, etc., can provide preschool facilities only for three days a week or less, can divide the preschool into two years. The preschool should then cover a total of at least 700 hours for five and six year olds.

2. All *children with special requirements*, arising from physical, mental, social and linguistic handicaps or from other reasons, shall be offered access to preschool from an early age as far as possible. This relates to the potential role of the preschool in expanded social activities of an outreach type. The necessary condition for this is teamwork between preventive social and medical-psychological child care and the preschool.

The term "children with special requirements" is used to broaden the somewhat narrow concept we often have today of a handicap. Handicapped children are those who are exposed to a greater strain, more difficult conditions, or obstacles in different activities and situations.

Those needing to attend preschool before the age of six often include children from immigrant families. Such children need support as much for their emotional and social development, as for learning Swedish.

Children in sparsely populated areas who lack contact with peers should also be provided with the opportunity to commence nursery school prior to six years of age.

The local authorities should run case-finding activities to obtain information about all children with special requirements and provide them with nursery school places. When fully developed, such case-finding activities should provide well-planned and coordinated social services to families with children. These activities should be such that they are experiences as a positive and desired support to parents and their children. The primary object of case-finding activities is to offer the children the services required by each child and its family. Examples include financial assistance, finding accommodation, referral to other bodies, etc. Also in many situations early preschool activities can be an advantage for the child and the family. For instance, a priority place at preschool can be necessary in sorting out a malfunctioning social situation. It can relieve the family of a burden, but it can also be a stimulus for the child and parents that will make possible a generally improved home environment.

The responsibility for case-finding activities in respect to children with special requirements lies with the local authority's social bodies. These should also bear the responsibility for the preschool, and its role in the total services offered as part of family policy.

In order to find out the best methods of case-finding activities, the King-in-Council has appointed a commission on case-finding activities in respect to children with special requirements. This commission will also analyze the question about the responsibility for preschool activities for these children, as the County Councils today are responsible for some of the handicapped children and their care, including nursery school. The commission on case-finding activities should test some of the proposals made by the Commission on Child Centres of 1968. (The Government Bill and the Preschool Act are both based on the proposals from the latter commission.)

To achieve general, positive case-finding activities, the Commission on Child Centres proposed experiments with cooperation centering around the preschool, primarily cooperation between the Child Welfare Committee and child care center. Municipal staff from the Child Welfare Committee/Social Services Committee is proposed to be attached to the child care centers where free supervision of the child's health is provided up to the age of seven, when the school health organization takes it over, for integrated socio-medical teamwork. An examination at the child care center in the spring of the year in which children reach the age of four is to be extended to cover all four year olds: at the same time, this examination can provide a basis for considering priorities to the preschool. The purpose of the "preschool examination" is primarily to find children in need of special support and stimulation, and to offer them priority to the preschool. This proposal should be seen as a first step towards increased cooperation between medical, pedagogical and social bodies.

The Commission on Child Centres further proposed experiments with direct cooperation between the Child Welfare Committee/Social Services Committee, maternity centers, child care centers, and the Mental Health Service for Children. Such cooperation would reinforce the various bodies concerned, in that they could utilize each others' resources. Different models for such cooperation are now being tested and evaluated in eight communities by the commission on case-finding activities. This commission also tries to find methods to establish a properly functioning system of parent training.

Finally, children with special requirements who cannot use their preschool places in a nursery school run by the local authority should be offered special preschool activities and play therapy, when they are at hospital, children's home or corresponding institution, from the earliest age possible. The responsibility for this lies with the principals of the institution in question, mostly with the County Councils.

3. *The children of gainfully employed or student parents* should as far as possible be offered access to day nursery places, family day nurseries or other kinds of day care, according to need. To create opportunities for a

continued fast expansion of day care facilities for children of gainfully employed or student parents, all local authorities should compile preschool plans, reporting the entire future need for preschool places in the area, and their location. The plan, which must be sanctioned by the local council, should present an account indicating the need for preschool activities and should indicate the extent and the manner in which the local government authority aims at satisfying the requirements for day nurseries, part-time groups, nursery schools and family day nurseries, play groups, care of sick children at home, etc. These plans should cover a five-year period and should take the form of a continuous program which is revised each year with regard to new production of dwellings, slum clearance, etc.

In this connection political, trade, and other local unions should have the possibility of delivering their views on the needs for preschool facilities to the local authorities working with this planning. This means that unions and the individual member of the community who are interested in these matters should obtain information that could easily be secured in good time before decisions are made in the local council. The local authorities should take measures in order to spread active information of the work with this preschool planning.

All communities in the country should report their plans of preschool facilities to the National Board of Health and Welfare, where they should be compiled to an outline of the preschool facilities of the whole country. This outline will be of great importance to the planning of training of preschool staffs.

4. *Governing Bodies.* In the general debate in Sweden, it has been discussed whether the preschool should continue to have the National Board of Health and Welfare as its central inspecting authority and be managed locally by the Child Welfare Committee/Social Services Committee, or whether the National Board of Education should assume central responsibility, with the Education Committee taking over the local level. By the Preschool Act it is decided by the Parliament that preschool is an integral part of the child welfare system. The Board of Health and Welfare should therefore continue being the central inspecting and advising authority. The main recommendation in respect to local administration is the Child Welfare Committee/Social Services Committee. In certain cases, however, administration by a special Child Centre Committee or by the Education Committee could have its advantage.

The preschool stands in an important relationship to both educational policy and social policy at large. There are many important tasks for cooperation. A common administration is particularly important in the solving of certain specific problems. The most essential thing however is to let the preschool merge, in its organization, with the various complementary services provided to support the family.

During a long period of construction, particular weight will have to be given to priority on social grounds in the allocation of preschool places. Case-finding activities by the authority responsible play a major role in this context. In many cases, such activities must be seen as an effort on behalf of the entire family, not simply for the child.

Here too, organizational integration is necessary with social policy. The local committee and central inspecting authority responsible for activities will cover all preschool facilities. The idea is therefore rejected of having day nurseries and family day nurseries run by the Social Services Committee, and other preschool activities, as nursery schools, etc. by the Education Committee.

For the purposes of collaboration between the preschool and school, the Government Bill proposes that joint bodies be set up by all local authorities to develop a practical system of coordination. Consultation on preschool matters is particularly important for the following local bodies; the Social Services Committee, Education Committee, Recreation Committee, Building Committee, Arts Committee, the child health organization, parents, staff organizations and unions, the local police force, and youth organizations. An interplay between the preschool and the lower level of the basic comprehensive will be important. The child must experience a continuity between the preschool and schooling proper. A certain interplay already takes place in various parts of the country, but a more intensive dialogue between the preschool and the lower level is necessary on various planes.

Centrally, cooperation and consultation should take place by a special cooperation body—the Preschool Delegation—that should be consultative to the National Board of Health and Welfare and to the National Board of Education. In this delegation questions concerning preschool and its future aims should be dealt with. Research and experimental activities for instance must be broadened and deepened.

Regionally the County Administration is the inspecting authority. The supreme authority for all preschool activities is the Ministry of Health and Social Affairs under the Minister of Health and Social Affairs. However, close collaboration takes place at all levels with representatives of the educational authorities, from the Ministry and Board of Education, which are responsible for the training of preschool teachers in the eighteen institutions existing for this purpose, to the local Education Committees, which are locally responsible for secondary schooling (gymnasieskolan). The latter incorporates the training of children's nurses on a two-year nursing line for the purposes of preschool.

NEW GOVERNMENT COMMITTEES ON
QUESTIONS CONCERNING CHILDREN

Since the government Committee on Child Centres of 1968 presented its main report, "The Pre-School," and its proposals were made, the proposals of the government autumn 1973 and passed by the Parliament, several new committees on children's conditions have been appointed in 1973 by the King-in-Council.

The Committee on Case-finding Activities is already mentioned above. Its proposals will be of great importance concerning the cooperation between the local social bodies and the child care centers in order to trace children and parents with special requirements. Experimental activities in some communities have shown that there are many children needing an early preschool place. In some activities almost every third four-year-old child, called to the above mentioned preschool examination, administered by the local welfare committee and the child care center, needed a preschool place and other social service. By cooperation of social workers and medical staff at the child care centers, the doctors and nurses taking part in the experimental activities, (as well as the social workers) report that they understand each other's work better and that they have become more observant of so-called hidden handicaps, such as social, emotional, and linguistic handicaps. They have also a new instrument to help children and parents by giving the children priority to a preschool place. The children then are always integrated in preschools where nonhandicapped children remain. In most cases, children with special requirements should be given places at a day nursery to afford adequate time both for participating with other children in games, meals, etc., and for the special stimulation that is usually necessary.

Another important committee that has just begun its work is *The Committee on the Childrens' Environment*, also appointed in 1973. This government committee should illustrate the long-term changes in the childrens' circumstances. The committee then should analyze the childrens' present circumstances and on-going changes. The future report from this committee aims at giving the basis of a broad discussion about what must be done concerning the children's circumstances.

In order to get a speedy analysis of the experiences from the above mentioned parents' insurance of 1973, a special government committee has been appointed at the beginning of 1974, *The Parents Insurance Committee*. This committee should thoroughly consider the question of the length of the parents' insurance, whether it will be possible to prolong the period of parenthood benefit in such a manner that the insurance will make it easier to parents with small children to be gainfully employed with reduced working hours during some period after the right to full parenthood benefit has ceased. The committee should also analyze the situation of the smallest children, the infant groups aged 6 months-2.5 years in the day nurseries. This investigation will be of great importance both to the children, their parents, the local authorities, and all people that are generally interested in these matters. Today we lack very much information of what influence day care in day nurseries has on the smallest childrens' personality development.

Finally, *The National Board of Health and Welfare* administers intensive experimental activities since the beginning of 1972, at the request of the Ministry of Health and Welfare, in the preschool field in connection with the reform of preschool. The activities refer to the organization and pedagogic patterns of preschools, to planning and extending the achievements of the communities to children in the preschool ages, and to case-finding activities to children with special requirements of support and stimulation.

At the beginning of 1973, the prime minister also called together a Delegation on Equality, with representatives for the employers' and employees' organizations, the political parties, and voluntary associations, with a view to promoting womens' opportunities on the labor market, and in Sweden's political and social life, thus offering also men the option of playing a greater part in the life of the child, and the home. This delegation has already done very much with laying stress upon the communities to build preschool activities.

Thus the rest of the 1970s will be a very interesting period concerning childrens' possibilities of a rich and good life. We will get more information on children and their circumstances. There may be several reforms at the beginning of the 1980s in the social field, but also in the field of compulsory basic school, where another government committee is trying to find solutions to improve the social and pedagogical situation in our compulsory school.

THE CONTINUED WORK OF THE GOVERNMENT COMMISSION ON CHILD CENTRES

For the Commission on Child Centres there remain present proposals on day care of children on the lower level of the compulsory basic school, i.e., on free-time centers and leisure activities for children of school age.

The commission presented its report in June 1974. It has concentrated its work on finding solutions to the problem concerning the ages 7-12. Children in these ages are a forgotten and exposed group. Many children have nowhere to go after school has finished. They have to get along quite by themselves and they are without contacts with any adult during the time after school until their parents will be at home after work. They are also often too small to be allowed to join the activities in the leisure time centers for youth, run by the local authorities. And they are too grown up to play in the playgrounds, where the small children play.

We have reason to believe that every fifth child aged 7-12 has no one at home after school has finished. A government commission presented these numbers of children being without contact with grownups in 1967. The commission on child centers has found the same by doing spot tests in some communities, although we have more places in free-time centers since 1967.

The main points which the commission has discussed are the following: Free-time centers are a valuable resource for children in the lower level of school, and for children with special requirements aged 7-12. They ought to be developed and must reach many more children needing care and constant contacts with adults. It is important to offer this complement of home and school to children with special requirements of support and stimulation. The children must also have the opportunities of activities outside the free-time centers within a wider framework and be able to have experiences in more distant areas, at the same time as they need to be rooted in the surroundings in their neighborhood.

One way of combining these needs is to organize free-time centers in the schools. Then the free-time center could take care of some thirty children aged 7-9 in its "domiciles," i.e., the rooms reserved for the enrolled children, but also hold an "open house" for other children in the residential area all day with different activities common to the enrolled children and the other ones in classrooms and workshops.

It is also necessary to introduce children in these ages in society activities and clubs of different kinds. We have had very few activities, run by societies and unions, for children aged 7-12. To guarantee the children enough contacts with adults, it will be necessary to activate societies and unions to all kinds through economic support from the state, to enroll children in the lower levels of school and run activities in the afternoon and during holidays.

The commission also underlines the needs for a continuous case-finding activity to children in these ages. One way is to try an examination when the child will be enrolled in the compulsory school, before school starts, in order to find out how many children there are who need places in free-time centers for different reasons, and especially to offer children and families with special requirements social services and also priority to a free-time center. Such an examination should be administered by the local social bodies in cooperation with the school health service.

In general the commission proposes a necessary cooperation between the same boards and services as concerns preschool. Every community ought to be divided into smaller districts and to have its own planning group for leisure time activities, consisting of officials from the different boards of health and welfare, of education, art, leisure activities, and of representatives of different societies and unions.

There ought also to be a central program group consisting of politicians from the social, educational, leisure time, and cultural sectors in order to make a total plan for leisure time activities for children and youth in the community.

The commission bases its proposals on experimental activities which have been run by the National Board of Health and Welfare concerning the need for activating societies and unions to work with children aged 7-12. Since 1971, 133 projects have been organized and 75,000 children have joined the activities. More than 4,000 leaders have been engaged. There is obviously a very big demand for activities and if societies and unions secure economic support by the state and the community, they can manage activities for children aged 7-12 very well.

QUANTITATIVE DEVELOPMENT OF DAY
CARE IN RECENT YEARS

During the 1950s very little was done to increase the number of day care places. The main reason was that the market for female labor then fell off. As we entered the sixties, a broad opinion made itself heard in favor of increased access to day nurseries. Increasing numbers of women took gainful employment. From the midst of the sixties, many institutions have been built. Table 13-2 shows the expansion of the social service to families with children, run by the communities.

According to the Labour Force Surveys, there were during the second quarter of 1972 approximately 410,000 children under eleven, whose mothers were gainfully employed for more than nineteen hours per week. Of these some 232,000 were preschool children. These figures should be compared with the facilities offered by the community in the form of day care and private families looking after the children of working parents. For preschool children, there was a total of 46,400 places in day nurseries, and about 37,500 places in family day nurseries. There were 11,900 places in free-time centers for children in the lower levels of the school, and about 6,000 places in family day nurseries. Thus day care facilities offered by society cater to only a minor proportion of parents who are already gainfully employed. If to this we add the day care requirements of parents who are studying or who apply for work, the discrepancy between supply and demand becomes still larger.

In its former report "The Pre-School," the commission discussed three alternatives of increasing the number of pre-school places. The trend up to now seems to be nearest the lowest of those three alternatives, 70,000 children in day nurseries in the year 1975. To 1980 the commission discussed two alternatives, full cover of the need and half cover. Full cover seemed unrealistic because of the preschool staff available. Half cover should require 150,000 places in day nurseries in 1980. The trend of the Budget and Finance Bill of 1974 concerning the years 1972-1974 means that there should be 112,000 places in day nurseries in the year 1980. This means that 37 percent of the need for day nurseries could be covered.

From July 1, 1974, the state operating grant will be increased to 6,500 Kr per place. Besides, the Parliament has decided that the operating grant shall be paid per number of children enrolled, instead of, as earlier, per number of places. This will mean a quite considerable increase of the operating grant. Therefore it seems probable that we will cover between 40 and 50 percent of the need for day nursery places in the year 1980.

Concerning the free-time centers, the number of places available in the year 1963 covered about 16 percent of the need together with the number of places in family day nurseries for school children. The trend of the Budget and Finance Bill of 1974 indicates that there will be about 41,000 children in

Table 13-2. Number of Places in Day Nurseries, Free-Time Centers and Family Day Nurseries, July 1, 1960-1974

Year	Day Nurseries	Free Time Centers	Family Day Nurseries	Total Number	Children in Nursery School
1960	10,300	2,400	4,000	16,700	38,400
1965	11,900	3,000	8,000	22,900	52,100
1970	33,000	6,500	32,000	71,500	86,000
1971	41,000	9,000	41,500	91,500	91,000
1972	46,400	11,900	43,500	101,800	96,000
1973[1]	54,600	14,500	44,500	113,600	101,000
1974[1]	62,800	18,200	51,000	132,000	108,000

[1] Estimated

Source: Budget and Finance Bill of 1974, appendix 7.

free-time centers, covering 28 percent of the need. A more ambitious trend is possible because of the increased state operating grant. But there is a heavy obstacle: We have and will have a big lack of free time centers' pedagogues and nurses, as well as of youth leaders/free time leaders of leisure activities until the year 1980. Therefore we will have to make extraordinary efforts to train people, for instance by training courses arranged by the Labour Market Board and otherwise.

COST AND FINANCING OF DAY CARE

Teaching is provided free in Sweden to children from the time they start the compulsory nine-year comprehensive school at the age of seven, the costs being met jointly by central and local government. From 1975 the general preschool will be introduced and subject to no charge.

The charge for use of a day nursery varies according to parents' income, the number of children in the family, and the number of days per week the child spends there. In 1972 the fee varied between Kr 1 and 34 per day, and it still does for a child to attend day nursery. On average, parents pay Kr 7 per day per child. The average is obtained by reason of the priority accorded by local authorities to the children of unsupported parents, and parents with small income. The costs of building a day nursery vary between Kr 12,000 and Kr 20,000 per place. In new areas, the costs of the outside environment in traditionally designed institutions are Kr 17 and 30 per square meter (about 11 square feet). In 1972 mean operating costs per child per year in a day nursery were about Kr 14,000. The figure for nursery schools was Kr 2,000 per year and for free-time centers Kr 7,800 per child per year.

The state is responsible for the following costs, otherwise the financial responsibility rests with the local authorities. An initial grant of Kr 6,000 per place, plus a loan of Kr 4,000 per place is made, unless the facility in question is built with a state housing loan, in which case only the initial grant is provided. A temporary increased initial grant was paid for those day nursery and free-time centers places which are built during the time October 15, 1973 and December 31, 1974, in order to stimulate the communities to develop day nurseries and free-time centers faster. From October 1, 1973 there is also paid an initial grant for nursery schools of Kr 3,000 per place.

Initial grants are approved and paid by the National Board of Health and Welfare. Loans are approved by the Board and Paid by the National Office for Administrative Rationalization and Economy.

The state operating grant for a child center is Kr 6,500 from July 1, 1974 per place per year for the supervision of children below school age, and Kr 3,250 for those of school age, i.e., free-time centers. The institution must be open for at least five hours per day. It is assumed that the center is under the management of properly qualified personnel, that it is housed in suitable premises equipped with a view to the children's need for rest and sleep, and that the children should receive the requisite number of meals, including cooked meals.

In total, the state answers for approximately 35 percent of the costs of preschool activities, the local authorities for approximately 50 percent, and the parents the rest. The Board of Health and Welfare establishes the number of places per department for which an operating grant shall be made, in the light of the center's available space and the children's age. Operating grants are approved and paid by the Board. No follow-up is made to check compliance with the Board's requirements and recommendations.

ORGANIZATION MODELS FOR DAY CARE

The following organization models for the pre-school can be applied.

Day Nurseries

Infant groups for children of six months through approximately 2½ years of age. Size of group is 8-12 children.

Mixed age "sibling" groups for children of approximately 2½-7 years of age. Different sibling group models can be formed, with 10-12 children.

Day nurseries could also be arranged in groups separated after ages, but the "sibling groups" are being organized more and more in newly built day nurseries.

Nursery schools or part-time groups

Children attending the preschool on a part-time basis (3-5 hours) should be integrated as far as possible in the groups of the day nursery. This recommendation, however, can be put into effect only gradually, owing to the great need for full-time places in the day nurseries, particularly in new residential areas. Separate *part-time groups* (3 hours per day), nursery schools should therefore be arranged for children who, while the day nurseries are being expanded, cannot be offered places in a full-time group. Such part-time groups will also continue to be arranged in districts where this is required by special circumstances, e.g., sparsely populated areas. The nursery school takes one group of twenty children in the morning, and another in the afternoon. Unlike the day nurseries and the free-time centers, nursery schools are closed during the school holidays.

Free-Time Centers

The free-time centers are day nurseries for school children, primarily those in 7-9 age group. Some free-time centers, particularly in Stockholm, are open to children up to the age of fourteen. Size of group is usually fifteen children. In Stockholm groups of twenty children are common.

Family day nurseries, run by
the communities

A family day nursery may not take care of more than four children, the family's own children included. The state operating grant is 35 percent of the operating costs. For the year 1974 it is temporarily increased to 50 percent in order to give more children places in family day care. The right to state operating grant begins, when the day care of children, run by the community, is developed to a special extent.

A NEW EDUCATIONAL PROGRAM

A *new educational program* has been proposed for the preschools and will be proposed for the free-time centers. The central points of this program are the ego development, conceptual development, and communicative capacity of the child. The educational program provides for the staff working in teams, in which all plan their work together and assume responsibility for common decisions, and in which all staff members have pedagogic duties. By their way of cooperating with each other, with the children and the parents, offering concrete examples of how problems and conflicts can be jointly resolved in a democratic manner, they could influence the children to a democratic human interplay. The child learns by imitation and identification. The adult, whether he likes it or not, functions as a model, so that it is important to stress the child's indirect learning process.

As a general characterization of the pedagogic pattern the term "dialogue pedagogics" has been adopted. This means that the educationist sees himself as an individual in an ongoing developmental process. This, in turn, affects the way in which he functions at work with the children. The mutual interplay between adult and child makes it possible to liberate the child's resources. This interplay can subsequently function as a model for the child, since it illustrates the terms of cooperation—namely, to give and take. The adult, the educationist, has in every situation the function of helping the child by structuring its learning opportunities, and expanding its environmental orientation. The child learns by acquiring concrete experience in different fields. The role of the adult is to stimulate and expand the child's growing interest, and to initiate that which is judged to be suitable, but which the child itself is incapable of realizing.

Finally, cooperation with and between parents is of decisive importance. A close contact with all parents is necessary, but there are still many problems how to cooperate and how to stimulate the parents' interest of taking an active part in the life of day nursery, nursery school, and free-time center. And still there are many parents, who for some or another reason won't have contact or don't dare to have contact with the staff. The dialogue and interplay still have to grow strong also with these parents.

THERE ARE STILL MANY PROBLEMS
TO BE SOLVED

After having presented its proposals this summer the Commission on Child Centres has to face two important problems. First it should analyze the programs of training and re-training of the staffs working in preschools and in free-time centers. What should a program look like in order to give people more social consciousness, a better ego comprehension, better communication ability, and an ability to understand how to work with parents not as specialists but as friends and together interested in the specific child? The commission is now experimenting with a training program for nurses in preschool who want to advance in their work and become preschool teachers. It has also built up a training program to people wanting to become nurses in day nurseries, with the framework of labor market training.

The other problem is as important. That is, what shall children of school age do in the summer? There are few summer camps in Sweden. Many children ought to be meanfully taken care of also in the summer. Here there are experimental activities ongoing. Communities, societies, and unions are trying to find ways to renew the older types of summer camps and also to integrate parents very much in the children's summer life.

Day care of children thus is a very complex field. We need money and people so that many more children could get better conditions of living; we need adults who want to work in a democratic way and who understand their roles in the interplay with each other and with the children. We are just in the beginning; but perhaps the children of the eighties will have much better circumstances than the children of the sixties and also the seventies.

Chapter 14

Sex Education in Sweden

Thorsten Sjovall

INTRODUCTION

It should be noted that Sweden, by the end of the nineteenth century, was a poor agricultural country in which malnutrition and infectious diseases, particularly tuberculosis, were killing a substantial part of a population which earlier during that century had been decreased by large-scale emigration. Thus, Sweden has never had a population problem of the kind we are faced with in the developing countries today. From conditions in many respects comparable to those prevailing in the presently developing countries, Sweden has reached its position of a highly industrialized welfare state within a rather short time-span, i.e., from the close of the last century through the first third of the twentieth century.

THE SWEDISH ASSOCIATION FOR SEX EDUCATION

Background, Foundation, and First Aims

When the Swedish Association for Sex Education (RFSU) was founded in 1933, it happened at a time when a strong and pioneer-spirited labor movement was for the first time coming into substantial political power. Various socio-political reforms and countrywide educational organizations covering all strata of the population were already in existence or in the making. Radical views in regard to the relations between the sexes and the status of women had been voiced in Sweden already some hundred years previously by a few writers, and literary proponents of a more honest and open approach to sex life multiplied around the turn of the century. A couple of them were sued, and the trials stirred up heated public debate. The writers were soon followed by some devoted and eloquent politicians, educators, and physicians.

Out of the debris of the First World War, an intellectual climate emerged which was considerably influenced by the theories of Marx and Freud, both of whom, although from different angles, were spokesmen of radical views in sexual matters.

Thus, by the early thirties the soil was well prepared for organizing the adherents of such opinions to concerted action. This was the first and main purpose behind the foundation of the RFSU, which was built as a nationwide organization on the pattern of such idealistic organizations as the Workers Educational Movement, the Movement for Adult Public Education, the Temperance Movement, etc. The RFSU was from the start financially self-supporting by operating a sales company for contraceptives in which the Association is the only stockholder, at a time when the sale and advertising of contraceptives were still prohibited by law making them difficult and humiliating for the general public to secure. Only for the last few years has a modest grant from public funds been received by the RFSU towards meeting the expenses for such clinical services which are not covered by the community.

It is worth noticing that the name given to the RFSU emphasized a rather broad approach to the whole field of applied sexology, with an explicit recognition of the basic importance of the educational element. The original formulation of aims comprised such proposals as the introduction of sex education in all schools including universities, the legal authorization of instrumental contraception, a broadening of the possibilities of obtaining legal abortion and sterilization, other law reforms as motivated by the findings of modern scientific sexology, and the establishment of centers for providing public advice and guidance in sexual matters all over the county.

Methods, Activities, and Later Development

In the early years the main method of promoting these aims was thousands of public lectures given all over the country, a good many of them literally in the bush, by the vivacious founder of the organization, Mrs. Elise Ottesen-Jensen. Thus, the movement was started very much by approaching the average man and woman in a direct and personal way. To this groundwork, carried on for several years, were later added formal seminars and courses for doctors, teachers, youth leaders, and paramedical personnel by an expanding cadre of lecturers from various professions. A correspondence service for education and advice was established, and a network of shops for selling contraceptives was developed, as well as a purchase system by mail order. A large series of publications have been issued through the years such as pamphlets, books, and a periodical, which first appeared under the name of "The Sexual Issue," later to be changed to the "Popular Journal of Psychology and Sexual

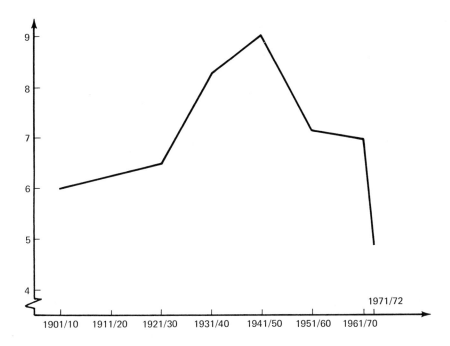

Figure 14-1. Marriage Rates per 1000 Mean Population

Knowledge." Many of these publications have stimulated public debate, and some of them have notably influenced socio-political reforms and authoritative decisions.

These activities were met by reactions ranging from enthusiasm to skepticism to indignation. Battles were fought, resulting in the stimulation of more debate, making the RFSU known all over the country, eventually to make it generally respected. The way was gradually opened for the RFSU to act as an efficient pressure group by being recognized as a consultant in official action within its scope of interest, making it possible to submit proposals directly to appropriate authorities.

During the first twenty-five years of its existence the RFSU had the satisfaction of seeing most of the aims put forward in the original program materialize. Legal restriction on advertising and selling contraceptives was repealed. Sex education was made compulsory by law at all age levels of the public school. Planned parenthood as a human right was accepted in principle by official authorities. So was the responsibility of such authorities to provide

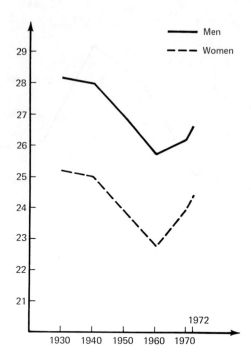

Figure 14-2. Median Age at First Marriage

services for advice and supplies. The abortion law was liberalized by several steps and the services for implementation of the law were taken over by the communities.

The original idea was for the RFSU to provide a nationwide network of clinics for sexual and contraceptive advice through its local branch organizations. At the height of this development, regular activities of this kind existed at eleven different places, mainly in the southern part of the country. Since this responsibility has now been recognized, at least in principle, by the public health services, the RFSU has retained only a couple of model clinics as a source of basic knowledge and experience for what is now felt to be the main task of the organization, namely to provide expert information and proposals within the field of general sexology and its social implications. One of these model clinics is in cooperation with the WHO worldwide scheme for the investigation of human fertility regulation.

Mrs. Jensen was one of the founders, and the RFSU one of the founder nations of the International Planned Parenthood Federation in 1952. Since then, mainly through personal initiatives of Mrs. Jensen, the RFSU, and

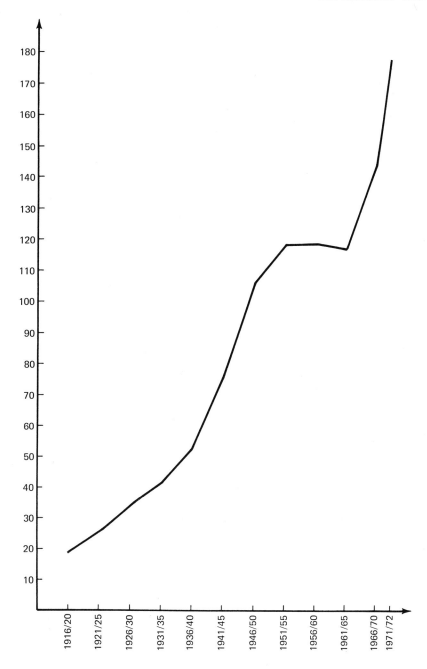

Figure 14-3. Divorce Rates per 100,000 Mean Population

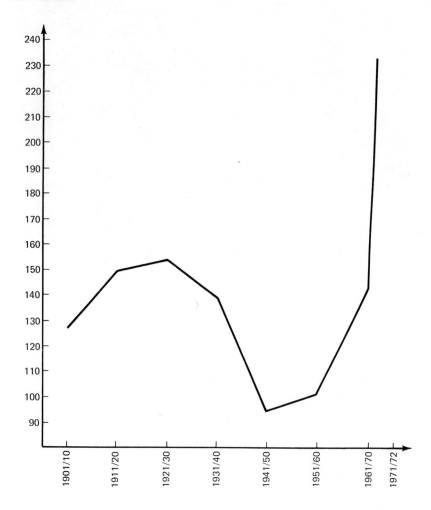

Figure 14-4. Out of Wedlock Births per 1000 Live Births
1901-1972

later the Swedish nation, have played a leading role in international planned parenthood work. At present, when the Swedish population is becoming increasingly aware of the international problems in this field, this development has considerably increased the respectability of the RFSU inside Sweden, thus broadening its possibilities for efficient action.

Rapid social progress, increasing engagement of public authorities, new contraceptive methods, etc., have considerably changed the original tasks and responsibilities of the RFSU. In early 1974, the following items were at the foreground of attention: A revision and reformulation of the ideological basis

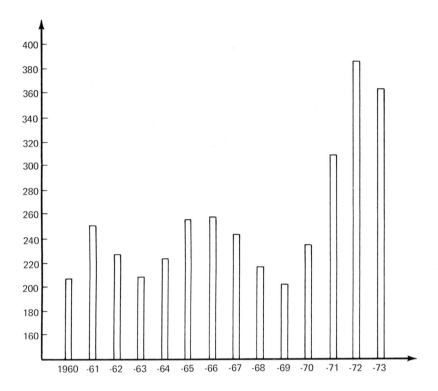

Figure 14-5. Import of Condoms
1960-1973

and the aims of the Association in order to provide clear and specific answers in a pluralistic and rapidly changing society on the RFSU standpoint in various controversial matters. And, closely related to this, a clarification of the relationship between such standpoints and aims on the one hand, and the business interests of a flourishing sales company on the other. At the clinical level, there is a shift of emphasis from giving just contraceptive advice to rendering qualified psychosexual services as well, for which there is an enormous demand, so far hardly approached by the public health system. These activities provide the Association with badly needed in-depth knowledge of current sexological problems in society. Training activities in cooperation with state authorities, aiming, for instance, at qualifying midwives for planned parenthood work, are expanding. Increasing attention is being devoted to certain neglected groups of the population and their sexual and intimate relationship problems. Such groups are, for example, the handicapped, the inmates of various institutions, and immigrants.

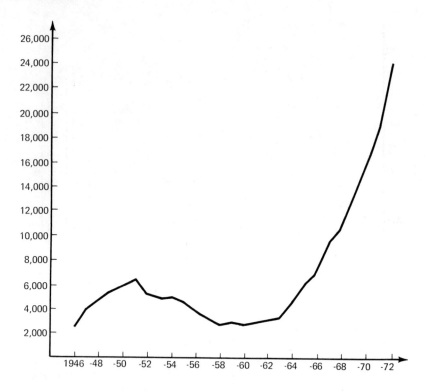

Figure 14-6. Total Number of Legal Abortions
1946-1972

SOME RELEVANT LAWS AND REFORMS

Emergence of "The Welfare State"

The Thirties and Forties. Not much happened in this area during the first three decades of the century. The last forty years, however, are conspicuous for an intense welfare reform activity most of which has some bearing on sex and family life. Two seemingly contradictory lines of thought underlie this policy. One was an increasing public awareness of the welfare and psychological aspects of sex in its own right stimulated by, inter alia, the radical ideology of the RFSU and aiming at individual sexual adaptability and satisfaction, voluntary birth control, and child spacing. The other was a concern, in authoritative circles, for a threatening underpopulation, pronounced in the thirties, then gradually waning into nonexistence at present. However, on the wave of this underpopulation concern a State Population Commission was

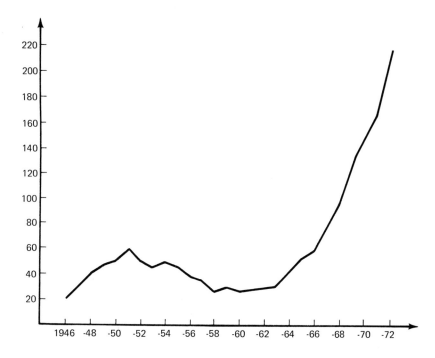

Figure 14-7. Legal Abortions per 1000 Live Births
1946-1972

appointed in 1935. During the following three years the Commission released seventeen publications, as a result of which the Parliament decided on state loans for young couples' settling expenses, the establishment of a nationwide network of centers for free maternal and child care, free obstetrical care, maternity allowance, and increased tax deductions for families with children.

In 1941 a new State Population Commission was appointed, which by 1947 had submitted another nineteen publications. In 1942 and 1943 the Parliament made provisions for certain home services for gainfully employed mothers and decided on state allowances for day nurseries. In 1946 free meals and free educational material at public schools were introduced, and also facilities for rest and recreation for mothers and children. In 1948 the tax deduction for families with children was exchanged for cash allowances for each child.

Although all these reforms were partly aiming at increasing birth-rates and faster population growth, no such effects are traceable when they have now been in force for some thirty years, a notable example of the complexities involved in population changes and the difficulties meeting demographic pre-dictions.

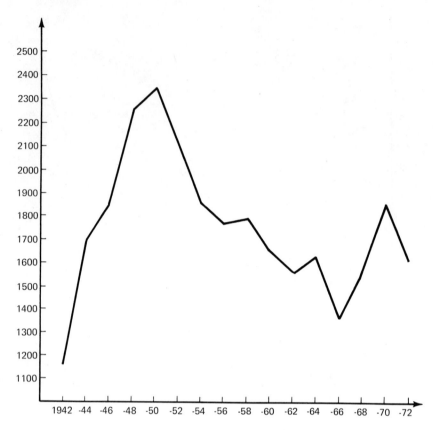

Figure 14-8. Number of Sterilizations
1942-1972

The Fifties and the Sixties. During these twenty years the reform work was mainly concentrated on the social insurance system. Obligatory health insurance was introduced and improved, national basic old age pensions and supplementary pensions as well as cash allowances for children increased.

In 1960 state allowances were allocated on a tentative basis for the establishment of community family guidance centers. These are designed for giving advice and guidance in matters of sexual, marital, and family relationships including problems of contraception and unwanted pregnancies under the leadership of a social worker with consultative support of doctors, psychologists, and lawyers. So far this possibility has been utilized by the communities to a limited extent only, mainly because of shortage of competent personnel.

In 1968 the National Board of Medicine and the National Board of Social Affairs were amalgamated into the National Board of Health and Welfare.

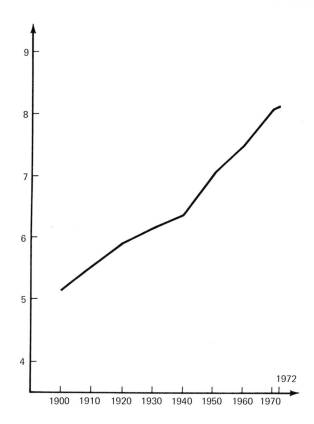

Figure 14-9. Total Population
1900-1972

This reflected, at an administrative level to begin with, the increasing awareness of the close connection between social welfare and public health.

WOMAN EMANCIPATION

The following list gives some of the important steps towards equal rights of Swedish women during this century.

1902 The National Association of Women's Vote founded.
1909 Women eligible for municipal bodies.
1919 Women given parliamentary vote and eligibility.
1921 First woman elected to Upper Chamber of Parliament.
1922 First three women elected to Lower Chamber.

1925 Competence Act, passed by Parliament in 1923, in force stating the principle, but not the implementation, of equal pay in civil service.

1939 Law prohibiting dismissal of women employees on account of engagement and marriage.

1945 Competence Act of 1925 superseded by new laws establishing equality for women in civil service.

1946 Law prohibiting dismissal of employees on account of pregnancy and/or childbirth.

1947 First woman Cabinet member (without portfolio).

1954 Ulla Lindstrom appointed Cabinet member, one of the main instigators of Swedish investments in international planned parenthood work.

1956 First woman ambassador (to New Delhi).

1960 First three women ordained to assistant curates in Swedish State Church.

1964 Woman allowed, if she so wishes, to keep her own family name at marriage.

1970 Law stipulating equal paternal inheritance rights for out of wedlock children.

1974 Family legislation reforms towards economical equalization of spouses as well as unmarried couples permanently living together.

RECENT DEVELOPMENT

In the early seventies the fusion of central social and medical administration started to extend to the periphery, mainly in terms of a more systematized teamwork organization being established at various institutions in the field. This development implies that a greater responsibility is being delegated to auxiliaries in an integrated care system.

In 1969 a State Commission was appointed to review marriage and family legislation. Some proposals of this Commission are in force from 1974 to the effect that various procedures for both marriage and divorce are simplified. Furthermore, most of the social and economic benefits for married couples and their children mentioned are extended also to couples living permanently together without being married and to their children.

MATERNAL AND CHILD CARE

In 1944 provisions were made for establishing a nationwide network of community maternal and child health centers. They are aiming at protecting the physical and mental health, free of charge, of children of preschool age and their mothers. The services include explicitly also guidance and advice in sexual and contraceptive matters for the mothers to be given by doctors and midwives. In 1965 an addition was made consisting of free specialist consultations considered to be of special importance for the prenatal care of mothers.

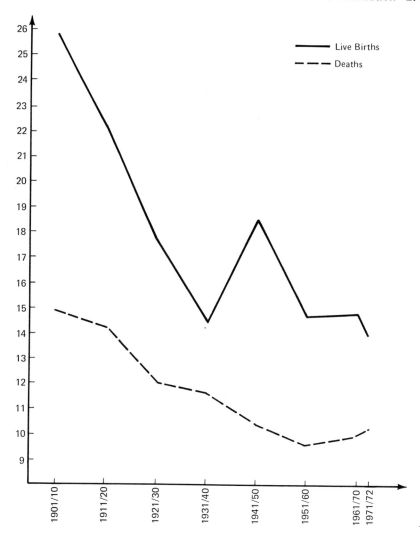

Figure 14-10. Births and Deaths per 1000 Mean Population

SEXOLOGICAL ASPECTS

Contraception

The legal ban on advertising and selling contraceptives stipulated by a law of 1910 was repealed in 1938. Before that, as in many other countries with a similarly restrictive legislation, this was circumvented in many ways with a more or less silent consent of the authorities, but the legalization represented a

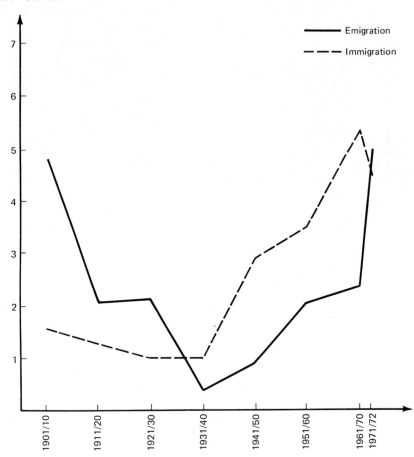

Figure 14-11. Emigration and Immigration per 1000 Mean Population
1901-1972

considerable ethical and practical improvement. Among other things, a responsible quality control was made possible, and testing of barrier rubber products was prescribed by law. Such products are, however, not manufactured in Sweden, so that state control has been added to the manufacturer's control. Since 1938, there has been extensive propaganda for contraception, particularly through the RFSU, in accordance with the principle that this is the matter of choice for avoiding unwanted pregnancies, and, as far as the condom is concerned, for diminishing the risk of contracting venereal disease. The main methods recommended and used were diaphragms and condoms until, in 1964, the hormonal drugs were legally accepted as contraceptives, followed, in 1966, by a legalization of the IUDs. The IUDs were to begin with less popular until recently when the introduction of the metal devices considerably increased the number of

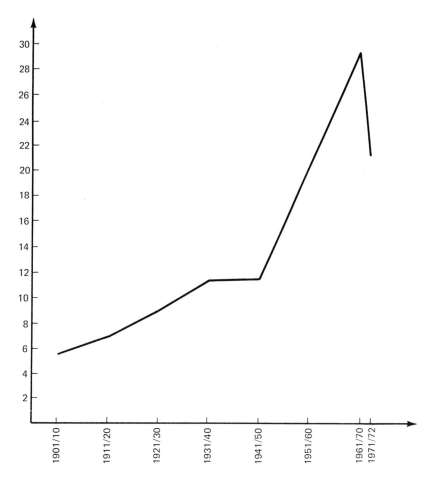

Figure 14-12. Delivered Girls under 18 per 1000 Deliveries
1901-1972

users. The condom has retained its position as the most widely preferred contraceptive, whereas the number of diaphragm users has dropped notably after the appearance of the orals. Those are provided by medical prescription only, and instruction for medical supervision is issued by the National Board of Health and Welfare.

However, the facilities for obtaining contraceptive advice and a method of individual choice are still far from satisfactory. This is particularly true of those methods requiring a direct involvement of physicians, i.e., orals and IUDs. In principle and by stipulation, such services should be obtainable at the maternal and child health centers, but this has so far remained more theoretical than real. Even in Stockholm a woman may have to wait months to start on oral

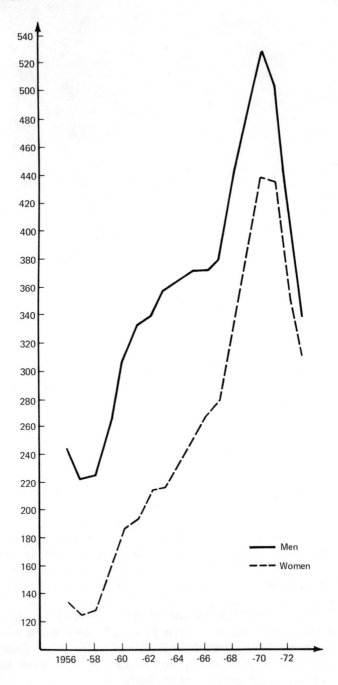

Figure 14-13. Incidence of Gonorrhoea per 100,000 Mean Population

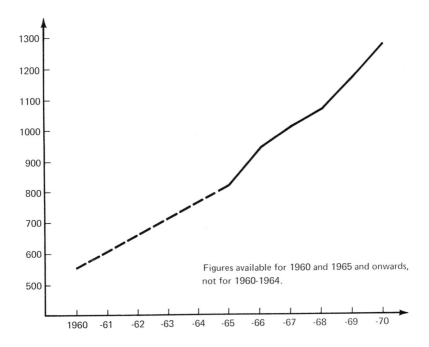

Figure 14-14. Total Admissions to Mental Hospitals per 100,000 Mean Population
1960-1970

contraception today. On the request of the RFSU the National Board of Health and Welfare appointed a committee which in 1971 submitted a proposal recommending that special clinic hours for contraceptive services should be organized, free of charge, within the framework of the maternal and child care system, these services to be open also for men. It was also recommended that greater responsibility in the field should, after appropriate training, be allocated to certain auxiliaries such as nurses and midwives. Since then a few courses in contraceptive techniques have been arranged for trained midwives.

Several years ago the municipal School Direction of the City of Stockholm established a separate clinic for sexual and contraceptive advice for pupils, and this initiative appears to have filled a great need and has, so far, aroused surprisingly little opposition.

The sale and distribution of contraceptives are regulated by a law of 1959. A stipulation that this could occur only after special authorization was repealed in 1970. The law permits the sale of condoms through vending machines in streets and public places and this way of distribution has expanded greatly during the last few years.

The RFSU sales company has achieved great experience and skill in marketing and advertising contraceptives within the country, and is now called on as a consultant to the IPPF for its recent worldwide project of community-based distribution of contraceptives.

Abortion

A matter of major concern for the Population Commissions during the thirties and forties was the steadily increasing number of clandestine abortions. To bring this problem under control was the main reason for a step-by-step extension of the possibilities for obtaining legal abortion with the explicit hope in this way to reduce the total amount of interruptions to a minimum. Under the present law of 1938, amended in 1941, 1942, 1946, and 1963, a pregnancy may be interrupted if:

1. childbirth would entail serious danger to life or health of a woman suffering from illness, a physical defect, or weakness as testified by medical and medico-social authorities.
2. there is reason to assume that childbirth and/or child care would seriously damage a woman's physical or psychic strength in view of her living conditions and other special circumstances.
3. a woman has become pregnant as a result of rape, other criminal coercion, or incestual sexual intercourse, or if she is mentally retarded, legally insane, or under fifteen years of age at the time of impregnation.
4. there is reason to assume that either parent of the expected child might transmit to the offspring hereditary insanity, imbecility, serious disease, or a serious physical handicap.
5. there is reason to assume that the expected child will suffer from serious disease or deformity resulting from injury during fetal life.

In 1946 state allowances were allocated, and instructions released, for community abortion advice centers, staffed by doctors and social workers, where advice and help are provided free of charge. There are at present some thirty of these centers distributed over the country.

As can be seen from the formulation of the law, particularly item 2 above, it allows for considerable flexibility of interpretation. This has been reflected by large variations in the yearly numbers of applicants as well as in the percentage of applications granted in different parts of the country. This again has been the subject of extensive public debate in which the opinion was loudly voiced that a free and personal choice of the woman concerned should be given priority in deciding the fate of her pregnancy. The number of applicants in 1960 was around 4,000, of which a little more than 60 percent were granted, whereas the corresponding figures for 1967 were about 10,000 and 90 percent, and for 1973 about 25,000 and 97 percent respectively. Such fluctuations in the

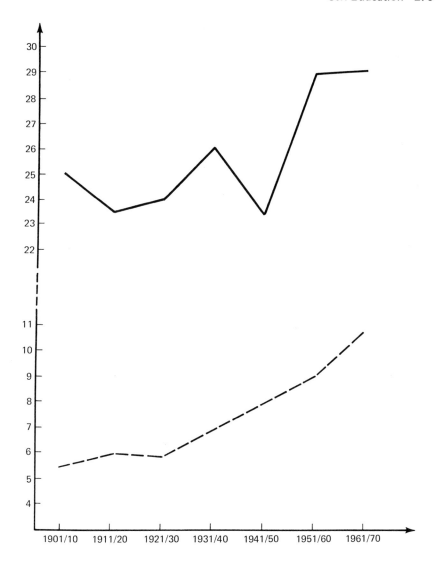

Figure 14-15. Suicides per 100,000 Mean Population

application of the law have caused the demand for a new formulation securing better uniformity and justice of implementation. In 1965 a State Commission was appointed for this purpose and a proposal was submitted to the Ministry of Justice under the title "The Right to Abortion" in 1971. As can be seen from the title, the idea was to decriminalize abortion and to state the right of the

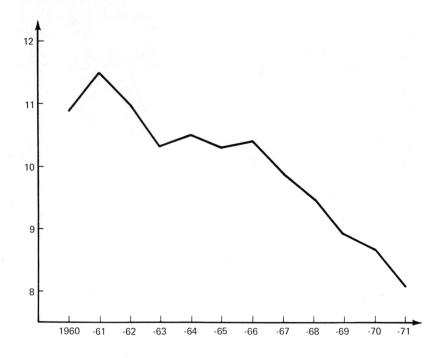

Figure 14-16. Cases Brought to Attention of Temperance Councils per 1000 Inhabitants

1960-1971

woman herself to the final decision. However, the proposal stirred a very heated public debate, and because of this, and pending the result of complementary deliberations and investigations, the matter has not yet been submitted for final decision by the Parliament.

Sterilization

Prevention of eugenic diseases was the main reason for the present law of 1941, stipulating that sterilization may be performed if:

1. there is reason to assume that the subject would transmit to his or her offspring hereditary mental disease, imbecility or another serious disease or physical handicap (i.e., blindness or deaf-muteness).
2. because of mental derangement or an asocial way of life the subject is found obviously unable to assume responsibility for the proper rearing of children.
3. pregnancy would entail serious danger to a woman's life or health.

In the last few years the law has been criticized for leaning too heavily on deficiency and illness, thus not making sufficient provisions for free choice and personal motivation on the part of the subject, or for male sterilization. Therefore, a State Commission for a revision of the law towards expansion and liberalization was appointed in 1972.

Castration

The castration law of 1944 is aiming at such forms of criminal or deviant behavior which presumably are connected with a too strong or abnormally directed sex urge. The law provides for the operation if:

1. the subject because of his sex urge may reasonably be assumed to commit such crimes that entail serious danger or damage to somebody else.
2. the subject because of abnormal direction or strength of his sex urge is the victim of severe mental suffering or other serious disadvantage.

This law has been executed in a very limited number of cases so far, and opinions are divided as to whether it has any real justification.

Sexual Deviations

In principle, sexual deviations are considered to be symptoms of a mental disturbance or retardation. Yet, some of them are subject to legal interventions under the Penal Code. Any sexual intercourse with children under fifteen years of age and homosexual activities with anybody under eighteen years of age are punishable.

To the category of sexual deviations, or the exploitation of such, belongs what in the present law is vaguely referred to as "offenses against a general sense of decency." To the extent that such offenses are subject to a more or less public display they are punishable. In 1969 two State Commissions released publications with some relevance to these problems under the titles "The Film Censorship and Responsibility" and "The Limits of the Free Word." A case in point here is pornography. The overall tolerance towards this phenomenon has increased considerably in later years. Pornographic publications can be obtained almost everywhere over the counter. According to recent information there are at present some 350 of them on the market, corresponding to a yearly turnover of about $30,000,000. In regard to pornography the present legal standpoint is that it is not forbidden but individuals should be spared from inadvertent exposure to pornographic displays. The latter stipulation has some legal bearing on what might be shown in shop windows, etc.

It should be emphasized that the unprecedently free display of sexual matters in word and picture during the last decade or so has not caused any significant increase in sexual offenses under the Penal Code.

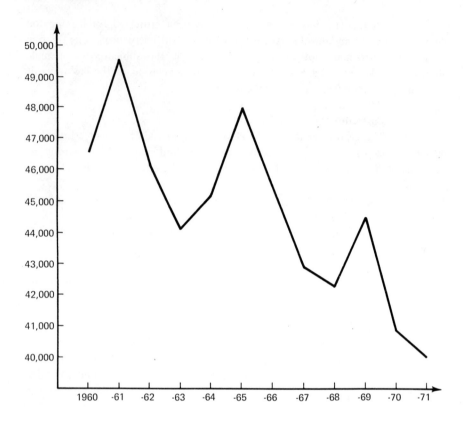

Figure 14-17.   Sentenced Offenders of Drunkenness Laws
Total Numbers—1960-1971

Venereal Disease

A law of 1918 stipulated that anyone who knows or suspects himself to be afflicted with venereal disease in a contagious stage is punishable for marrying and having sexual intercourse, as well as for refraining from seeking medical treatment which is free of charge. Special clinical services were established for this purpose. The doctor is legally obliged, in cooperation with the patient, to trace and disclose the source of contagion. Since 1969 this "lex veneris" is incorporated in a general law dealing with such contagious diseases which require special intervention on the part of society.

In Sweden gonorrhea is by far the most common venereal disease. As in many other countries the incidence has fluctuated considerably during the last fifty years to reach a summit in 1970 with nearly 40,000 reported cases, of which about a third were teenagers. Since then there has been a decrease to about 27,000 reported cases in 1973. The reasons for this are presumably

Figure 14-18.   Beds and New Admissions to Public Institutions for Alcoholics

intensified information, more efficient treatment methods, free sale and increased use of condoms and, coinciding with the falling incidence, an intense
advertising campaign by the RFSU sales company under widely and conspicu-
ously posted slogans such as "Tonite 86 Swedes contract gonorrhea. Use the
condom."

EDUCATION

The School System
The beginning of an organized public school system dates back to

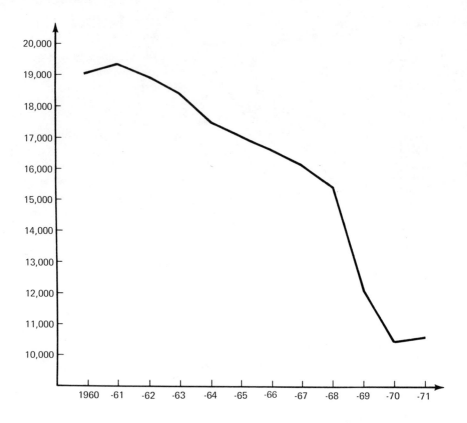

Figure 14-19. Total Numbers of Individuals Subject to Qualified Interventions by Temperance Councils

1960-1971

the eighteenth century leading up to the first public school ordinance of 1842. This stipulated six years compulsory school and the establishment of public schools in every primary community. Out of a set of school reforms the most important of which took place in 1905, 1927, and 1962, the present school system developed. This is based on the comprehensive public school divided into a lower, an intermediate, and an upper stage each of three years duration. After this, alternatives for further noncompulsory education are a two years preparatory vocational school with social, economic and technical branches, and a three years gymnasium school with some twenty different branches aiming at studies at university level. The present curriculum plans for the comprehensive public school and for the gymnasium school were issued by the National Board of Education in 1969 and 1970 respectively.

It should be noted that the administration of the entire social welfare and the medical care system, and of the educational system up to the university level is the responsibility of the communities with state financial support.

Among the aims set for the comprehensive school the following may be quoted: "In a changing society it is not possible and not appropriate to determine precisely and in detail either scope or form of the school work. Therefore, the tasks and responsibilities of the school must be reviewed continually so that they are in accordance with contemporary development." It is within the responsibility of the school "to help and stimulate each pupil to develop, in the best possible way, his inherent propensities both as an individual and as a citizen in a democratic society. This implies putting a strong emphasis on the role of the school in personality development." The school shall provide for each pupil "a basic education which transmits such skill, knowledge, habits, attitudes and values which are of importance for his maturation and personal development, and for his ability to adapt to the present and future society, and to function therein both as a professional individual and as a citizen." Furthermore, the school shall "stimulate the pupils to debate, and to query prevailing conditions."

Sex Education at School

The above presentation of the legal and reformatory background and development pertaining to sex and family life in the Swedish society may give a fair impression of the complexities and responsibilities involved. This, in connection with some of the just quoted aims of the comprehensive school, should make it quite clear that such a crucially important domain of human relationships as sex could not simply remain left out of the school curricula. Consequently, the decision on compulsory sex education in schools was taken by the Parliament in 1956, and guidelines for implementation were issued by the National Board of Education in 1956. This "Handbook on Sex Instruction in Swedish Schools" has the following chapter which reads: The need for sex instruction in Schools; General considerations on sex instruction in schools; Sexual problems of the pre-school child; Preliminary sex instruction at the junior stage with lesson examples; Sex instruction for ages 11-13 with lesson examples; Sex instruction for ages 14-16 with lesson examples; Sex instruction for ages 17-20; Advice and direction on dealing with pupils engaging in undesired sexual practices; Measures by the school in proved cases of intercourse between pupils and when a school-girl becomes pregnant; Survey of teaching material.

The curricula at different levels are outlined as follows:

Age 7-10: How the sexes differ, where children come from, and how they develop before they are born, how children are born, how children depend on their mothers and fathers and their homes.

Age 11-13: Differences between the sexes, structure and function of the sexual organs, puberty, menstruation, "wet dreams," masturbation, conception, pregnancy and development of the fetus, labor, determination of sex, twins, "traumatic experiences" during pregnancy.

Age 14-16: Revision of previous items as required, sex and youth, moral considerations, abstention from sexual relations during adolescence, illegitimate children, spontaneous and induced abortion, venereal diseases, contraceptives, sterilization, the menopause, sexual abnormalities.

Age 17-20: Revision of previous items as required, menstruation and hormones, moral and social aspects of sex, welfare measures to help setting up a family, welfare measures during pregnancy, confinement and nursing, welfare measures for the care and upbringing of children and adolescents, impotence and frigidity, sex education at home.

The implementation of this educational program did not correspond to the expectations of the reformers or to those of an even more sophisticated population. The teachers were found to be badly prepared for the task. In view of what became gradually known about the actual sex behavior of Swedish youth as well as the increasing candor by which intimate human relationships were exposed in easily available verbal and pictorial material, the handbook was criticized for being old-fashioned and moralizing.

These and other circumstances resulted by 1964 in the appointment of a State Commission for a revision of the whole field of general sex education, both at school and at the adult level. This Commission, after nearly ten years at work, is expected to submit its final proposals to the Ministry of Education soon.

THE 1964 STATE COMMISSION
ON SEX EDUCATION

Aims

The full Swedish name given to this Commission is in English: "The Commission on Aspects of Sex and Living Together in Teaching and Educational Work." It seems appropriate to describe it in order to give a correct impression of the scope envisaged. Below it shall be referred to as the Commission.

From the directives given the Commission by the Ministry of Education the following passages may be quoted:

The Commission shall consider experiences so far gained about sex education in schools and about educational work among young people and in public education movements as well as findings and experiences within this and related fields from medical, psychological and social research. In their deliberations about what kind of

values on which this teaching should be founded . . . the Commission
shall observe that such values must be in accordance with those on
which the over-all ethical education at school is built.

In the course of its work the Commission has published a series of
investigations, referred to below, and they have been called upon as consultants
on a number of issues within their field of competence. In this way a continuous
dialogue has been carried on between the Commission and various outside
experts as well as with the public over mass media.

On the basis of this material the Commission has formulated, in their
final publications, the aims of sex education at school as follows:

The pupil shall by being taught about sex and human relationships:

a. achieve knowledge on anatomy, physiology, psychology, ethics
and social conditions in order to obtain a better basis for experiencing sex life as a source of happiness and joy in relation to another
human being, and for achieving a feeling of living together in a spirit
of mutual responsibility and concern for one another.

b. obtain a factual and comprehensive orientation as to different
values and ways of living relevant to sex life, both basic values which
according to aims and guidelines for the comprehensive school shall
be emphasized and promoted, and controversial values which,
according to the same aims and guidelines, shall be illuminated
without any standpoint being taken on the part of the school.

c. develop a capacity for understanding that sex is an integrated part
of human life which is inextricably interwoven with personality
development, relations of human mutuality, and social structure.

d. achieve a greater degree of general awareness and thereby a better
possibility of taking a personal standpoint at different levels of
maturity and sexual experience.

Investigations

The Commission has organized five investigations in its field of
interest and has reported about them in five separate printed publications. These
investigations were regarded as a necessary source of information for the work as
well as for a reference for the final publications. Space does not permit a full
review of them, but titles, year of publication and some figures from each of
them are presented below.

On Sex Life in Sweden, 1969. This investigation aimed at giving
some broad information about attitudes, knowledge and behavior with regard to
sex life in a statistically representative sample of the total Swedish population
between eighteen and sixty years of age.

Ninety-five percent of the total sample had had sexual intercourse. The median age at first intercourse was 17.5. This age had decreased by one year between 1920 and 1950. Two percent with, as compared with 4 percent without heterosexual experience, admitted to having homosexual desires.

Eight-five percent of the total sample felt that "being in love" legitimizes premarital intercourse. Sixty-two percent were in favor of premarital sexual experience for men, and 54 percent for women. In contrast, about 90 percent felt that faithfulness in marriage is absolutely essential, and 90 percent of those married also reported faithful behavior throughout married life. Eighteen percent of married men and 45 percent of married women said that their respective spouses were their only sexual contact.

A question about the number of sexual partners within the last month gave the result that 87 percent reported one partner, 6 percent two, 4 percent three to five, and 2 percent more than five.

Questions about the last intercourse revealed a negative correlation between subjective sexual satisfaction and lax contraceptive habits, promiscuous habits, lack of emotional involvement with the partner, and consumption of pornography. Of last intercourses, only 9 percent were aiming at conception.

Seventy-one percent of the total sample felt that the use of a contraceptive is mandatory at each intercourse not aiming at conception. Twenty-seven percent reporting on their last intercourse did not take contraceptive precautions although conception was not desired. Nineteen percent of those practicing contraception at this occasion used non-reliable methods.

It requires 1,100 intercourses to produce one Swedish baby!

By certain criteria defining "sexual restrictedness," there was a positive correlation of this factor with female sex, rural residence, lower income, less education, and regular church attendance.

Eighty-six percent of the total sample were in favor of sex education at school. Eighty-nine percent felt that young people should be taught the use of contraceptives. Among those 18-20 years old the median age for achieving such knowledge was 13 years. Sixty-five percent of the boys and 36 percent of the girls received it from their contemporaries. Only 11 percent of the age brackets falling within the time-span of compulsory sex education received such education at school. Thirty-five percent of those which, by this criterion, should have had sex education at school said they had none. Seventy-five percent of the total sample felt that the main responsibility for sex education lies with the parents.

Given four alternatives as to the desirable attitude of the school in regard to sexual behavior in adolescence the result was as follows:

The school should:	Age 18-23	Age 24-60
Teach abstinence, fight other attitudes	4%	20%
Teach all attitudes, recommend abstinence	33%	47%
Teach all attitudes, leave conclusions to pupils	60%	31%
Teach all attitudes, recommend "freedom	3%	2%

Sexual Knowledge at the Upper State of the Comprehensive School, 1969. In the comprehensive school all teaching in the lower and intermediate stages is in principle assigned to the class teacher, whereas in the upper stage it is divided in the different subjects with a different teacher for each of them. Sex education at school has never been conceptualized as being condensed, at any stage, into a separate subject, say "sexology," in the curriculum. The idea has been to integrate a rather vaguely defined area of experience and knowledge into already existing subjects in roughly such a way that "the facts of life" or factual sex instruction belong to biology, the sexological aspects of social life to civics, and the ethical and normative aspects to religion. The individual teacher of different subjects is given considerable freedom as to his personal choice of approach to sex education in consultation with fellow teachers and the headmaster.

This investigation was an inquiry to a representative sample of ninth-graders as to their experience and opinions of sex education in general and what they had received in this respect in particular. They were not questioned about their actual sexual behavior.

Ninety-three percent of the total sample said they had had no information on sexual matters in biology, 53 percent in religion, and 42 percent in civics. Eighty-three percent reported about information on contraceptives.

Ninety-eight percent were in favor of being taught about sexual facts at school, and 82 percent wanted more of such teaching than they had actually received. The corresponding figures for sexual aspects of social life were 96 percent and 82 percent respectively. Sixty-five percent said they wanted more discussion on norms and ethics.

Asked whether different opinions regarding sex relationships at their own age level had been discussed at lessons the answers were as follows: Yes extensively; 5 percent; Yes to some extent: 38 percent; No: 46 percent.

There was a definite correlation between the quantity of sex education reported and the sexual knowledge achieved as measured by a specially constructed knowledge test.

Among various sources of information outside school, parents, contemporaries other than schoolmates, and books ranked highest, the parents topping the list of girls and contemporaries other than schoolmates that of boys. A preference for the parents was expressed by both sexes. As to the choices of instructor at school, 31 percent would prefer a teacher and 43 percent an extramural expert. Fifty-four percent would like the opportunity to discuss sexual matters confidentially with some authoritative adult (61 percent of the girls and 49 percent of the boys).

Sixty-five percent of the total sample felt that "going steady" is a legitimate basis for sexual relationships. Only 6 percent were adherents of sexual abstinence in adolescence. There was no correlation between such normative attitudes and the amount of sex education received at school.

Fifty-five percent were of the opinion that the school does not condemn sexual relationships in adolescence, but encourages personal responsibility and individual decision.

To the question at what age level instruction about the items of intercourse and contraceptives should occur the answers were as follows:

	Lower	Intermediate	Upper
Intercourse	8%	38%	49%
Contraception	1%	22%	74%

It should be noted that, at the time of the investigation, the instruction on sex education at school stipulated that the bulk of such information should be provided in the ninth grade.

Sexual Knowledge at the Gymnasium School, 1969. Sex education in the gymnasium school is provided in "hours at disposal" and five to six of these hours are, according to the plan, envisaged to be devoted to the subject in each of the three grades.

This investigation was made on a representative sample of the second gymnasium grade. Procedure and results were essentially similar to those of the previous investigation. The extent of information obtained was reported as follows:

"Facts of life"	74%
Social implications of sex life	36%
Sexual norms	15%

Overall sexual knowledge was found to be somewhat better at this stage than among the ninth-graders of the comprehensive school, better for girls than for boys, and better for those "going steady" than for others.

An attitude of "freedom" was more pronounced here (26 percent) than in the comprehensive school. Sixty percent felt that the gymnasium school recommended personal freedom of choice in sexual matters. However, the average gymnasium pupil envisaged his schoolmates as being more "free" in their attitude than he considered himself to be. Thirty-one percent felt that information on contraception, and 47 percent that information on sexual intercourse should be given at the first or intermediate stage of the comprehensive school. Books were reported as the main source of information by both boys and girls.

Inquiry to Teachers at the Ninth Grade of the Comprehensive School About Sex Education, 1969. This inquiry was submitted to all teachers in biology, civics, and religion teaching in the ninth grade of the comprehensive school during the school year 1967-68. Only a few figures can be given here.

	Teachers in:		
	Biology	Religion	Civics
Had training in sex education	60%	36%	30%
Read the Manual for teachers on sex education	88%	48%	45%
Taught about sex	96%	76%	69%
Taught about premarital relationships	85%		
Taught about contraceptives	94%		
Taught about pornography	34%		
Demonstrated contraceptives	28%		

As can be seen, the teachers in biology had taken by far the most of the responsibility on themselves. The information given by them corresponds closely to what was reported by the ninth-graders.

The teachers were asked to what extent they considered sex education difficult and interesting, respectively, and the answers were as follows:

Teachers	Difficult	Interesting
Biology	13%	92%
Religion	36%	86%
Civics	25%	72%

The alternatives regarding the desirable attitude of the school given to the total population were presented to the teachers and this was the result:

The school should:

	Biology	Religion	Civics
Teach abstinence, fight other attitudes	2%	7%	2%
Teach all attitudes, recommend abstinence	46%	55%	39%
Teach all attitudes, leave conclusions	47%	32%	52%
Teach all attitudes, recommend "freedom"	1%	1%	2%
None of the above	1%	2%	2%

This inquiry was sent to a representative sample of some 28,000 relevant teachers. Practically all of these had taught something they themselves categorized as sex education. A survey of the prevalence of such teaching through the entire comprehensive school, according to the information given by the teachers, shows a concentration at the beginning of the lower and at the end of the intermediate and the upper stage. Thus, the majority of pupils were instructed on sexual anatomy at the lower stage, and 75 percent of the teachers reported that they had given instruction on contraceptives to grade six pupils. A scarce majority of lower stage teachers felt that sex education should be given under home and family knowledge, whereas 80 percent of the intermediate stage teachers would prefer to give it under instruction on natural sciences. All lower stage teachers feel that boys and girls should be taught together, whereas about 25 percent of intermediate stage teachers are of the opinion that part of the teaching should be given separately for boys and girls. Large groups of lower stage teachers feel that sex education should start much earlier than do the majority of intermediate stage teachers, but all agree that the emphasis should lie in the upper stage. About two-thirds of lower and intermediate stage teachers feel that the school shall recommend sexual abstinence during adolescence. Among upper stage teachers there is no clear-cut opinion in this matter.

The lower and intermediate stage teachers were asked whether they would consider, in explanatory connection with more neutral terms, using the "four letter words" in front of the children with the purpose of addressing them in their own language. About half of the teachers expressed doubt, 40 percent were definitely against, and only between 10 and 20 percent were positive.

Some Inferences

In the 1920s 7 percent of the Swedish school population had sex education at school as compared to 90 percent in the late sixties. There is no evidence that correct knowledge about sexual matters is harmful at any age, whereas there is considerable evidence that lack of such knowledge exposes youngsters to unnecessary hazards. About half of the present day school population say that they had no kind of sexual information through their parents. The effect of the information given at school on the overall sexual knowledge of the pupils is considerable. In spite of the information given at school, about half of the pupils finishing comprehensive school today say they heard nothing about menstruation and wet dreams at school before experiencing these phenomena themselves, and were not sure whether masturbation is harmful or not. The same proportion of these pupils had coital experience. Sex education at school is in great need of further improvement.

Two Outside Investigations

These investigations are of interest in terms of aiming at the actual sex behavior of the subjects than were above.

The first one was made in a provincial town on students at a gymnasium, a girls' school, and several vocational schools, age 16-20, average age about 18.

Fifty-seven percent of the boys and 46 percent of the girls had had coital experience. About the first coitus the following was reported: Only 12 percent of the boys and 2 percent of the girls were under the influence of alcohol. Ninety-five percent of the boys and 80 percent of the girls said they themselves wanted their first experience when it happened. Ninety-eight percent of the boys and 93 percent of the girls said their first coital experience effected a desire for repetition which actually happened in the following patterns:

Coital frequency after first experience	Boys	Girls
None	8%	4%
Occasionally	55%	34%
Regularly	37%	64%

About sexual satisfaction the following was reported:

Satisfied	Boys	Girls
Sometimes	14%	32%
Usually	35%	46%
Always	43%	12%
Don't know	6%	10%

The other investigation was made at the RFSU clinic in Stockholm on the assumption that teenage girls coming to the clinic differ from the average teenage girl population. One hundred and sixty-four consecutive cases visiting during a period of twenty-three days in the spring of 1969 were compared to reports about an average teenage population in Stockholm. It was found that the RFSU visitors had their first menstruation, their first steady relationship, their first coital experience, their first experience with alcohol and smoking earlier than the average teenage girl. Furthermore, it was found that the RFSU visitors to a larger extent than their contemporaries decide on their first sexual experience in cooperation with their partner, rather than being "seduced," and that they do to a larger extent prefer orals to condoms as a contraceptive at their first intercourse. Finally, it was found that the RFSU visitors have no more steady relationships, no more sexual partners, and no higher coital frequency than those having their first coital experience at a later date. The overall conclusion was that there is no relationship between an early coital experience and the intensity of later sexual activities.

Manual and Survey for Teachers

One of the main tasks for the State Commission was to prepare a Manual and Survey of basic sexology for teachers to replace the present one of 1957. The latter is a rather thin book in which the two parts are covered in about 70 + 20 pages. The proposed one, now in print, is much larger, about 150 + 225 pages.

The new manual differs from the old one in several respects of which the following may be mentioned: Factual knowledge as such is considered harmless at any age. There is no warning for using visual aids at the lower stage of the comprehensive school. There are no attempts at circumventing the fact that sex generally is conceptualized and experienced as pleasurable, neither the fact that it may be unpleasant. Premarital sex relations are dealt with in an honest view of its prevalence in our society, at the same time due respect is given to those who feel that sex belongs to marriage only. Sex relations among adolescents are treated in the same way. Statements in the present manual to the effect that abstinence during adolescence is the best guarantee for a happy and harmonious marriage are not repeated in the proposed one because their truthfulness appears more doubtful in the light of present experience. This does not mean that very early sex relations are not cautioned against and the reasons for this given. Class discussions on these matters are encouraged. Attempts at avoiding an over-idealized image of marriage are recommended in favor of a more true and honest one describing both lights and shadows.

A general recommendation is to give a rather broad orientation at an early stage and then to expand and elaborate on this basis as required by increasing maturity and broadening interests in the upper grades. The following are some items recommended to be dealt with in the lower stage of the comprehensive school (7-9 years of age): Living together; Differences between sexes; Sex organs, anatomy and function; Menstruation; Intercourse; Masturbation; Conception; Pregnancy; Sterility; Adoption; Exhibitionists and pedophiliacs.

At the intermediate stage (10-12 years) are added such items as preliminary information on contraceptives, gonorrhea, puberty and elementary puberty psychology, some information about homosexuality.

At the upper stage (12-15 years) the proposed manual recommends more information on social, psychological, and ethical aspects than does the present one.

The manual contains fairly detailed recommendations for how the material could be transmitted at various stages, from preparatory to gymnasium school. Beyond this there are separate chapters on Aims and Guidelines from the point of view of the Committee proposals: The Need for Sex Education; On Normative and Objective Teaching; Teaching Material and Cooperation between Home and School.

The Survey on Basic Sexology for teachers was published as a pocket edition in 1971, under the title "Sexuality and Living Together." It had the following chapters: Anatomy and Physiology; Teaching about Living Together; Social Aspects; Psychological Aspects and The Role of the Home. This book is now going to be added to the manual in a revised, separate edition.

Part III:

Implications for the United States

Chapter 15

Maternal and Child Health in a National Health Service: Implications for the United States

Helen M. Wallace

INTRODUCTION

It is likely that in the 1970s there may be a national health service or a national insurance program in the United States in some form. It may cover all or some of our population, such as high risk, more vulnerable groups, such as the elderly, mothers and children, the chronically ill, the handicapped, etc. It may cover comprehensive health care for everyone or be more limited to those requiring care for catastrophic illness. It may include efforts to improve the health care delivery system for all or some of our population, or it may still be largely an insurance, bill-paying program, as it is at present for the elderly and the indigent. It may cover the broad range of services needed to provide comprehensive care, or it may be restricted to selected aspects, such as inpatient care, ambulatory care, home care, etc. Many choices and options are open to our country. In anticipation of a new national health insurance program or a new national health service in our country in some form in the 1970s, it is timely, and in fact imperative, that all of the existing fields of public health study and analyze existing services and programs, begin to define their future roles, and make plans now for the future. Steps are taken in this article to do this, using the field of maternal and child health[a] as the example.

SOME MAJOR ISSUES AND QUESTIONS

There are many major issues and questions, requiring public, civic, professional,

---

[a]Whenever the term "maternal and child health" is used, this includes the sub-areas of maternal health, child health, school health, handicapped children, adolescence, family planning, abortion, and the care of children and youth in special settings or circumstances such as day care, foster homes, institutions, courts, camps, and other children's and youth settings.

and legislative debate, discussion, agreement, and planning. One issue is the role and interrelationships of government (federal, state, and local), the voluntary health agencies, and the professional societies. A second issue is concerned with the extent of coverage of the population—the types of recipients of care, the volume of the population to be covered, and the need to provide more even geographic distribution of health services for the total country. A related issue is the need to develop a regional plan for the delivery of services.

One set of issues is concerned with the health delivery system itself. Should there be one monolithic system of health care, or will there be opportunity for a pluralistic plan using several approaches, including the opportunity to experiment with innovative ways to deliver care? Who will provide primary care? Will this be done by an individual, or by a group, or a team? Should it be done only by a physician, or can it be done mainly by one or more nonmedical personnel? Can preventive, treatment, and rehabilitative care be integrated and coordinated? What interrelationships can be developed between those providing primary care, and those who are specialists or consultants? How can inpatient and ambulatory care be integrated?

Issues pertaining to the content of patient care include what should be provided. What should be included in the screening of children for health problems? Will it be possible to identify high risk groups, and to provide special and more intensive services for them? What will quality control consist of?

There is a series of manpower issues including the need for a plan for the number required, their qualifications, and the need for a plan for their recruitment, preparation, and distribution.

Issues in regard to funding are crucial. They include the sources of funds; the question of channeling funds to improve the health care delivery system versus a bill-paying program only. Methods of reimbursement of providers are an important issue; will physicians and dentists be reimbursed on a fee-for-service, salary, or capitation method, or a combination? What is the role of government, and of possible other intermediaries such as health insurance companies? What methods of cost control can be applied? Is there a need for separate funds for special services for special population groups? How much will the total program cost? Which groups of the population will bear the major cost of the program? The working poor? Employers?

GENERAL PRINCIPLES

In making plans for a national health service or a national health insurance program, certain basic principles will need to be kept in mind. These include the following: Health care is considered to be a right of everyone [1]. The government has the responsibility to see that it is provided. Access to health care needs to be equally available to all, regardless of socioeconomic status, ethnic group, or geographic location. Barriers to health care need to be eliminated.

Preventive services need to be included and provided free of charge. Quality control and cost control need to be built into the health delivery process and system. Public accountability is essential.

There is need for the drafting of a *national plan* which will include a blueprint for health manpower needs and their distribution. It should also include a plan for the construction, staffing and utilization of hospitals, ambulatory care facilities, extended care facilities, and home health care. A plan is needed to provide basic primary health care for the entire population, with provision to experiment with alternate methods to deliver primary health care—through group practice, the health maintenance organization concept, or other form of team care. The quality of primary health care needs to be safeguarded so that the usual and minor health problems of the total population may be quickly handled; there will be screening for more serious problems; and rapid referral of those suspected of serious health problems to specialists or consultants for more specialized diagnosis and treatment.

DIFFERENCES BETWEEN A NATIONAL HEALTH SERVICE AND A NATIONAL HEALTH INSURANCE PROGRAM

There is a fundamental difference between a national health service and a national health insurance program. These are not synonymous terms or similar programs.

A national health service consists of planning to meet the health manpower needs of the country on a national basis—recruitment, education and training, licensure, and distribution. It consists of providing the health delivery system—the provision of basic primary health care for everyone, of specialists or consultants services, of hospital and ambulatory care, and of the chain of related services (extended care facilities, home health care, rehabilitation services). It is concerned with the delivery of health care to all of the people.

A national health insurance program consists of the plan to collect funds, provide the financing, and pay the bills for health care of some or all of the population.

Both a national health service and a national health insurance program are needed to deliver comprehensive health care to the people of a country. The one does not substitute for the other. Both the United Kingdom and Sweden provide a national health service and a national health insurance program. The provision of national health insurance without a national health service will direct more money into the present health care delivery system in the United States, which is not functioning well, and which is unevenly distributed. It will tend to overstrain the present system, and is likely to raise the cost of health care under the present system.

REGIONAL PLANNING

There is need to adopt the principle of regional planning for the delivery of health services in the United States. The principle of regionalization can be applied to such specialized services as diagnostic, treatment, and rehabilitation services for handicapped children and youth; perinatal centers for selected high risk pregnant women and infants; genetic diagnostic and counseling centers; and other selected highly specialized services.

There is evidence that the MCH leadership in the United Kingdom and Sweden has been taking steps to implement the principle of regionalization and regional planning.

In the United Kingdom, there has been projected a plan for the development of at least one assessment center for handicapped children for each of the eight regions of the country. So far seven already exist, and an additional thirteen are projected as needed. Each would serve a population of about three million. Within each region, it has been recommended that there be a number of district assessment centers for handicapped children, based in district general hospitals, each one serving a population of 200-400,000 [8]. In the United Kingdom there is also some beginning regional planning for special care units for the newborn of high risk in hospitals. A formula has been suggested of 6 cribs per 1,000 total beds [4].

In Sweden, which is divided into seven regions, the plan is for each region to have a major central pediatric clinic or center for handicapped children. The purpose is for each center to provide diagnostic, treatment, and rehabilitation service on an inpatient and outpatient basis; physical therapy; social work; training in activities of daily living; special education. Because of the organization of maternal health services in Sweden, it has been possible to implement to some extent the concept of regional perinatal care. For example, the fact that a maternity patient with a complication can be placed under the care of an obstetrician means that she can potentially be delivered in a hospital with special services both for herself and her baby. In addition to this, some intensive care units for the newborn have been developed on a regional basis, with some transport services.

PROVISION OF BASIC PREVENTIVE SERVICES

The area of MCH is the single most strategic area in which to apply preventive health services. Children and youth, mothers with young children, and pregnant women not only represent a large part of the total population; they are also the group who are most vulnerable, and the group which responds most readily to preventive measures. Basic preventive health services include maternal health services—prenatal care, hospital inpatient maternity care, postpartum care, contraceptive services, abortion counseling and services. They include child health services—continuous health supervision of growth and development, health assessment and screening for disease, immunizations, advice to parents regarding feeding, safety and accident prevention, behavior, and anticipatory guidance, and dental health. They include school health services, including services for adolescents. Family life education and sex education are important components of basic preventive services.

In both the United Kingdom and Sweden, where a national health service and a national health insurance program exist, basic preventive health services for mothers and children have been maintained as a strong foundation for health care. By and large, they have been provided free of charge by the local unit of government.

Basic Preventive Services in Sweden

In Sweden, the country is provided with a network of maternal health centers at local level [2]. Maternal health centers type 1 (99 in number) are connected with a hospital department of obstetrics and gynecology, and headed by an obstetrician. Maternal health centers type 2 (183 in number) are headed by a district medical officer or some other physician. They are sometimes combined with a child welfare center. Almost all pregnant women receive prenatal care and postnatal care, including family planning, at these centers. The basic maternity care is provided by nurse midwives, reinforced by obstetricians. Thus, any patient with an early complication can quickly be placed under the care of an obstetrician. Delivery of normal patients is done by nurse midwives; of abnormal patients by obstetricians. The country is provided with a network of child welfare centers [2]. They see 99 percent of all babies born during the first year of life, and continue to supervise 69 percent of them from 2-7 years of age. The basic preventive services consist of health education; advice in child rearing, nutrition, anticipatory guidance, safety and accident prevention; immunizations; health assessment of the child; screening for handicapping conditions. A new special health assessment of four-year-old children has recently been introduced. The school health service provides health services to all pupils in the school system, including pupils in the first nine grades of compulsory schools, and in the secondary schools. Health examinations are provided in grades 1, 4, 7, and 9. The examinations in grades 7, 8, and 9 are looked upon as having an important vocational component. School lunches are provided to all children in grades 1-9, and to some youth in secondary schools. There is a considerable emphasis on sex education in the schools. Family planning information is available in schools, and in hospital maternity services. The availability of family planning services varies among the counties. Abortion service is generally available, performed only by obstetricians in hospitals. It is estimated that 20 percent of preschool children in Sweden are receiving some form of day care at present (212,000 children).

The local health authorities operate child welfare centers in the

United Kingdom. In 1965, they saw 76.7 percent of all infants born in England and Wales; 69.6 percent of children aged 1-2 years; and 20.7 percent of those aged 2-5 years. A higher proportion of children of the three lowest social classes (3,4,5) attend the child welfare centers. One of the emphases in the child welfare centers has been early identification of handicapped children [5]. The school health program in the United Kingdom is currently providing a pattern of surveillance as follows: (1) Entrance medical examination; (2) Follow-up visits to the schools by the doctor and nurse; (3) Subsequent medical examinations on referral; (4) Periodic parent questionnaire; and (5) Periodic screening of vision, hearing, height, and weight [6]. The school health program in the United Kingdom is looked upon as the first step of an occupational health program. Family planning was originally provided largely by the Family Planning Association. Gradually, general practitioners are playing an increasing role in providing patient care. On April 1, 1974, the responsibility for family planning was turned over to the general practitioner and the local health authority, to be incorporated into general health care. One of the interesting parts of the family planning program is the domiciliary family planning program for poorly motivated women. This consists of a visit to the home by a health visitor, nurse, and/or general practitioner. Advice and contraception service are provided the woman in the home. In 1972, it was estimated that 150,000 abortions were done in the United Kingdom; two-thirds were estimated to have been performed on women from the United Kingdom; of the U.K. group, one-half were done in the National Health Service under the care of an obstetrician. In 1948, legislation was enacted to make day care available for everyone. During World War II this had increased considerably, and then declined. It is about to increase due to expansion of preschool children. It is estimated that 12 percent of preschool children receive some form of day care. The new expansion of day care about to occur will be planned by each local authority, and it is expected that there will be concentration of services in districts of special need [7].

SPECIAL CARE OF HIGH RISK
MOTHERS AND CHILDREN

Regardless of the sources of funds and methods of payment of health and medical care of any population, there will always be certain groups of the population at higher risk and in greater need of more extensive and specialized services. Within the MCH field, responsibilities include the identification of high risk groups; the development, provision and supervision of special services for them; the evaluation of such services. Examples of high risk groups include: (1) Families with a history of continuum of reproductive loss; (2) Families and/ or youth in trouble; (3) Infants and children of high risk, such as low birth weight, the abused child, etc.; (4) Handicapped children and their families; and (5) Families with serious social, financial, health or marital difficulties.

In both Sweden and the United Kingdom, there is evidence that high risk mothers and children do have special needs and require special care. One example of this is the effort to make prenatal care easily available to pregnant women, to identify early those with special problems; those with special health needs can then be immediately referred to and kept under the care of the obstetric specialist. A second example in both the United Kingdom and Sweden is the development of regional perinatal centers for high risk mothers and newborn infants.

A third example in both countries is the development of a regional plan and regional centers for handicapped children—for evaluation, diagnosis, counseling, treatment, and rehabilitation.

A fourth example in both countries consists of the steps being taken to further develop services for preschool children (day nurseries, etc.). Within these programs, there is effort being made to give high priority to sections of communities with special needs, and to give high priority to individual families with special needs, e.g., children of working mothers, one-parent families, etc.

ORGANIZATION OF SERVICES FOR NATIONAL AND CHILD HEALTH IN THE UNITED KINGDOM AND SWEDEN

At present, in both the United Kingdom and Sweden, there are visible and identifiable MCH services and personnel. These personnel provide the leadership in the field of MCH in the country, along with the professional societies and organizations, and the universities. In each of the two countries, there is a clear public policy which recognizes the special needs of mothers and children. Special provision for the needs of mothers and children is made within the framework of the national health care system. Each country has a designated agency responsible for making health services available and accessible to all mothers and children without cost.

Organization of MCH Services in the United Kingdom

At the national level in the United Kingdom, within the National Department of Health and Social Security, there is a separate unit responsible for MCH, including child health services, handicapped children; responsibility for school health is just being placed in this MCH unit. MCH is also partly responsible for some children at high risk, such as child abuse. One person has just been appointed in a separate unit, but closely associated with MCH, for maternal health.

At the local level, the local health authority is responsible for the MCH services. Most local health authorities have a medical officer of health in charge of MCH services. The local health authority provides midwifery, health visiting, home nursing, child health services, family planning, immunization, health centers, welfare food services, care of premature infants. The local education authority operates school health services, and there are some local medical officers in charge. The local authority operates personal social services through local social service departments.

Organization of MCH Services in Sweden

In Sweden at the national level the National Board of Health and Welfare has a separate unit on child health services with a pediatrician as full-time director. There is a separate unit responsible for mental retardation. Responsibility for maternal health and family planning is separate, with a very part-time obstetric consultant. The National Board of Education has a pediatrician in charge of school health.

At the local level, each of the twenty-five counties and three large cities is responsible. Each county has a head doctor for child health, a pediatrician recruited mostly from the Department of Pediatrics of a hospital. At the local level there are maternal health centers and child welfare centers. At county level, there is a county medical officer who serves as a medical advisor to the County Board of Education.

In the United States, this would mean that there would be one strong, clearly identifiable unit in the federal government, which would be responsible for planning, implementing, and evaluating the health and social care and needs of mothers and children, and for their advocacy. The many-splintered units presently existing would be pulled together to make it possible for the federal government to have strong leadership in the MCH field, in order that there be national planning for services, research, and manpower needs. A cadre of MCH personnel in a clearly identifiable unit is also needed in state government in each state, responsible for planning, promoting, and evaluating the health care and needs of mothers and children, including handicapped children, in each state. Each large city, or each large county, or city-county, or multi-county local health department in the United States also needs a unit responsible for planning, providing, and evaluating the health care of mothers and children at local level. In order to provide for the MCH manpower needs for the country, a national plan is needed for the recruitment, education and training, and deployment of MCH personnel throughout the country.

DEVELOPMENT OF STANDARDS, RECOMMENDATIONS, AND GUIDELINES

Both the United Kingdom and Sweden MCH leadership have been active in developing materials which contain standards, recommendations, and guidelines. These materials have been used in a variety of ways to upgrade the quality of delivery of health care to mothers and children in the country.

In Sweden, the National Board of Health and Welfare in 1970 developed "Model Regulations for Maternal and Child Health Service" [2]. This material describes the responsibilities of the county. It classifies maternal health and child health centers into types 1 and 2. It describes the content of prenatal and postnatal care, including family planning. It describes the content of child health care, including mention of the new special examination of four year olds. Another document in Sweden "Essentials of the Swedish National Program for Preventive Child Care," describes the plan and content of child health care [10]. Another document "Health Screening for Four-Year-Olds" describes the purpose and content of the special evaluation of four-year old children in Sweden [11].

The United Kingdom has had a long-standing pattern of setting up special government committees and working parties to study and make recommendations concerning special problems of MCH care. In the past, this technique was used for babies with hemolytic disease of the newborn [12], and babies with congenital malformations [9]. More recently, this technique was used to consider child welfare centers [5], care of the child with spina bifida [13], human genetics [14], screening for the detection of congenital dislocation of the hip in infants [15], deafness in early childhood [16], domiciliary midwifery and maternity bed needs [17], and special care for babies of high risk [4]. Each of these reports when completed is intended to represent the consensus of scientific, technical and administrative summary of facts, thinking, application to patient care, and planning for the future. Each then becomes a reference report for personnel providing patient care, in an effort to improve the quality of care.

In the United States, this principle of developing standards, recommendations, and guidelines has been carried on more through the aegis of professional organizations (American Academy of Pediatrics, American Public Health Association, American College of Obstetricians and Gynecologists) than through the use of expert committees by the MCH leadership in the federal government. This difference needs to be analyzed to determine if there might be value in the use of this method in the United States.

PROVISION OF SPECIAL SURVEILLANCE AND MONITORING

There is evidence of this in both the United Kingdom and Sweden. The United Kingdom has had a program of notification of congenital malformations for some years [9]. This consists of voluntary reporting on a special form to the local medical officers of health. The data are transmitted to the Office of Population Censuses and Surveys for analysis and surveillance. In 1970, 14,019 babies were reported to have a total of 17,293 malformations, a rate of 15.7 per 1,000 live births. In the United Kingdom, a register of handicapped children is in operation by local health authorities.

In Sweden, a register of infants reported with congenital malformations is kept by the National Board of Health and Welfare. Reporting is done by maternity services with a pediatrician. Data are sent monthly from the maternity service to the NBHW. The purpose is surveillance. A register for handicapped children is just beginning in Sweden. There is also a special one for children with mental retardation, with special doctors who follow the children.

Principles in this which would apply to the United States consist of the use of the birth certificates, which contain information on reported congenital malformations and birth injuries. This could be used by local health departments for epidemiological surveillance and to provide follow up to bring care to the infants and their families. A national plan is needed for the network for reporting and for services.

USE OF FUNDS FOR CURRENT NEEDS AND EMPHASES

Both the United Kingdom and Sweden have applied the principle of use of special funds to reorient and redirect the emphasis in the delivery of health care, to meet current needs.

In the United Kingdom, there is evidence of providing financial incentives to physicians in general practice to form medical groups. Special funds are available to help them establish and equip physical facilities. Local health authorities are providing special physical facilities in health centers for general practitioners in groups, in an effort to bring together the general practitioners services with the overall general community health services, in order to coordinate preventive and treatment services. Health visitors employed by local health authorities are being attached to general practitioners for this same purpose. Special funds are being provided by the government for new full-time positions for "community pediatricians." These are well-trained younger pediatricians, with a concern for "community" or "social" pediatrics, who are appointed full time to Departments of Child Health of medical schools (or to Departments of Pediatrics of hospitals) to extend hospital services into the community; to bring together community MCH services with hospital care; to upgrade the community MCH services; to attempt to integrate preventive and curative medical care of mothers and children. Special funds have been used to pay general practitioners extra on a fee-for-service basis for immunization of infants and children, for antenatal care, and for family planning. All of these examples are illustrations of the use of funds to introduce more emphasis on certain aspects of patient care.

In the United States, flexibility of funding is needed to be able to redirect funds for new problems quickly. Not only are funds needed for demonstration purposes; they are also needed to apply successful demonstration programs throughout the country to those requiring assistance and care. For example, in the United States, this might include teenage pregnant girls and their babies, youth in trouble, families with child abuse, the extension of Maternity and Infant Care Projects and Children and Youth Projects to all high risk mothers and children, and the provision of a network of perinatal centers and genetic centers on a regional basis covering the country.

THE QUESTION OF PROVIDING SEPARATE SPECIAL FUNDS

Frequently, when there is discussion of a national health service or of a national health insurance program, the statement is made that separate special funds will no longer be needed. The evidence is clear from the United Kingdom and Sweden that their experience indicates that there is still need of support of certain specific services for patient care. These include:

1. The basic preventive services of prenatal care, postnatal care, infant and preschool health supervision, contraception, abortion, the school health service, with emphasis on health assessment, screening, health teaching, and health care.
2. Special diagnostic, treatment, and rehabilitation services for handicapped children and their families.
3. Special services for high risk mothers and infants, through the development of regional perinatal centers.
4. Special health and social services for mothers, children, youth, and families in trouble.

Special health and social services for mothers and children have not been disbanded or terminated. To the contrary, it is clear that as our scientific knowledge has developed, there is evidence of further development of specific services to apply the information to the community. Examples of this are mass immunization with new vaccines as they become available; inclusion of the genetic aspects of MCH, through genetic histories, diagnostic studies, counseling, family planning, and abortion when indicated; prevention of mortality and brain damage associated with iso-immunization due to the Rh factor, etc.

Tables 15-1 and 15-2 from Anderson [28] would tend to confirm his statement that "the system in the U.S.A. concentrates on care for the elderly relative to children, while the British and Swedish systems do the reverse."

Based upon the experience in Sweden and the United Kingdom, the principle is that, even in the presence of a national health service and a national health insurance program, special funds would continue to be needed for selected services for mothers and children. These would include the maintenance and strengthening of basic preventive services; special services for handicapped children and youth; special perinatal centers for the care of high

Table 15-1.   Age-Specific Mortality—1965

Age	Deaths Per 1,000 Population		
	U.S.A.	Sweden	England
Under 1 year	24.1	13.3	20.5
1-4 years	0.9	0.7	0.8
5-14 years	0.4	0.4	0.4
15-24 years	1.1	0.7	0.8
25-34 years	1.5	1.0	0.9
35-44 years	3.1	1.9	2.1
45-54 years	7.4	4.4	5.8
55-64 years	16.9	11.3	15.1
65-74 years	37.9	32.3	32.0
75 & over years	101.7	110.9	111.1
Overall	9.4	10.1	11.1

Source: O.W. Anderson, *Health Care: Can There Be Equity?* (New York: John Wiley and Sons, 1972), page 151, table 27.

Table 15-2.   Age-Specific Death Rates—Sweden, Utah and Minnesota

Age	Rate Per 1,000 Population		
	Sweden (1968)	Utah (1969)	Minnesota (1969)
Under 1 year	12.4	16.6	19.8
Under 5 years	3.2	4.1	4.1
5-19 years	0.5	0.5	0.6
20-44 years	1.2	1.6	1.6
45-64 years	7.4	9.0	9.6
65 and over	57.6	55.4	56.3
All ages	10.1	6.4	9.2

Source: O.W. Anderson, *Health Care: Can There Be Equity?* (New York: John Wiley & Sons, 1972), page 158, table 30.

risk women and infants; genetic services; day care for children; other high risk mothers and children, such as teen-age pregnant girls, families with child abuse and other serious family problems.

REFERENCES

1. Smith, D.C. *Report on Cross-National Study of Health Care Delivery Systems.* Washington, D.C.: U.S. Dept. of Health, Education, and Welfare, March 1972.
2. National Board of Health and Welfare. *Model Regulations for Maternal and Child Health Service.* Stockholm, 1970.

3. Rosengren, B. *Preschool in Sweden.* Stockholm: The Swedish Institute, 1973.

4. Department of Health and Social Security. *Report of the Expert Group on Special Care for Babies.* London: Her Majesty's Stationery Office, 1971.

5. Ministry of Health. *Child Welfare Centres.* London: HMSO, 1967.

6. Report of The Chief Medical Officer of the Department of Education and Science. *The Health of the School Child.* London: HMSO, 1972.

7. Jessel, S. "34M Building Programme Will Provide at Least 70,000 New Places in Nursery Schools." *London Times,* Aug. 14, 1973, page 2.

8. Court, D. and Jackson, A. *Pediatrics in the Seventies.* London: Oxford University Press, 1972.

9. Ministry of Health. *Congenital Malformations.* London: HMSO, 1963.

10. National Board of Health and Welfare. *Essentials of the Swedish National Program for Preventive Child Care.* Stockholm, 1971.

11. National Board of Health and Welfare. *Health Screening for Four-Year-Olds.* Stockholm. 8 pages mimeographed. Undated.

12. Ministry of Health. *Haemolytic Disease of the Newborn.* London: HMSO, 1961.

13. Department of Health and Social Security. *Care of the Child with Spina Bifida.* London: HMSO, 1973.

14. Department of Health and Social Security. *Human Genetics.* London: HMSO, 1972.

15. Department of Health and Social Security. *Screening for the Detection of Congenital Dislocation of the Hip in Infants.* London: HMSO, 1969.

16. Department of Health and Social Security. *Deafness in Early Childhood.* London: HMSO, 1971.

17. Department of Health and Social Security. *Domiciliary Midwifery and Maternity Bed Needs.* London: HMSO, 1970.

18. Ministry of Health. *Enquiry Into Sudden Death in Infancy.* London: HMSO, 1965.

19. Department of Health and Social Security. *Confidential Enquiry into Postneonatal Deaths 1964-1966.* London: HMSO, 1970.

20. Department of Health and Social Security. *Report on Confidential Enquiries into Maternal Deaths in England and Wales 1967-1969.* London: HMSO, 1972.

21. Department of Health and Social Security. *Report on the Working Group on Risk Registers.* London, 1970. 19 pages mimeographed.

22. Department of Health and Social Security. *The Battered Baby.* London: HMSO, 1970.

23. RFSU Statistik. *Befolkningen, Sexualvanor Aborter, Gonorré, Sexualbrott, Internationellt.* Stockholm, 1973.

24. Association of the Blind. *Swedish Blind Welfare–72.* Stockholm, 1972.

25. Grunewald, K. *The Mentally Retarded in Sweden.* Stockholm: The Swedish Institute, 1969.

26. The Family Planning Association. *41st Report and Accounts 1972-73.* London, 1973.

27. National Council for the Unmarried Mother and Her Child. *Annual Report April 1971-March 1972.* London.

28. Anderson, O.W. *Health Care: Can There Be Equity?* New York: John Wiley and Sons, 1972.

Chapter 16

Child Health Care in the United States: Expenditures and Extent of Coverage With Selected Comprehensive Services

Helen M. Wallace and Hyman Goldstein

INTRODUCTION

With the possible enactment of a national health insurance program of some type in the near future in the United States, it is essential that current expenditures for health care be studied. Analysis of current expenditures will tell us how much funds are being expended for the health care of children and youth, the sources of such funds, the recipients of such funds, services provided, and recent trends. It is possible to compare overall national expenditures for the health care of children and youth with the average cost of child health care in selected special community programs for children and youth. It should be possible to use such fiscal and program data as a basis for the future planning of health insurance for children and youth in the United States.

RECENT NATIONAL EXPENDITURES FOR HEALTH CARE OF CHILDREN AND YOUTH IN THE UNITED STATES

Comparison of Age Distribution of the Population with Health Expenditures

Table 16-1 shows that while children and youth under nineteen years of age represent 36.9 percent of the total population in the United States, they are the recipients of only 15.9 percent of the expenditures for health care. By contrast, individuals aged sixty-five years and over comprise 9.5 percent of the population, but their health care represents 27.5 percent of total expenditures. The intermediate aged group (19-64 years) constitute 53.6 percent of the population and represents 56.6 percent of the expenditures for health care.

Table 16-1. Percentage Distribution of the Population
and Health Expenditures, United States, Fiscal Year 1972

Age (in years)	Population	Health Expenditures
Under 19	36.9%	15.9%
19-64	53.6	56.6
65 and over	9.5	27.5
Total	100.0	100.0

Source: B.S. Cooper and N.L. Worthington, "Age Differences in Medical Care Spending, Fiscal Year 1972," *Social Security Bulletin*, May 1973, pp. 3-15. DHEW Pub. No. (SSA) 73-11700.

Personal Health Care Expenditures

In fiscal year 1972, total national spending for personal health care amounted to $71,862 million. Of this, $11,459 million was expended for children and youth under nineteen years of age (Table 16-2).

From 1969-1972, there was a 36.5 percent increase in expenditures for personal health care for children and youth under nineteen years of age. This was an increase similar to that for individuals in the intermediate age group (19-64 years), but a smaller increase than that for individuals aged sixty-five years and over (42.7 percent), (Table 16-2).

In fiscal year 1972, of the total $11,459 million for health expenditures for children and youth, $8,235 million (71.9 percent) came from private sources and $3,221 million (28.1 percent) came from public sources. From 1969-72, expenditures for health care for children and youth from public sources increased 52.6 percent, while those from private sources increased 31.0 percent (Table 16-2).

Sources of Public Funds for
Expenditures for Health Care

For children and youth under nineteen years of age, in fiscal year 1972, 57.9 percent of the public funds for health care were federal, and 42.1 percent were state and local (Table 16-3).

The proportion of public funds for health care for children and youth in fiscal year 1972 came from Medicaid (40 percent); from the military dependents' medical care program (24 percent), and from the general hospital and medical care programs (13 percent). The remaining public outlays (23 percent) came from maternal and child health programs, school health, vocational rehabilitation, and the Office of Economic Opportunity Programs (mainly neighborhood health centers).

Almost half of the state and local health expenditures for children and youth from public funds came from the Medicaid program.

Table 16-2. Estimated Personal Health Care Expenditures by Source of Funds and Three Age Groups, United States, Fiscal Years 1969-72

Age (in years)	(In Millions)				% Increase 1969-72
	1969	1970	1971	1972	
Under 19					
Total	$ 8,397	$ 9,598	$10,755	$11,459	36.5
Private	6,287	7,226	8,040	8,236	31.0
Public	2,110	2,372	2,714	3,221	52.6
19-64					
Total	29,825	33,796	37,218	40,654	36.3
Private	22,681	25,730	28,078	30,084	32.6
Public	7,144	8,065	9,136	10,571	48.0
65 and over					
Total	13,838	15,710	17,699	19,753	42.7
Private	4,380	5,593	6,334	6,787	55.0
Public	9,457	10,115	11,366	12,966	37.1
All Ages					
Total	52,057	59,101	65,670	71,862	38.0
Private	33,346	38,549	42,455	45,105	35.3
Public	18,711	20,522	23,215	26,757	43.0

Source: B.S. Cooper and N.L. Worthington, "Age Differences in Medical Care Spending, Fiscal Year 1972," *Social Security Bulletin*, May 1973, pp. 3-15. DHEW Pub. No. (SSA) 73-11700.

Table 16-3. Source of Public Funds by Three Age Groups, United States Fiscal Year 1972

Age (in years)	Percentage Distribution		
	Total	Federal	State and Local
Under 19	100	57.9	42.1
19-64	100	51.2	48.8
65 years	100	80.8	19.2
All ages	100	66.3	33.7

Source: B.S. Cooper and N.L. Worthington, "Age Differences in Medical Care Spending, Fiscal Year 1972," *Social Security Bulletin*, May 1973, pp. 3-15. DHEW Pub. No. (SSA) 73-11700.

Per Capita Expenditures

In 1972, the per capita expenditure for health care for children and youth was $146.86. This is about 40 percent of that spent for individuals in the intermediate age group (19-64 years), and it is about 15 percent of that spent for the elderly (Table 16-4).

The per capita expenditure of $146.86 for health care for children and youth in 1972 represents a rise of 32.3 percent from $111.03 in 1969 (Table 16-4).

The per capita expenditure of $146.86 for health care for children and youth in 1972 represents approximately two-thirds ($105.55) from private sources, and one-third ($41.28) from public sources (Table 16-4).

Of the per capita expenditures for children and youth in 1972 of $146.86, about one-third each was for physicians' services (31.1 percent) and for hospital care (31.0 percent). The remaining expenditures were for drugs and drug sundries (13.6 percent); dentists' services (9.7 percent); other professional services (3.2 percent); eyeglasses and appliances (2.9 percent); nursing home care (0.8 percent); and other health services (7.7 percent), (Table 16-5).

From 1969-72, the largest increase in per capita expenditures for children and youth was for hospital care (68.4 percent), (Table 16-5).

The United States per capita expenditure of $146.86 for health care for children and youth in 1972 can be compared with fiscal information from other programs:

Program	Annual Per Capita Expenditure for Health Care of Children and/or Youth	Year
Job Corps [2]	$344.00	1967-68
Medicaid [3]	301.87	1971
Children and Youth Projects [5]	128.00	1972-73
Head Start [6]		
Screening & Immunization	$ 27.00 - 44.00	
Treatment	73.00 - 98.00	
Total	$100.00 - 142.00	1972-73
United States—All Sources	$146.86	FY 1972

The U.S. per capita expenditure of $146.86 somewhat approximates that of Children and Youth Projects and Head Start health care, and also is close to North's prediction of $100-200 per child per year [4].

EXTENT OF COVERAGE WITH SELECTED COMPREHENSIVE SERVICES

Table 16-6 presents data on estimates of the population as a whole, the high priority population, and the population of children and youth presently served.

Table 16-4.   Estimated Per Capita Expenditure for Personal Health Care by Source of Funds for Three Age Groups, United States—Fiscal Years 1969-72

Age (in years)	1969			1972			Percentage Increase—1969-1972		
	Total	*Private*	*Public*	*Total*	*Private*	*Public*	*Total*	*Public*	*Private*
Under 19	$111.03	$ 83.13	$ 27.90	$146.86	$105.55	$ 41.28	32.3	27.0	48.0
19-64	270.76	205.90	64.86	358.25	265.10	93.15	32.3	28.8	43.6
65 and over	710.22	224.80	485.42	981.42	337.21	644.21	38.2	50.0	32.7
Total	253.61	162.46	91.16	339.56	213.13	126.43	33.9	31.2	38.7

Source: B.S. Cooper and N.L. Worthington, "Age Differences in Medical Care Spending, Fiscal Year 1972," *Social Security Bulletin*, May 1973, pp. 3-15. DHEW Pub. No. (SSA) 73-11700.

Table 16-5. Estimated Per Capita Personal Health Care Expenditures by Type of Expenditure for Three Age Groups, United States—Fiscal Years 1969-72

	1969 Age (in years)			1972 Age (in years)			% Increase—1969-72 Age (in years)			Percentage distribution of per capita expenditures for those under 19 years of age, 1972
	Under 19	19-64	65 & over	Under 19	19-64	65 & over	Under 19	19-64	65 & over	
Hospital care	$ 27.04	$124.93	$336.17	$ 45.54	$168.92	$483.83	68.4	35.2	43.9	31.0
Physicians' services	37.50	59.18	127.64	45.64	79.63	176.53	21.7	34.6	38.3	31.1
Dentists' services	11.68	24.00	15.14	14.23	31.35	17.79	21.8	30.6	17.5	9.7
Other professional services	4.08	6.46	13.91	4.67	8.17	18.09	14.5	26.5	30.0	3.2
Drugs	16.85	33.45	78.06	19.97	40.02	89.98	18.5	19.6	15.3	13.6
Glasses & appliances	3.85	9.79	19.25	4.31	11.15	21.66	11.9	13.9	12.5	2.9
Nursery home care	0.82	2.80	107.52	1.13	3.86	147.81	37.8	37.9	37.5	0.8
Other health services	9.22	10.15	12.52	11.39	15.15	25.74	23.5	49.3	105.6	7.7
Total	$111.03	$270.76	$710.22	$146.86	$358.25	$981.42	32.3	32.3	38.2	100.0

Source: B.S. Cooper and N.L. Worthington, "Age Differences in Medical Care Spending, Fiscal Year 1972," *Social Security Bulletin*, May 1973, pp. 3-15. DHEW Pub. No. (SSA) 73-11700.

Table 16-6. Extent of Coverage of Population With Selected Comprehensive Care Programs

Program	Total Population	High Priority Population	Population Presently Served	Year	Number of Programs
Children & Youth Projects	77,000,000	15,400,000	487,000	June 1972	76
Maternity & Infant Care Projects				1973 Estimate	56
Maternity	3,500,000	700,000*	140,000		
Infant	3,500,000	700,000*	47,000		
Official Crippled Children	11,116,000[1]		500,000	FY 1972	54
Mental Retardation	5,400,000[2]		71,182	FY 1972	177
University Affiliated Centers			Approx. 16,000	FY 1971	21
Community Clinics			60,859	FY 1971	156
Head Start	3,500,000	700,000		FY 1972	
Full year			269,500		1,605
Summer			86,400		434
Neighborhood Health Centers					
Total			330,000	FY 1973	113
Maternity					
Children			115,500		

*There are other high risk groups, using criteria other than income.

[1] C.G. Schiffer, and E.P. Hunt, *Illness Among Children* (Washington, D.C.: U.S. Gov. Printing Office, 1963).

[2] President's Panel on Mental Retardation, *A Proposed Program for National Action to Combat Mental Retardation* (Washington, D.C., 1962).

Sources: D.A. Trauger, Special communication to the authors, Jan. 2, 1974, for all sections of table except:

(1) Head Start data from Head Start Office

(2) Mental Retardation data from Mr. Rudolf P. Hormuth.

It is clear from Table 16-6 that the extent of coverage of even the high priority population with comprehensive care services is extremely limited. For example:

— The 76 Children and Youth Projects serve only 487,000 of the 15,400,000 high priority children and youth.
— The 56 Maternity and Infant Care Projects serve only 140,000 of the 700,000 high priority mothers, and only 47,000 of the 700,000 high priority infants.
— The 54 official state Crippled Children's Programs serve only 500,000 handicapped children and youth.
— The 177 University-affiliated and other community centers for the mentally retarded serve approximately 77,000 of the retarded.
— The 2,039 Head Start Programs offer service to approximately 356,000 of the 700,000 high priority children.

DISCUSSION

It is significant that the per capita expenditure from all sources for health care of children and youth in the United States ($146.86) is similar to that of Children and Youth Projects ($128), one federally-supported program. The Children and Youth Projects provide comprehensive health and social care through the use of an interdisciplinary team for a relatively small proportion of the childhood population who are from low income families. Health care of all children and youth in the United States is largely provided through the existing system of private practice, predominantly of a "solo" pattern. Thus, from a fiscal point of view, it would be possible to provide comprehensive health care to children and youth, without any increase in funds, but via the use of existing funds through a different pattern of delivery of health care, i.e., through organized group practice or interdisciplinary team care. The team approach, which has been successfully used in several types of comprehensive care programs (handicapped children, children and youth projects, maternity and infant care projects, neighborhood health centers, etc.) has recently been endorsed by Gillespie, president of the American Academy of Pediatrics [7].

It is clear from the above estimated data that the extent of coverage of children and youth by comprehensive health services is currently limited. Much more careful planning is needed, if all children and youth or even those of high priority are to be provided with comprehensive health care.

Probably the largest current public medical care program for children is that of Medicaid. In a recent study [3], it was reported by sixteen of the fifty-four states that the Medicaid Program in 1971 covered care for approximately 2,500,000 children; it was reported by those sixteen states that almost $700 million was spent that year for their care. One of the first steps to be taken in redirecting the use of existing funds is to channel Medicaid funds into the development, expansion, and strengthening of present comprehensive care programs for children and youth. Medicaid funds need to be made available as an addition and a supplement to existing funds used for comprehensive care programs, and not as a replacement for the funds which those programs have.

Another early step for consideration is to devise means of channeling funds now used to pay for episodic, discontinuous service, into a system which will provide more continuous and comprehensive care, combining preventive, treatment, and rehabilitation services. Recently enacted legislation establishing Health Maintenance Organizations represents one approach. Pediatricians and other child health experts need to play a prominent role in planning HMO's to insure an improved quality of health and social care for children and youth.

SUMMARY

This chapter summarizes pertinent data on national health expenditures for children and youth. In fiscal year 1972, the average expenditure per child per year for health care from all sources in the United States was $146.86 for children and youth under nineteen years of age, an amount slightly (14 percent) above that for the Children and Youth Projects ($128 per child per year). The extent of coverage of children and youth, even those in high priority groups, is still very restricted. Some implications are suggested for future planning for the use of existing funds currently available for the health care of children and youth.

REFERENCES

1. Cooper, B.S. and Worthington, N.L. "Age Differences in Medical Care Spending, Fiscal Year 1972." *Social Security Bulletin*, May 1973, pp. 3-15. DHEW Pub. No. (SSA) 73-11700.
2. Bicknell, W.J.; Macht, L.B.; Scherl, D.J.; and English, J.T. "Evolution of a Health Program: The Job Corps Experience." *American Journal of Health* 60 (May 1970):829-837.
3. Wallace, H.M.; Goldstein, H.; and Oglesby, A.C. *The Health and Medical Care of Children Under Title 19 (Medicaid). American Journal of Public Health* 64 (May 1974):501-506.
4. North, A.F. "Research Issues in Child Health: A Head Start Research Seminar. I. Introduction and Overview." *Pediatrics* 45 (April 1970):690-701.
5. Weckwerth, V. Personal Communication, December 1973.
6. Randolph, L. Personal Communication, December 1973.
7. Gillespie, J.B. Quoted in *Pediatric News* (December 1973):1.

Index

Aberdeen, 80; adolescents, 137, 141
abortion: Act, 1966, 20; overview, in
    Sweden, 196–201; 278–280; and U.K., 21
Ackral, M. et al., 144
administration: Health Service, 71; hospital/
    services, 173; in Mitchell, 52; National
    Health Service structure, 5; procedure for
    handicapped, 42; staff training, 62
adolescents, 29; defined by Morton and
    Kolvin, 135; sex life statistics, 287–292
Akademiska, 172
Alberman, E.D. and Goldstein, H., 166
Anderson, E.M., 163
Anderson, O.W., 307
Annesley, P.T., 140
assessment: centers, 162, 164; defined by
    Holt, 159

Barter, J.T. and Langsley, D.G., 147
Beveridge Report, 4
Black, J.M. M. et al, 161
Birmingham, 68; Local Welfare Authority,
    96
Brandon, S., 136, 137
Bristol, 100
British Pediatric Association, 23; assess-
    ment cetners, 42; "Pediatrics in the
    Seventies," 57; report on premature
    babies, 99
British Pregnancy Health Service, 91
Brook Advisory Service, 21
Bruggen, P., et al, 148
Burbridge and Sickel, 144
Butler, Neville, 117; National Childrens
    Bureau Study, 35; and Alberman, E.D.,
    104; and Bonham, D.G., 156

Caldbeck-Meenan, J., 139
Capes, M., 139, 140, 148
Central Health Services Council, Report
    of, 101
Central Midwives Board, 105
Chamberlain Study, 35
child health: the blind or partially sighted,
    225; department activities, 72; mortality,
    28; Pre-School Act, 247; Scotland's Chil-
    dren's Hearing, 57; U.K. overview, 22–29;
    university department, 69; welfare centers,
    in Sweden, 208
Child Health Service: features, 58; treatment
    and benefits, 59
Children's Act of 1948, 53
Children's Charter, 1907–08, 52
Children's Tuberculosis Service, 75
Child Welfare Centers, 28, 29, 302
Child and Youth Project, ix, 317–319
1970 Cohort-British Births Study, 117
Commission on Child Centers, 252
costs: FPA income, 90; of medical policies
    in U.K., 53; for patient in Sweden, 190,
    191; preventive services, in Sweden, 181;
    Seven Crown Reform, 179; in Sweden,
    170
County Council: authority, 173–176
Court, Donald, 57
Cranbrook Report, 101, 104
Cross, Kenneth, 105
Crosse, Mary, 96

Davies, B. et al, 139
Dawes, Geoffrey, 105
day care, 210; Commission on Child Centres,
    253; organization models, 257; philosophy,

244; program expansion, 33; in social context, 241

dental care: County Council in Sweden, 181; and National Health Service, 6; service overview, 31

Dept. of Education and Science, 13

Dept. of Health and Social Security (DHSS) 23; and adolescents, 148; assessment centers, 160; Better Services for the Mentally Handicapped, 44; Report of Expert Group on Special Care for Babies, 27; school health service, 36

Douglas, J.W.B.: study, 34

Dudgeon, J.A., 156

Economic Opportunity Act, 1964, ix

Edinburgh: adolescents, 137; Psychiatric Adolescent Service, 145

Education Act, 1944, 36, 144

education: of doctors and family planning, 21; and effect on low infant mortality, 237; for family planning, 86; FPA fertility training, 88; for handicapped, 44; intensive baby care training for nurses, 108; medical, in Sweden, 181, 182; philosophy of FRSU, 265-267; program for day care, 258; provisions for handicapped, 219; psychiatric training, 144; role of Child Welfare Centers, 29; school system overview, 283-285; sex manual for teachers, 293, 294; Social Pediatrics, culture and diagnosis, 77; for Special Care Baby Units, 102; special in U.K., 45; Spence program, 69; Swedish university as base for research, 172; training and care of handicapped, 164; training in preventive pediatrics, 61; undergraduate curriculum, 62

Egan, D. et al, 159

Eisenberg, L., 149

Emergency Hospital Service, 4

employment, 242; and daycare statistics, 254

England: infant mortality, 24; maternal mortality, 16; special education, 45

epidemiology, 60; and adolescents, 136-147; Children's Tuberculosis Service, 75; and child's ecosystem, 65; clinic services, 87

evaluation: and adolescent services, 140; and adolescent strategies, 149; of child examination, 209; issues in National Health Service, 11

Evans, J. and Acton, W.P., 142

family planning: contraception, 273-277; fertility in U.K., 13; history of in U.K.,

20; landmarks in U.K., 86; and school health program, 214; sex education statistics, 287-292; in Sweden, 196

Family Planning Act, 20; clinic service, 88; financial structure, 90, 91; and handicaps, 157; overview, 21, 22

fertility, 86

funding: and County Council, 176; day care, 256; economic support for families, 242; for handicapped, 163; maternity grant, 20; strategy, 306; in Sweden, 186-190; U.S. data, 312

Garside, R.F. et al., 137, 140, 141, 143, 146, 149

Gath, D., et al., 145

Geijerstam, G., 204, 206, 237

Gillespie, J.B., 318

Glass, David, 113

Goldberg, D.P., 136

government: Acts for handicapped, 155; Acts of Parliament, 70; Acts of Parliament and child health, 53; Castration Law, 1944, 281; economic assistance, 242; Expert Group on Special Care for Babies, 105; family planning landmarks, 86, 87; and family planning in U.K., 85; jurisdiction in PreSchool Act, 249; legislature for handicapped, 217; Ministry of Health and Social Affairs, Sweden, 171; National Board of Education and School Health, 212; National Insurance Act, 184; National Labor Market Board, 222; organization for newborns, 97; Preschool Act, 245-250; regulations for Child Welfare Centers, 209; "The Right to Abortion," 59; role of Swedish municipalities, 177, 178; Royal Regulations, 1864, 172; State Commisson on Sex Education, 286, 287; State Population Commission, 269; U.S. per capita expenditures, 314

Graham, P., 141

group practice: and Health Visitor, 54; and issues in National Health Service, 6, 10; service teams for handicapped, 260

Hammersmith Postgraduate Institute, 105

handicapped: assessment centers, 76; in daycare, 212; defined by Holt, 155, 156; mentally retarded, 223; overview of services, 41-46; 216-219; Pre-School Act, 247; regionalization of services, 303; services for, in Mitchell, 59

Hansen, S., 147

Health Authority, 62

health care: abortions in Sweden, 196-201; administrative organization in Sweden,

174; adolescents, 141; assessment centers, 76; community medicine, 62; concept of delivery in Wallace for U.S., 299; delivery issues, 10; expenses and benefits, 184; and handicapped, 41; impaired hearing, 224; long-term, 180; manpower for adolescents, 143; maternity and child, defined by Wallace, 297; prematurity, 32; prenatal, 19; and primary care, 78; school program, 214; service and insurance program, 299; and "Social Pediatrics," 66; solo pattern, 318; U.S. data, 312; venereal disease, 282; Wales and Northern Ireland, 57

Health Insurance Plan of New York, x
Health Visitor, 54; and perinatal care, 96
Henderson, A.S., 136, 137, 138, 141; et al, 137, 147
Hill-Burton Act, ix
Holt, K.S., 161; and Huntley, 164; and Reynell, J.K., 161
hospital: access, 99; adolescent admissions, 138; as basis of health care in Sweden, 170; care of children, 29; childrens, establishment of, 53; concept of rooming-in, 73; role in infant mortality, 27; role in National Health Service, 5; size, in Sweden, 181
infant care: battered babies, 32, 210; factors behind mortality rate, 230–232; handicapped identification, 41; intensive for newborns, 107; issue of high risk, 11; mortality issues, 26; mortality in Sweden, 202–206; screening, 208
Infant Life Protection Act, 1872, 52
insurance: national health, x
issues: delineated in Wallace, 10

Joseph, Keith, 91

Kaiser Permanente Plan, x
Karolinska Hospital, 172
Kidd, C.B., 143; and Dixon, G.A., 137, 138; and Caldbeck-Meehan, J., 139
Kolvin, I., 136, 139

Lambeth Conference of Church of England, 86
legislation: Abortion Act of 1967, 91
Levitt, E.E., 149
Lindon, R., 166
London Hospital, 105
London: maternal and child care organizations, 13; pediatrics, 68

McCulloch, J.W., 141; et al, 137
management: and handicapped, 159; inter-

agency and handicapped, 59; National Health Service reorganization, 10
Masterson, J.F., 136, 139, 140
Maternal and Child Health Division, 13
maternal care: in England, 16; exposed in World War I, 52; grants and allowance, 34; indicators of risk, 103; overview in Sweden, 195, 272; place of hospital, 73; sterilization, 280
Maternity and Child Welfare Act, 1918, 53
Maternity and Infant Care Projects, ix
Medicaid, 318
methodology: and adolescent population, 139; behind Social Pediatrics in Miller, 66; case-finding, 248; 1964 National Survey, 115
midwifery, 19; and perinatal care, 96
Miller, F.J.W., 100
Mitchell, S., and Shepherd, M., 140
mortality: causes of maternal in England, 19; decline and role of Medicare, 234; indicators of risk, 103; infant, 24, 229–231, 206; infant sudden death, 27; maternal in Sweden, 196; maternal in U.K., 16; neonatal and improved pediatrics, 58; prematurity, 69

National Birth Control Council, 85
National Birthday Trust, 102
1958 National Child Development Study, 116
National Council for the Unmarried Mother and Her Child, 1918, 53
National Health Insurance Act, 1912, 3; organization in Sweden, 182
National Health Service: consultants and funding, 9; dental care and schools, 32; Family Planning Act, 1967, 85; Health Visitor, 54; maternal and child health reorganization in Wallace, 13; organization in Sweden, 170; overview of 1946 Act in Wallace, 4; reorganization, 10, 108; Reorganization Bill, 85; school health service, 36; special benefits, 33; team provisions for handicapped, 162
National Nursing Board, 144
National Society of Prevention of Cruelty to Children, 32
National Survey of Health and Development, 1964, 113
Newcastle upon Tyne, 66; adolescence, 137, 141; Maternity Survey, 80; prematurity in Miller, 100; regional organization, 72
Nuffield Foundation, 69
nursing: and childrens hospitals, 54; home service, 74, 100; manpower distribution, 144; role of, 180

Offer, D. and Offer, J., 136, 139
ophthalmic care: and National Health
  Service, 6
organization: medical structure for handicapped, 161; move to reorganization,
  300; National Survey, 1964, 114; pediatrics and child health, 71; regionalization
  of hospitals, in Sweden, 170; restructure
  of National Health Service, 108; and
  Social Pediatrics in Miller, 66
Ottesen-Jensen, Elise, 260-265
Overseas Development Administration, 88
Oxford University, 105

parents insurance: concept of, 244, 251
payment: dental health, 31; general practicioners, 8; and speciality lists, 99
pediatrics: and Child Health Service, 58; form
  of practice in United Kingdom, 71; growth
  of specialty, 54; and newborns, 96; in
  U.K., 22
perinatal care: in U.K., 95
physicians: family practicioners and child
  care, 53; generalists and child health in
  U.K., 22, 27; role in contraception availability, 275; role in National Health
  Service Act, 4; and specialists in new
  child health service, 60
Platt Report, 1959, 119
Plowden Committee, 117
Plymouth, 85
policy: abortion in U.K., 91; for adolescent
  care, 138-142; conversion of maternity
  allowance, 243; DHSS, 97; family planning training courses, 89; for handicapped
  in Sweden, 220, 221; influence, 69;
  maternity service reports, 101; national
  and wartime, 80; nutritional, 70; segregation of handicapped, 57; to upgrade MCH
  care, 304, 305
"polyclinic," concept of, 170
Poor Law, 4
Power, M.J., et al, 145
Pregnancy Advisory Service, 21, 91
prenatal care: and handicapped, 157
prevention: and adolescents, 143-148; "at
  risk" concept in Holt, 158; cervical
  cancer screening, 19; Committee on Case-
  Finding Activities, 251; and decline in
  infant mortality, 235; effect on infant
  and mother mortality rates, 208; and
  issues in National Health Service, 11;
  MCH in Sweden, 181; network in Sweden,
  301, 302; and pediatics, 55; and prematurity, 15, 32; school health program,
  214; student health surveys, 37
Pringle, Kelmer, 117

Pritchard, C., 145
public health: curricula revisions, 164;
  university department and community
  work, 74

Regional Health Authorities, 56
Rehin, G.F., 149
research: adolescent services, 138, 139;
  Commissions of Inquiry, 171, 172; 1958
  national survey, 117; in Newcastle, 145;
  on prematurity, 100; reorganization, 109;
  social and operational, 79
Reynell, J.K. and Huntley, R.M.C., 161
RFSU (Swedish Association for Sex Educa-
  tion), 261-266; survey of habits, 293
Rietz, E., 232
Rinsely, D.B., 136
Rogers, M.G.H., 159
Rosen, B.M. et al, 142, 143
Royal College of Psychiatrists, 143
Royal Medico-Psychological Association,
  143
Rutter, M., 137; et al, 136, 138, 139, 140,
  142; and Graham, P., 136, 139, 141,
  142
Ryle, A., 139, 141, 145

Schonfeld, W.A., 142, 146
schools: dental program, 31; health, 36,
  212; program overview, 214-216
Scotland: approach to juvenile delinquency,
  57; "Towards an Integrated Child Health
  Service," 57
screening: and adolescents, 138-147; analysis and surveillance, 305; and assessment
  center for handicapped, 59; case findings
  of handicapped, 218; case-finding under
  Pre-School Act, 248; cervical cancer, 19;
  for four year olds, 209; growth of and
  Health Visitors, 55; and handicapped,
  41; health defect identification, 40; identification of high risks, 302; maternal
  care, in Sweden, 195; for PKU, 15
Seebohm Report, 156
Serafimerlasarettet, 169, 172
services: alteration, 56; district and mentally retarded, 44; integration, 59; national
  health, x; National Health Service special
  benefits, 33
Seven Crown Reform 170
sex education, 215; curricula at school,
  285; deviations and penal code, 281;
  evolution of commitment, 270; overview,
  262-266; sex life statistics, 287-292; in
  U.K., 40
sexism: elimination in child care benefits,
  244; woman emancipation, 271, 272

Sheldon Report, 55
Sheridon, M.D., 158
social class: child welfare centers, 28
socioeconomic class: and infant mortality, 230–232; and health status, 35; and malnutrition, 68; and Social Pediatrics, 78
social care: concept of, 169
Social Insurance System, 179
social needs: and adolescent services, 141
Social Pediatrics: defined in Miller, 65, 79
Social Security of 1935, ix
Sorrento Municipal Maternity Hospital, 96
specialties: and adolescents, 145–148; and consultant pediatrics, 72; and National Health Service, 6; pressure for within pediatrics, 56; R.S.C.N., 54; in Sweden, 179
Spence, J.C., 68
Stockholm, 196; contraception availability, 275–277; infant mortality, 232; RFSU survey, 293
Stopes, Marie, 85
survey: and adolescent population, 139; deaf population, 47; disease incidence, 76; maternity in Miller, 79; perinatal care in U.K., 98; sex life statistics, 287–292; student population, 37
Sweden: abortions, 196–201; birthrate, 193, 194; development of services, 169; The Government Bill, 245–260; infant mortality and factors, 230; low perinatal mortality, 238; MCH services, 304; pension insurance overview, 185; regionalization, 300; RFSU, 266–269; school system overview, 283–285; services for handicapped, 218; sex education, 215; socioeconomic development, 233
Swedish State Committee for Sex Education, 215

taxation: and National Health Service, 8; in Sweden, 170
Titmuss, R.M., 70
Tizard, Peter, 105

Umea, 196
United Kingdom (U.K.): abortions, 92; birth rate, 15; Child Health Service pattern, 58; finances and National Health Service, 6; handicapped, in Holt, 156; maternal grants and allowances, 34; MCH services, 303; 1964 national survey, 114; overview of health care, 3–9; political overview in Mitchell, 51; postwar, 69; regionalization, 300; serivce organization, 13; survey of the deaf, 47
United States: birth rate, 15; health care distribution, 311; issues of health delivery, 298; need for funding strategy, 306, 397; organization for MCH services, 304
Uppsala, 209; perinatal mortality, 236

Wadsworth, Mr., 116
Wales: infant mortality, 24; maternal mortality, 16; special education, 45
Wallace, H.M.: definition of maternal and child health, 297
Warren, W., 140, 146, 147
WHO Report on Prematurity, 99
Wing, J.K. et al, 139
Wolfson Centre, 160

About the Editor

Helen M. Wallace, M.D., M.P.H.

Dr. Wallace is a graduate of Wellesley College, Columbia University College of Physicians and Surgeons, and the Harvard School of Public Health. She is a diplomate of the American Board of Pediatrics and of the American Board of Preventive Medicine. She has served in positions of high administrative responsibility in the New York City Department of Health and in the U.S. Children's Bureau, in the field of maternal and child health. She has served as Consultant to a number of governmental and voluntary health agencies in the U.S.A. concerned with the care of mothers and children, and as Consultant to the World Health Organization in Uganda, the Philippines, India, and to the South East Asia Regional Office. She is the author of 230 articles and two textbooks in the field of maternal and child health.

About the Editor

About the Contributors

Dr. Beryl D. Corner. M.D., FRCP. Senior Consultant Pediatrician, United Bristol Hospitals, and Clinical Lecturer in Child Health, University of Bristol, Bristol, England

Dr. J.W.B. Douglas. Director, MRC Unit on Environmental Factors in Mental and Physical Illness, London School of Economics, London, England

Dr. Hyman Goldstein. Ph.D. Research Biostatistician, Maternal and Child Health Program, University of California School of Public Health, Berkeley

Dr. Kenneth S. Holt. M.D., FRCP, DCH. Director, The Wolfson Centre and Department of Developmental Paediatrics, Institute of Child Health, University of London, London, England

Dr. I. Kolvin. M.D., Dip. Psych., FRC Psych. Physician in Psychological Medicine, Newcastle University Hospitals, Nuffield Child Psychiatry Unit, Hospital for Sick Children, Newcastle-On-Tyne, England

Dr. Fred J.W. Miller. Professor of Social Paediatrics, Department of Child Health, The University of Newcastle-Upon-Tyne, Newcastle-Upon-Tyne, England

Dr. Ross G. Mitchell. Professor and Chairman, Department of Child Health, University of Dundee, Dundee, Scotland

Dr. S.T. Morton, M.B., Ch.B., M.R.C. Psych., D.P.M., D.C.H. Consultant in Child Psychiatry, Nuffield Child Psychiatry Unit, Newcastle University Hospitals. Clinical Lecturer in Psychological Medicine, University of Newcastle, Newcastle-On-Tyne, England.

Mrs. Bodil Rosengren. Chief Secretary of the Government Commission on Child Centres, Ministry of Health and Social Affairs, Stockholm, Sweden

Dr. Stig Sjolin. Professor and Chairman, Department of Pediatrics, University of Uppsala Medical School, Uppsala, Sweden

Dr. Thorsten Sjovall. Settervallsvag.15, Nacka, Stockholm, Sweden

Dr. Michael Smith. Chief Medical Officer, The Family Planning Association, London, England

Dr. Malcolm Tottie. Head, Division of Information and International Cooperation, Swedish Committee on International Health Relations, Socialstyrelsen, Stockholm, Sweden

Dr. Helen M. Wallace. M.D., M.P.H. Professor and Chairman, Maternal and Child Health Program, and Family Health Program, University of California School of Public Health, Berkeley, California

book is due on the last date stamped